TEN
SECRETS

TEN
SECRETS

The Hidden Prophecies
of Medjugorje
and the
Path to Peace

THOMAS W. PETRISKO

St. Andrew's Productions

Pittsburgh, Pennsylvania   Ave Maria, Florida

First Edition: January 2024

Hardback ISBN: 978-1-891903-62-5
Paperback ISBN: 978-1-891903-63-2
eBook ISBN: 978-1-891903-64-9

Distributed by:
St. Andrew's Productions
PO Box 746
Imperial, PA 15126

Telephone: 412-787-9735
Web: saintandrew.com
Email:standrewsproductions@yahoo.com

Books are available at special discounts for bulk purchases in the United States for individuals, organizations, institutions, bookstores and corporations. Call or email for details.

Special thanks to all the publishers that granted permission to quote their works. The author and publisher are grateful to all whose materials have been used in one form or another in this book. If any materials have been inadvertently used in this work without proper credit being given in one form or another, please notify the publisher in writing so that future printings of this work may be corrected accordingly.

TABLE OF CONTENTS

To Emily: wife, mother, hero

Also by Thomas W. Petrisko

Twilight of Marxism

The Miracle of the Illumination of All Consciences

The Fatima Prophecies

Call of the Ages

The Last Crusade

The Prophecy of Daniel

St. Joseph and the Triumph of the Saints

The Sorrow, Sacrifice and Triumph: Visions & Prophecies of Christina Gallagher

Glory to the Father

In God's Hands: The Miraculous Story of Little Audrey Santo

The Kingdom of Our Father

Inside Heaven and Hell

Mother of the Secret

The Ideal You

Inside Purgatory

Fatima's Third Secret Explained

False Prophets of Today

The Face of the Father

For the Soul of the Family: The Apparitions of the Virgin Mary to Estela Ruiz

Living in the Heart of the Father

P.S. Your Sandwich May Be Killing You

St. Philip and the Apostles of the Father

Original Separation

The Mystery of the Divine Paternal Heart of God Our Father

What They Say About the "Ten Secrets"

"Yes, people will come from everywhere. And, there will be a reason why. I am no prophet. but if anything should happen at all…It will only happen through Medjugorje, through the Mother of God. The world will be shown where lies authentic power. I am thinking here, among other things, in the Sign that was promised in the Ten Secrets."

—FR. SLAVKO BARBARIC, Ph.D., Author

"We find ourselves before a prophecy that announces a radical and extraordinary change in the world, an overthrow of the mentality dominating the modern world, probably following dramatic events for humanity…The Third Secret of Fátima could coincide with events contained in the Ten Secrets of Medjugorje."

—ANTONIO SOCCI, Vatican Correspondent,
Internationally Acclaimed Author

"The plans of the seers, the tears of some of them, after having the Ninth, and Tenth Secrets, assures us that these (the Ten Secrets) announce the wages of sin…Medjugorje has an apocalyptic, even eschatological flavor. Terrible trials have been unveiled. If men do not convert, these trials will occur as surely as night follows day."

—FR. RENE LAURENTIN, Renowned French Theologian,
Papal Advisor, Author of 150 Books

"At Medjugorje, Our Lady has imparted more Secrets than at Fátima or any other well-known Marian shrine… The message is that the world is undergoing a crisis of faith. Because of that crisis the world finds itself on the edge of catastrophe."

—FR. JOSEPH PELLETIER, Marian Theologian and Author

"The Marian apparitions at Medjugorje have strong apocalyptic elements, perhaps more than Fátima…The Ten Secrets tell us we can have hope in the future. They console us because we do not know what the future holds, but we do know *who* holds the future—the Lord."

—FR. ROBERT FARICY S.J., Author, Professor of Mystical Theology, Pontifical Gregorian University, Rome

"What of the Ten Secrets? Is it not strange that, with the whole apparatus of Church government publicized as never before, with all the public relations—successful or failure—of Vatican II, with incessant assemblies, meetings, seminars, renewal courses, committees, commissions—the Mother of the Church should pick out some unsophisticated children in a remote Yugoslav village to talk to them about matters affecting the future of the whole human race?"

—FR. MICHAEL O'CARROLL, CSSp, Renowned Irish Theologian, Author of 30 Books

"By now, everyone certainly knows that Mary has given Ten Secrets. The ten are not identical, but some involve warnings and some catastrophes. Mary implies that all who know of the Secrets have a strong motivation given them to pray much for unbelievers, who are not aware of them and will learn only too late…She who is still Our Lady of Fátima, has explained Fátima and its apocalyptic message at Medjugorje."

—FR. ALBERT HEBERT, Theologian, Expert on Mysticism, Author

"The Ten Secrets involve predictions of future catastrophes which will overtake the world if it fails to turn to God. Ominously, the Madonna declares that Medjugorje represents the last such appeal to mankind... The first three Secrets appear to be warnings in the form of dire events..."

—GABRIEL MEYER, Correspondent,
National Catholic Register, Author

"There is a marked apocalyptic significance in the ten Medjugorje secrets, even stronger than was the case at Fátima."

—FR. RICHARD FOLEY S.J., British Theologian,
Former *EWTN* Host/Commentator, Author

"The Ten Secrets represent the strange—to many people, repellant—apocalyptic aspect of Medjugorje. With its emphasis on the cosmic struggle between Good and Evil, God and Satan; apocalyptic has always held an important place in the Christian worldview, though in the latter twentieth century it has come to be unacceptable...The Secrets refer to the future of the world."

—MARY CRAIG, British Journalist and Award Winning Author,
BBC Radio and TV Host.

NOW AVAILABLE:
TWILIGHT OF MARXISM

- 'PULITZER PRIZE' Submission, 2022
- "A remarkable book, a work of erudition and breadth…"—**Roy Abraham Varghese**, Author/Editor of over 20 books, including *Cosmos*, *Bios*, *Theos*, which **Time Magazine** called "The year's most intriguing book about God."
- "Inspiring, marvelous, and opus magnum work…"—**D. Brian Scarnecchia, M.Div., J.D.**, Ave Maria School of Law. Author of *Bioethics, Law and Human Life Issues*.
- "A masterpiece, an extraordinary work of storytelling…an enthralling look at the fraught times at hand."—**Gerard Beer**, former Cyber-Security, Bio-Terrorism, Chemical and Nuclear Triad Senior Command and Control Officer for the U.S Air Force.

Author's Note

This book examines the story of the ten secret prophecies being given by the Virgin Mary at Medjugorje to six visionaries, beginning in 1981. The "Ten Secrets of Medjugorje" are related to the fulfillment of Mary's historic prophecies at Fátima, which were also termed "Secrets."

The complete histories of Fátima and Medjugorje are not addressed in this work. Those accounts can be found in my book, *Twilight of Marxism* (St. Andrews Productions, 2022).

I have written three other books on Fátima and Medjugorje: *The Call of the Ages*, *The Fatima Prophecies*, and *The Third Secret of Fatima Explained*. These are available on the website of St. Andrews Productions (saintandrew.com) or by calling 412-787-9735.

An extensive list of hundreds of recommended books, videos, and other materials on Fátima and Medjugorje can be found in the bibliography of *Twilight of Marxism*.

Preface

On June 24, 1981, an apparition of the Virgin Mary was reported in the rustic hamlet of Bijakovići, located ninety-six miles southwest of Sarajevo in what was the nation of Yugoslavia at the time.

By the end of the following day, six youths emerged as the visionaries at what is known today as Medjugorje, a Marian shrine visited by pilgrims from throughout the world. Some sixty million have traveled to the quaint little village in Herzegovina over the past forty-two years, where the miraculous is said to be on display every day.

As with the 1917 visions of the Virgin Mary at Fátima, Portugal, an appeal to renounce sin and return to God is reported to be the primary message of the apparition. And, like Fátima, confidential prophecies—known as the "Ten Secrets of Medjugorje"—have been received by the six visionaries from Mary. The futuristic foretellings are said to involve world transforming events of a considerable magnitude, believed greater than Fátima, where both World War II and Communism were predicted.

As of this writing, three of the Medjugorje visionaries have received the ten secrets, the other three have nine. Upon each of the six visionaries receiving all of the Secrets, the events foretold in them are reportedly to begin to unfold—one by one.

On March 17, 2010, Pope Benedict XVI empaneled a seventeen-member board, known as the Ruini Commission, to study the events at Medjugorje. It completed its work on January 17, 2014.

Though not officially approved by the Church yet, a pre-released copy of the commission's report in 2020 disclosed the majority of the panel concluded the first seven apparitions at Medjugorje were "*constat de supernaturalitate*"—determined to be supernatural. *

---

* Andrea Tornielli, "The Conclusions of the Ruini Report on Medjugorje," *The National Catholic Register, nc.register.com*. Posted by Andrea Tornielli / CNA/ EWTN News on Wednesday, May 17, 2017, at 9:02 p.m.

In May of 2019, the Holy See sanctioned official Church pilgrimages to the shrine.

On August 2, 2020, Archbishop Luigi Pezzuto, the Vatican's apostolic nuncio to Bosnia-Herzegovina, addressed for the first time the yearly gathering of youth in Medjugorje on behalf of the Pope. Since then, the Pope has continued to address the Annual International Youth Conference in Medjugorje.

No judgment as to the veracity of the succeeding visions at Medjugorje has been rendered primarily due to their volume and to the fact that the reported supernatural events there have not concluded.

The Ten Secrets remain secret.

The Path to Peace

"Turn from evil and do good, seek peace and pursue it."
—Ps 34:15

With World War I raging and millions perishing, three shepherd children in the rustic village of Fátima, a hamlet in the Serra de Aire Mountains of central Portugal, reported an apparition of the Virgin Mary in the spring of 1917.

Mary previewed to the visionaries, in a three-part prophecy known as the "Secret of Fátima," a worrisome future.

Out of Russia would spread a malignant scourge and a second world war was looming, the children were informed by the vision. There would be martyrs, persecution, famine, and even the "annihilation of nations."

But if the Catholic Church responded to the Virgin's requests and humanity stopped "offending God"—if the world corrected its "sinful" course—Mary foretold there would come instead a "triumph" of good over evil and an "era of peace."

There would be no course correction.

As the twentieth century unfolded, the harsher prophecies of Fátima scaled the horizon. World War II exploded with all its horror and devastation, the specter of nuclear weapons arrived, and the greatest systematic evil in history, Marxism, methodically infested not just Russia, but every nation and culture on Earth.

By the 1980s, a Pandora's Box of afflictions—communism, nuclear annihilation, practical atheism, moral relativism, Islamic terrorism—would come to haunt the world.

The ungodly forces behind these malevolent movements—deterred at times but never disheartened—proved resolute in their efforts.

And so, she would come again.

In a bucolic hamlet named Bijakovici, located in the Alps of the former Yugoslavia, the Virgin Mary appeared on June 24, 1981, to six more children. Internationally known today as "Medjugorje," a plea to humanity to reject sin and return to God was heard once again.

Most significantly, the Madonna revealed that she had come to "fulfill Fátima"—to honor her word that God will guide the world to a "triumph" over evil and into an age of peace—providing, as she requested at Fátima, that people change.

But after 42 years, no "change" has been seen…and no "triumph" has come.

<hr>

The visions at Fátima were a preeminent moment in history.

It was an extraordinary, miraculous appeal to all peoples, not just Catholics, to recognize the intrinsic repercussions that emanate from sin.

The insufferable war raging at the time, World War I, was a result of such consequences, the Virgin Mary said. World War II and Communism, both forewarned at Fátima, would further illuminate this tacit, immutable truth.

Today, an even stronger divine overture is heard at Medjugorje.

It is in response to the pandemic of sin in the world and the exponentially greater consequences now posed, consequences that are undeniably apocalyptic.*

The roots of the present crisis at hand are identifiable: systematic atheism infects all humanity; evil is not only glorified but evangelized; abortion has canceled two billion lives; and numerous mutations of Marxism now delude, subjugate and pervert the masses, debasing Judeo-Christian precepts while forwarding the preeminence of man—the long-suffering, indefatigable quest of Babel.†

---

* From artificial intelligence to designer viruses, from climate architecture to bio weaponry, from a new generation of nuclear armaments to the unpredictable repercussions of genetic engineering, today's technological threats to the human race are menacing, omnipresent, and very capable of what scientists call a "civilization changing event." They are all evidence of the ongoing consequences of original disobedience, of continuing to experience the effects of partaking in the fruits of the " Tree of the Knowledge of Good and Evil" (Genesis 2:15-17).

† While there are a host of Cultural Marxist aberrations now invading all societal interaction, a venomous Orwellian ideology known as "Wokeism" is said to be the most pervasive and intrinsically deranged, regarded by many as a cult/religion. Wokeism seeks to redefine human biology, traits, and characteristics; it pits races and sexes against one another, replaces meritocracy and language, promotes selective violence, and reengineers an array of former Soviet and Maoist dystopian evils. Wokeism is, in essence, an authoritarian, weaponized, antichristian ideology that strives to regulate not only how people act but how they think. Pope Benedict XVI warned in 2010 that such "ideological currents"—such "winds of change"—were the "crisis of our age." Such ideologies, Benedict said, were "intolerant, and seek to create in society a culture within which religious belief is hard to find, to hold and to proclaim." They desire, Benedict warned, to "build a false reality, based on false truth." Elon Musk, the noted entrepreneur, writes: "The Woke mind virus is triggering civilizational suicide."

Most threatening, however, remains the nuclear sword of Damocles that hangs over the planet—unsheathed and ever menacing—an ominous harbinger of a world playing Russian roulette with not just its future, but its very existence.

"Modern man", Mary warned at Medjugorje in 2023, teeters on "perdition."‡

〜∞〜

As far back as 1987, the Virgin Mary cautioned that humanity was again straying too far for its own good, that its immoral excesses were still "offending" God, infringing on the limits of divine patience.

Like she did at Fátima, the Virgin intimated at Medjugorje that global calamities now hovered over the planet—as if in a holding pattern—waiting to land.

But by the time the direness of the situation would be apparent, she added, "It will be too late."§

"Too late"?

What did Mary mean that it would be "too late"?

In the same revelation that the Virgin delivered those portentous words, she referred again to the greatest mystery surrounding her apparitions at Medjugorje: Ten confidential prophecies being given by her to the six visionaries.

---

‡ On January 25, 2023, the Virgin Mary said at Medjugorje: "…The future is at a crossroads, because modern man does not want God. That is why mankind is heading to perdition." See various Medjugorje websites for the message of January 25, 2023.

§ On Wednesday, January 28, 1987, the Virgin Mary delivered the following message to Mirjana Dragićević in Sarajevo: "… I warn you. There are Secrets, my children; one does not know what they are; when they learn, it will be too late. Return to prayer. Nothing is more necessary. I would like it if the Lord had permitted me to show you just a little about the Secrets, but He already gives you enough graces." Laurentin and Lejeune, *Messages and Teachings of Mary at Medjugorje*, 1988, p. 291.

Known as "The Ten Secrets of Medjugorje," the hidden foretellings are believed to hold the perils that Mary cautioned were fomenting: Trying events that mankind will ultimately bring upon itself.

"The Ten Secrets [of Medjugorje] announce—to a large extent—impending destruction which are not extrinsic punishments, but immanent justice; the 'self-destruction' of a world which entrusts itself to evil," said renowned French Scholar Fr. René Laurentin.[1]

Laurentin identifies the exacting future foretold in the Secrets as "retributive justice"—a groundswell of intrinsic punishment invariably destined to hemorrhage due to the collective sin of the present day.

In their own way, the Medjugorje visionaries concur.

As at Fátima, Mary has given them to understand that the wages of sin hold serious consequences, as alluded in the Bible (Lv 24:19-22; Dt 19:18-21; Mt 5;38-40), consequences that unfailingly invoke the age old principle that people "reap what they sow" (Gal 6:7; Eccl 10:8, Prv 1:32, 26:27, Ps 7:15-16).[2]

But while this principle is true, both biblical law and biblical narrative reveal that "retributive punishment" is not necessarily required to satisfy justice.[3] Alternatives to retribution—such as repentance, reproof, forgiveness, and restitution—were constantly solicited and celebrated in the Old Testament.[4] Theologians say these alternatives to punishment do not contradict the demands of justice but serve to restore relationships and thus vindicate the true character of justice.[5]

This is especially revealed in the New Testament, where believers are to forego retribution and retaliation, and to refrain from seeking "ultimate justice" (Mt 5:38-48, Rom 12:17-21; 1 Pt 2:21-23).[6]

The Church teaches that God uses this approach with his sinful children.

He is willing to forego punitive justice if we appeal to His mercy, as in the Biblical account of the city of Nineveh, whose citizens escaped destruction by responding to Jonah's call to turn back to God and away from their evil ways.

In essence, "mercy triumphs over justice,"[7] which is the heart of the Gospels[8] and the approach Mary brought to Fátima and continues to pursue at Medjugorje, despite the long shadow cast by the looming Secrets.

～∞～

At Fátima, Mary sought "to prevent" God's "punishment" by offering an alternative path to assuaging God's justice. Her requests for the "Consecration of Russia" and the "Communion of Reparation" were prescribed remedies to help satisfy retribution, though not timely enacted.

At Medjugorje, it is no different today.

The six visionaries all report the events in the Ten Secrets are to come, but the degree of hardship they carry depends on penance, prayer and conversion, or lack of it.

Once again, God's mercy is readily offered to the world, a world few can deny is immeasurably worse than in 1917.

Indeed, the world of today is drowning in sin, submerged in darkness, and *completely* under the *deception* of Satan (Rv 12:9); it is a world so consumed by evil that it appears to visibly embody Babylon the Great, which the *Book of Revelation* described as a "haunt for demons" where "sins were piled up to the sky."

But though God's mercy is still readily available ("For whoever shall call upon the name of the Lord shall be saved" (Acts 2:21), as at Fátima, time remains a factor in the unfolding of the Secrets.

A "period of grace" is at hand, Mary repeats over and over at Medjugorje, but it will give way to the time of the Secrets.

～∞～

The Secrets.

The events contained in the Ten Secrets, the visionaries insist, will unfold.

But it is important to note that the role of the Secrets of Medjugorje is significantly different from the Secret of Fátima.

While both apparitions reveal prophecies designed to forewarn God's permissive justice and the coming of Mary's "triumph" in the world, the divine impetus behind the Secrets of Medjugorje involves more—and for a significant reason.

The mysterious events contained in the Ten Secrets—both the wondrous and the trying—are meant to be seen in retrospect someday as the pivotal catalysts God utilized at this interim in history to birth a universal revival of faith, one in which humanity moves from an age of conflict and rebellion to an age of peace and spirituality.

Through the Ten Secrets—by way of their *strategic* pre-announcement and subsequent "one by one" unfoldment—mankind is to be convicted of the truth of God, of His indisputable existence, a reality most of the world today denies by word or deed.

Thus, the Secrets are to precipitate an epiphany in the souls of people—an "exalted horn" rousing of the glorious Creator as celebrated in Psalm 148—one that resoundingly validates Mary's opening and repeated cry at Medjugorje:

"God exists!"

￼

But the Secrets of Medjugorje are to not only tear the veil off humanity's eyes so it may acknowledge the Creator.

They are to do more, much more.

They are to reportedly trigger a divine reset in the way life on Earth is perceived and lived, one that will totally realign humanity's priorities.

"We find ourselves before a prophecy that announces a radical and extraordinary change in the world, an overthrow of the mentality dominating the modern world," wrote Vatican correspondent and author Antonio Socci about the Secrets of Medjugorje.[9]

It is an overthrow, Socci says, that began with the epic 20th century events foretold and fulfilled "in the Secret of Fátima,"[10] and will conclude, he writes, through the events "belonging to the Ten Secrets of Medjugorje."[11]

Socci foresees, in essence, that the Ten Secrets and their aftermath are going to spur a shift in the focus and direction of the world, moving humanity out from under its incessant quest for the material and into a reawakened hunger for the spiritual.

Others voice a similar understanding.

"What will happen at Medjugorje will be a complete paradigm shift in world affairs," said Ted Flynn, a Catholic author and columnist, about the Ten Secrets. "It will make the parting of the Red Sea seem insignificant as a miracle and will be the equivalent of a polar shift for the world. It will be that significant."[12]

The coming new world will be, some say, as much about the past, as the future. The world is to slow down, and be more as it once was, God-centered and faith-filled.

"Life in the world will change. Afterwards, men will believe as in ancient times," writes Father Joseph Pelletier A.A., echoing one of the Franciscan friars stationed in Medjugorje who frequently spoke with the visionaries about the Secrets and the times to come.

"Those few words: *'men will believe as in ancient times,'* said Pelletier, " imply a lot about the extraordinary events that lie ahead and for which Our Lady came to prepare the world for at Medjugorje."[13]

⌒∞⌒

The reason why so many see a new way of life coming is based upon one fundamental understanding: The Ten Secrets are to bring into the world what Mary promised at Fatima, and continually speaks of at Medjugorje: a reign of peace in the world.

At Fátima, Mary foretold the coming of *a time of peace* (referred to in most Fátima writings as the "Era of Peace"), and "*peace*" is what she set out to herald at Medjugorje, beginning on just the third day.*

"Peace, peace, and only peace," the Virgin told a stunned 16 year-old Marija Pavlovic, one of the six visionaries at Medjugorje, that day. "Reconcile yourselves. Peace must reign between God and men, and between men!"[14]

Indeed, the call for "peace" is found at the center of a countless number of Mary's messages at Medjugorje over the past 42 years.

It is the reason why she proclaims her title at Medjugorje to be "Queen of Peace."

It is the reason she is in the world.

Thus, it is "peace" that will allow the world to shift direction, why life on Earth is to radically change, and why it will be through the *fulfillment* of the Ten Secrets that this peace will finally come.

"The Blessed Mother has told the visionaries that she would confide in them Ten Secrets," explained Father Slavko Barbaric, one of the Franscican priests stationed in Medjugorje during the 80s and 90s. "There are both nice and difficult things. The *primary importance* is the road towards peace, and this is the primary message for us. Regarding the question of an apocalyptic dimension [to the Secrets], certainly

---

* At Fátima, a commission of six experts appointed by the Bishop of Fátima to interpret the message of Fátima rendered the opinion that the "Era of Peace" promised by Mary implied a true "reign of Christ" on the Earth. This was because, the panel said, "there could be no other meaning of the word peace on the lips of the Mother of Christ" and "no other meaning to her words, "'My Immaculate Heart will triumph.'" Numerous mystics and visionaries over the centuries have concurred with an understanding that there was coming , after a great victory of God over Satan, an extended period of peace on Earth. It will be a peace, many write, in the true sense of the word "shalom"—"peace amongst men, and peace between men and God." Some see this coming period of peace to be directly related to passages in the Old Testament (*Numbers, Ecclesiastes, Isaiah, Micah*). At Medjugorje, the Virgin Mary has often implied there is coming a time of peace in relation to her "Triumph," especially in her messages over the last two decades. On Christmas Day, 1992, Mary said at Medjugorje, "Today is a day of peace, but in the whole world there is a great lack of peace. That is why I call you all to build *a new world of peace* with me..."(December 25, 1992).

we understand the possibility for catastrophe to occur. But the Blessed Mother did not come primarily to speak about catastrophes; she came to show us the way to peace."[15]

Yes, the Ten Secrets—both the welcome and the trying ones—are to be the path to peace in the world. It is a reality Mary has repeatedly noted at Medjugorje.

"I invite you little children," the Virgin Mary said at Medjugorje on June 25, 1995, "to be joyful carriers of peace in this troubled world . Pray for peace so that as soon as possible *a time of peace*, for which my Heart patiently waits, may reign."

~∞~

In 1948, Archbishop Fulton Sheen voiced a poignant observation:

"It is a characteristic of any decaying civilization that the great masses of the people are unaware of the tragedy. Humanity in a crisis is generally insensitive to the gravity of the times in which it lives…Only those who live by faith really know what is happening in the world."[16]

Sheen's astute words strike a resounding chord with the Secrets of Medjugorje.

Life on Earth today is undergoing a divinely crafted metamorphosis.

The last forays of a demonic war are moving towards a climax.

A new world and a new time of peace stand at the doorstep of the world.

But only those with *faith*—especially those with a "sensus fidei " of the Virgin Mary's apparitions, her mission in the world, and the role of her "Secrets"—are aware and recognize what is happening…and understand what is coming.

~∞~

This book attempts to take an in depth look into the Ten Secrets of Medjugorje.

It carefully documents the Virgin Mary's and the six visionaries' words concerning them.

It examines the context in which they were given, explores what is known about their content, and emphasizes how the more menacing sounding of the Secrets can still be mitigated through penance and prayer.

Most importantly, this work stresses how the Ten Secrets need to be embraced in a positive way.

The prophecies are not to be awaited with trepidation, anxiety and fear, for God intends to permit the events contained in the Secrets to fulfill His promise to purify and transform the world for the better; to bring to an end an age of sin, and to usher in a time of true peace—an era of "shalom."

Conjecture, assumptions, and especially sensationalism are avoided in this work.

No predictions are made.

Finally, this writing seeks to be true to the essence of the message of Medjugorje: Mary's preeminent quest for the salvation of souls, and for the fulfillment of Fátima's promise—the long awaited and glorious "Triumph of the Immaculate Heart of Mary."

PART I

DEADLINES AND DESTINIES

"When the people of Nineveh believed God; they proclaimed a fast. And all of them, great and small, put on sackcloth, from the greatest to the least. When the news reached the king of Nineveh, he rose from his throne, laid aside his robe, covered himself with sackcloth, and sat in the ashes."

—Jonah 3:5-7

"Keep converting and clothe yourselves in penitential garments and in personal, deep prayer; and in humility, seek peace from the Most High...Little children, keep looking at my Son and follow Him towards Calvary in renunciation and fasting..."

—The Virgin Mary,
Medjugorje,
February 25, 2023

CHAPTER ONE

"The Secrets Are Their Destiny"

"If you belonged to the world, the world would love its own; but because you do not belong to the world, and I have chosen you out of the world, the world hates you."

—Jn 15:19

"All the Secrets force me to pray."[1] It was a disclosure by Marija Pavlović, one of the six Medjugorje visionaries, that Father René Laurentin struggled to understand while pondering the clarity of the gaze in her eyes.

Marija had been transformed, Laurentin noted, by something he had not seen in any young girl before. She was deeply affected, he thought, by the knowledge of what was contained in the Secrets.[2]

The Secrets.

The six visionaries—Ivanka Ivanković [Elez], Mirjana Dragićević [Soldo], Vicka Ivanković [Mijatovic], Marija Pavlović [Lunetti], Ivan Dragićević, and Jacov Colo—who never discuss the Secrets among themselves—say the Ten Secrets of Medjugorje involve warnings, signs, and chastisements that will bring all of mankind to a renewed awareness that God exists.[3]

Most significantly, their unfolding centers on the Third Secret—a revelation by its number alone—that immediately recalls the daunting history of Fátima's celebrated Third Secret in a way that appears to be no accident. Moreover, their disclosure will occur in a way that vastly differs from Fátima or any other apparition before.

Each Secret is to be publicly preannounced to all mankind—one by one.[4]

⁓⌑⁓

But if mysterious describes the coming arrival of the Ten Secrets, apocalyptic defines their nature, even more so than the Secret of Fátima, according to theologians.

- "There is a marked apocalyptic significance in the Ten Medjugorje Secrets, even stronger than was the case at Fátima," wrote British Theologian Father Richard Foley.[5]
- "The Marian apparitions at Medjugorje have strong apocalyptic elements, perhaps even more so than the apparitions at Fátima in 1917," asserted Father Robert Faricy, a professor of Mystical Theology Emeritus at the Pontifical Gregorian University in Rome.[6]
- "At Fátima, Our Lady prophesied World War II as a punishment for the sins of that era. At Medjugorje, she tells the world that its lack of faith and consequent sinfulness are about to extract a costly toll," said theologian Father Joseph Pelletier.[7]
- "She, who is still Our Lady of Fátima, has explained Fátima and its apocalyptic message at Medjugorje," opined mysticism expert and prolific author Father Albert Hebert.[8]

Father Luigi Bianchi—an Italian author and an acknowledged expert on Fátima—noted an undeniable, symbolic lesson unfolding through the Virgin Mary's major apparitions.

"The hours of the apparitions follow a progression," explains Bianchi, "At Lourdes, they took place in the morning. At Fátima, at noon. At Medjugorje, in the evening. Is it the end of a long day, and the announcement of the Eighth Day?"[9]

~~~

Father Bianchi poses a rhetorical question, but its answer is "yes.

"It is "yes" because it appears that God is indicating at Medjugorje that our trouble-filled world has reached a critical point. Unlike at Fátima, where the future could still be determined by a proper and substantial response to the Virgin's requests, no such precise conditions are associated with the Ten Secrets of Medjugorje.

The Pope and the bishops are not known to play requested roles in a prophetic drama. The faithful, while asked to pray and do penance, can only mitigate the intensity, not prevent, the unfolding of the Secrets.

God's plan, say the visionaries in regard to the Secrets, will be realized by a series of future events.[10] A climax, therefore, to what Mary began at Fátima and is concluding in Medjugorje, is a fait accompli.

Why?

Because the Virgin has announced that God desires to bring to an end an era of conflict and for the world to enter an era of peace. Therefore, through Mary's intervention, through her words at Fátima and Medjugorje, she has announced that He Himself will guide its arrival.

~~~

All of this means one thing: the world cannot outrun the future that is posed to descend through the unfolding of the mysterious Ten Secrets of Medjugorje.

Down through the years, the visionaries have been consistent with this message. The following statements range from 1983 to 2015:

- "First, some of the Secrets will be revealed—just a few," said Mirjana in Medjugorje on January 10, 1983, "then, the people will be convinced the Madonna was here. Then, they will understand the Sign."[11]
- "The Secrets and their revelation—the happenings that are tied with the secret messages—are going to happen for sure," Ivan told Father Zoran Ostojich on November 19, 1989, in Chicago. "Our Lady said that the beginnings of these happenings and the revelation of each Secret *will* be proclaimed."[12]
- "Our Lady talked to me about the Fifth Secret," revealed Ivanka on June 25, 1997, after her annual apparition at her home in Medjugorje, "and then spoke the following message, 'Dear children, pray with the heart to know how to forgive and how to be forgiven.'"[13]
- "Our Lady spoke to me about the Secrets," stated Jacov after his annual apparition of the Virgin Mary on December 25, 2010, "and, at the end said, 'Pray, pray, pray.'"[14]
- "I have nine Secrets. I was only talking about the Third Secret earlier," Vicka disclosed in a 2015 interview. "The only thing I can say is the Seventh Secret was half reduced, because of our prayers and sacrifices."[15]

~⌘~

"The Secrets are their destiny," observed Irish Theologian Father Michael O'Carroll, about the six visionaries at Medjugorje.[16]

Yes, they are.

But the Secrets are also mankind's destiny.

It is a destiny—if we take the visionaries at their word—that will have a dramatic bearing on history in a way never seen before.[17]

"They say that with the realization of the Secrets entrusted to them by Our Lady," offered one of the Franciscan friars at Medjugorje, "life in the world will change. Afterwards, men will believe like in the ancient times. What will change and how it will change, we don't know given that the seers don't want to say anything about the Secrets."[18]

Unlike the Secret of Fátima—which foretold the Second World War and that a universal evil would emerge out of Russia—no significant clues are found as to what to expect.

Rather, their content is shrouded in mystery.

Mary's own words concerning the contents of the Ten Secrets, however, are delivered in a tone that reflects their rather pressing and grave nature:

> The Sign will come; you must not worry about it. The only thing that I would want to tell you is to be converted. Make that known to all my children as quickly as possible.
>
> No pain, no suffering is too great to me in order to save you. I will pray to my Son not to punish the world; but I beseech you, be converted. You cannot imagine what is going to happen nor what the Eternal Father will send to Earth. That is why you must be converted…[19]

CHAPTER TWO

"Never Tell the Secret to Anyone"

"No one can receive anything except what has been given him from heaven."

—Jn 3: 27

"You could write down the Secrets, put them in an envelope, seal them, and leave them with me," a Church official told ten-year-old Jacov Colo in the early days of the Medjugorje apparitions. "I could write down the Secrets, put them in an envelope and leave them at home," Jacov replied.[1]

Adroit in countering any attempt to dislodge their contents, Jacov—as did all the young visionaries at Medjugorje—knew from the very beginning that the Secrets were *secret*.[2] And, their determination to protect them has been well noted by many.

Historically, this has been true with the Secrets the Virgin Mary has revealed to her chosen ones, especially children.

In 1932, at the Church approved apparitions in Beauraing, Belgium, three of the five visionaries claimed they received Secrets that not even the Pope could be told. One of the visionaries—an 11-year-old boy named Albert Voisin—upon examination, did say his Secret was sad, which was in itself enough to spark concern.[3]

During another Church-approved apparition in Belgium the following year, this time in the town of Banneux, Mary gave 12-year-old Mariette Beco two Secrets that she would not reveal during interrogations.

Again, curiosity filled the air.

Mariette is alleged to have even told her father, while pointing to her chest,

"Papa, even if you would place your gun here, I would not tell!"[4]

The same kind of thinking with young visionaries was found at Fátima, as Lúcia's *First Memoir* reveals how little Jacinta said to her shortly before she died,

"Never tell the Secret to anyone, even if they kill you."[5]

Anyone aware of the Ten Secrets of Medjugorje and their mysterious contents cannot help but be curious a little, wondering what the fate of the world is to be. But this has always been part of awaiting the fulfillment of prophecy, especially when *secrets* are involved.

﹏

In Scripture, the idea of divine secrets is prefigured in Saint Paul's *Letter to the Ephesians* when he speaks of God's secret plans.[6] Theologians say that Mary's secrets exist in this same context because they involve what Saint Paul declared to be the "mystery of Christ."

But when did the Virgin Mary start giving Secrets?

Mary has been reportedly appearing since the first century. In A.D. 40, she is believed to have manifested before her death to the Apostle James the Greater in Zaragoza, Spain. However, many consider this event a bilocation, not an apparition.

Her appearance to St. Gregory the Wonderworker (A.D. 213-270), according to St. Gregory of Nyssa, is said to be the earliest recorded vision of Mary, while her first "classic" apparition is believed to have occurred in Syro-Malabar, India, to three young boys at a spring in A.D. 335.

While the Virgin may have given secrets to other visionaries over the centuries, it was during the nineteenth century apparitions at Rue de Bac, Paris, that the mystery of her secret messages begins to clearly unfold. It all started here, say Mariologists, when a nun named Catherine Laboure revealed that she had been given:

"Several things I must not tell."[7]

Saint Catherine's words are the starting point for this mystery.

But it was with the Church-approved apparitions in 1846 at La Salette, France, in the diocese of Grenoble, that this element of the Virgin's revelations piques significant interest, not just to the faithful, but also to Church hierarchy.

And it's not surprising why.

Once the presence of secrets at La Salette was known, public speculation about their content and nature became rampant. Everyone wanted to know if the "special knowledge" in the secrets concerned them in any way, and if so, what could be done to escape harm.

At La Salette, public figures, institutions, different interest groups, members of religious orders, clerics, bishops, cardinals, and even the Pope became involved in a drama surrounding the secrets—one that stretched all the way into the twentieth century.

∽∝∾

It all began when two children, 14-year-old Francoise-Melanie Calvat-Mathieu and 11-year-old Pierre-Maximin Giraud, reported that when the Virgin Mary appeared to them on a mountain in the French Alps near the village of La Salette on September 19, 1846, she gave each of them a secret message.[8]

At first, the children apparently made no reference to the secrets in their accounts of the apparition. But upon repeated interrogations during the first week, Maximin and then Mélanie revealed that personal secrets were confided to them.

On October 12, 1846, Father Melin, a priest from the village of Corps, composed a letter to Victor Rabillou, a librarian in Bourgoin, that briefly noted the secrets' existence. This was the first document to cite their presence, but at this point, the secrets were considered to be of a personal, not public, nature.[9]

The earliest written account of the apparition in mid-October 1846 again disclosed the secrets. This came from the notes of Father Louis Perrin, the newly appointed pastor of La Salette who interviewed the children.[10]

According to available documentation, the visionaries initially refrained from even speaking of the secrets for fear of revealing them. But once they were known to exist, an almost ceaseless investigative effort was begun to dislodge them.

Over time, the children repeatedly outmaneuvered their interrogators, but this did nothing to inhibit the efforts. Threats of punishment and death, bribes, tricks, and pretense all failed to get the children to reveal the secrets.[11]

On the positive side, their determination was seen as evidence of their integrity—and thus, increased the probability that the apparition was authentic.

As the months went by, the pressure on the children continued.

When asked if the secrets concerned Heaven, Hell, the world, religion, or other matters, Mélanie replied:

"It concerns that which it concerns; if I tell you this you will know it, and I don't want to tell it."[12]

In the spring of 1847, a report written by Dr. Armand Dumanoir, a Grenoble lawyer, suggested for the first time the possibility of the children's secrets being of public relevance.

"After these words," wrote Dumanoir, "the Lady gave each of them a secret which appears to consist in the announcement of a great event, fortunate for some, unfortunate for others."[13]

With this document, a new stage in the mystery of Marian apparitions was upon the world.

Church officials now began to intensify the investigative process. The public also began to voice its interest, especially given the great social and political turmoil in France in 1848.[14] Many began to speculate that the children's secrets were vital for understanding the unfolding contemporary events.

At this time, Church officials also began to write letters of inquiry to the priests involved with the children. By 1849, rumors were running amok, with the contents of the secrets at the center. Various scenarios were being outlined, with even the Second Coming of Christ foretold to be at the culmination.[15]

Reported efforts involving two future Saints, Catherine Laboure, the visionary at Rue du Bac, and then an actual visit to little Maximin by the Cure of Ars, Jean Vianney, all contributed to efforts to encourage the children to reveal the secrets.

But they would not budge.

Finally, in June of 1851, Pope Pius IX was informed that the children were willing to transmit their secrets to him.

The Pope agreed to the arrangement.

On July 2, Maximin sat down and recorded his secret, after which he reportedly said:

"I am unburdened. I no longer have a secret. I am as others. One no longer has any need to ask me anything. One can ask the Pope and he will speak if he wants."[16]

The next day, Mélanie wrote down her secret. Claiming she forgot something; she repeated the action on July 6th.

The children said that they finally agreed to tell the secrets because they now understood the Pope's position within the Church. But further information disclosed that both children believed they were graced with special signs from Heaven that permitted the disclosures.[17]

The Secrets of La Salette were given to Pope Pius IX on July 18, 1851.

The Pope opened and read them in the presence of the Grenoble officials. Ironically, this series of events—which finally brought the secrets to the Pope—also exacerbated speculation that they were apocalyptical in content.[18]

Reports and rumors about the audience with the Pope further fueled this speculation. Other reports from a handful of clerics who read the secrets also emerged. Together, the public began to piece together a picture that fit in with their apocalyptic suspicions.

Some of the rumors, nevertheless, were true.

Witnesses who observed the children write their secrets reported their facial expressions and other behavioral aspects. One witness noted that Mélanie asked how to spell "Antichrist." The length of the texts was also noted as to which of the two secrets was longer.

In addition, Pope Pius IX's reaction upon reading the secrets seemed to convey more information.[19] According to the representatives present, the Pope stated after reading Maximin's message:

"Here is all the candor and simplicity of a child."[20]

However, while reading Mélanie's secret, the witnesses said that the Pope's face changed and reflected strong emotion. Upon finishing, he reportedly stated:

"It is necessary that I reread these at more leisure. There are scourges here that menace France, but Germany, Italy, all Europe is culpable and merits chastisement. I have less to fear from open piety, than from indifference and from human respect. It is not without reason that the Church is called militant, and you see here the captain."[21]

Afterwards, further comments were attributed to the Pope by respected sources.

Cardinal Lambruschini, First Minister to Pius IX and Prefect of the Congregation of Rites, said:

"I have known the fact of La Salette for a long time and, as a bishop, I believe it. I have preached it in my diocese, and I have observed that my discourse made a great impression. Moreover, I know the Secret of La Salette."

Cardinal Fornaric, Nuncio to Paris, remarked:

"I am terrified of these prodigies; we have everything that is needed in our religion for the conversion of sinners, and when Heaven employs such means, the evil must be very great."[22]

Upon returning home from Rome, Father Perrin told Mélanie that he was unsure of what she had written, but judging by the Pope's reaction, it wasn't flattering. He then asked the girl if she knew what the word "flattering" meant. She replied, "To give pleasure," and then Mélanie added, "but this (the secret) ought to give pleasure to the Pope—a Pope should love to suffer."[23]

And that is what the Secrets of La Salette apparently brought to Pius IX—considerable suffering.

Asked years later about the contents of the Secrets, Pius said:

"You want to know the Secrets of La Salette? Ah, well, here are the Secrets of La Salette: If you do not do penance, you will perish."[24]

─━◦◦◦━─

As the years went by, the Secrets of La Salette became irrevocably present in the public realm.

This knowledge convinced many Catholics that to know the contents of a secret revelation was crucial to understand the critical times in which they lived.

The Church also found itself in a most uncomfortable situation after La Salette.

While wanting to reap the fruits of authentic events, the presence of secrets placed its very trustworthiness on the line. Church officials were torn between understanding the public's desire to know, and its mission to protect sound doctrine from contamination and confusion.

This problem has not gone away.

According to one investigative writer, thirty-one alleged apparition sites in two dozen countries in the course of the twentieth century alone have been discovered to have secrets given to visionaries.[25]

In short, there is no limit to the ramifications of what the Secrets of La Salette have meant to the drama of many later Marian apparitions—especially to those that have also revealed secret messages, such as at Lourdes, where the Virgin gave Bernadette Soubirous three secrets she never revealed,[26] and at Fátima and Medjugorje.

Like with Pius IX and La Salette, the anguish brought upon the popes of the twentieth century due to the Secret of Fátima is evident and well documented. From Pope Pius XI through Benedict XVI, every pope for almost a century labored under the controversies surrounding the prophecies of Fátima.

But even after the Secret was revealed—and the 20th century was over—the controversies remained.

As did the troubled world it was meant to help.

"The tragedies foretold in Fátima did not come to an end with the demise of Communism," bemoaned Pope Benedict XVI, "The crisis has not been resolved."[27]

CHAPTER THREE

The Winter of Tomorrow

*"He answered them, 'It is not for you to know the times or
seasons that the Father has established by His own authority.'"*
—Acts 1:7

At La Salette, two Secrets were given by Mary, one to each of the
visionaries.

At Fátima, there were three parts to what Sister Lúcia termed to be
one Secret.

But now, at Medjugorje, there are Ten Secrets being given to each
of the six visionaries.

What is Mary doing at Medjugorje with so many Secrets?

"It is certain that the Secrets of Medjugorje contain impetus for us,"
advised Father Slavko Barbarić, a Franciscan assigned to the St. James
parish at Medjugorje in September of 1985. "The messages tell us what
we have to know for now. The fact of secrets is found again and again in
Marian apparitions; obviously they belong to the educational method
of the Blessed Mother, which trains one to patience and an ability to
wait. We must wait for much until the time for it has come."[1]

"The word 'secret' has a magical effect on people," said Mariologist
Father Joseph Pelletier, "it arouses curiosity and stimulates interest.

God makes use of this to draw attention to the message He wishes to transmit through His heavenly messenger."[2]

Father René Laurentin says it's apparent that Mary is giving so many Secrets to her visionaries at Medjugorje because the times are urgent, and the future is threatened:

"The world is destroying itself. It is vehemently preparing its own destruction for having struggled, forgotten, or relegated the essential: God and His law of love, which the messages of Medjugorje recall."[3]

Laurentin—a renowned scholar on the subject of apparitions—can be seen to be addressing the fact that the apparitions at Medjugorje have strong apocalyptic elements, as seen at Fátima, and are reminiscent of passages found in Scripture.

Examples of the apocalyptic in the Bible are many, but predominantly recalled in the Old Testament books of *Daniel, Ezekiel*, and *Zechariah*, along with certain books in the New Testament, most notably *The Book of Revelation*.[4]

Theologians say that Jesus's most apocalyptic statements in the Gospels are found in *Mark*, Chapter 13, Luke 21, and especially in *Matthew*, Chapters 24-25:

"Nation will rise against nation, and kingdom against kingdom; there will be famines and earthquakes from place to place."[5]

Apocalyptic, though, is not only about content, but also style, and the two cannot be separated.

Apocalyptic style embraces symbols, images, and visions to express religious concepts.

In *Daniel*, Chapter 7, the mysterious Son of Man figure is used by Jesus in His teaching on the end of the world.[6]

In *Matthew*, Chapter 25, Jesus speaks of the separation of the sheep from the goats to symbolize the Last Judgment.[7]

The Book of Revelation abounds in symbolism and allegorical language that is comparable to that of the Old Testament.

Apocalyptic is also different from prophecy.

Prophecy calls us to change, to convert our lives to God.[8] It condemns sin and infidelity to the Lord. Most of all, prophecy calls us to faith and leads us to prayer, to confession. It calls us to reconciliation with God and with one another. This will bring peace, Mary's chosen ones tell us, that God wants His children to experience in their lives and in the world.

At Medjugorje, what is occurring is both "apocalyptic and prophetic," says mystical theologian Father Robert Faricy.[9]

Faricy states that this is found at Medjugorje in a variety of ways: The Ten Secrets and their implied content; the many references to the Devil; the promised Sign that is to appear on Podbrdo and the mysterious wonders witnessed in the village—strange lights, solar miracles, visions experienced by visitors, and the many miraculous healings.[10]

Most of all, the apparitions announce that the future belongs to the Lord, which is a strong confirmation of the prophetic makeup of the revelations. Writes Faricy:

> The messages are prophetic, but many elements that make up the content of those messages are apocalyptic. Prophecy tells us what to do. Apocalyptic tells us what God intends to do. It sees history as completely under the Lordship of Jesus Christ. The future belongs to God. He is the Lord of history, in charge of the world and everything in it. The future lies hidden in the Lord's hands because it belongs to Him. He holds the future, and He makes it present to us now in a mysterious and hidden way, through signs and symbols.

> Furthermore, apocalyptic confronts evil squarely. Its strong vision of God's power and lordship makes possible a clear vision of evil in this world. Belief in the reality of Satan, in fact, comes from the Old Testament apocalyptic tradition. In the New Testament, the apocalyptic victory is already present in Jesus, He defeats sin, death, and Satan, triumphing by His Cross and Resurrection.[11]

We especially find much of this in the Ten Secrets of Medjugorje, says Faricy.

The Secrets, from what is known about them, are to confront the evil of today with the power of God, who completely tells us what He is going to do, that He is the Lord of history and that He will defeat sin, death, and demonic influence.

As the Virgin has said at both Fátima and Medjugorje, we see God's intent to change the world through the apparitions of Mary *will* come.[12]

"The Ten Secrets tell us we can have hope in the future," assures Faricy. "They console us because they say to us that we do not know what the future holds, but we do know who holds the future—the Lord…True, the future holds some terrible things. But it belongs to the Lord. The *terrible things* coming do not dim His Lordship or His victory. We can trust in Him."[13]

⟞⟝

"I have chosen you; I have confided in you everything that is essential. I have also shown you many *terrible things*," said the Virgin Mary to a stunned Mirjana on December 25, 1982, the day she received her Tenth and last Secret. "You must now bear it all with courage. Think of me and think of the tears I must shed for that. You must remain brave."[14]

Mary's words of encouragement in discharging the final Secret to Mirjana are revealing. Something incredibly challenging awaits her, and—for that matter—the whole world.

So, the obvious question stands before us: What kind of *terrible things* was Mary speaking of, in giving such consoling yet serious advice to her official mouthpiece, the one chosen to reveal the Ten Secrets to the world?

In an age when no one has to be told that nuclear missiles can flash through the air like Zeus throwing lightning bolts, there is no need to strain the imagination as to what could come upon mankind. The potential divine justice of tomorrow's world certainly has already been crafted by the hands of today's man.

"We didn't need an apparition to convince us that nuclear war is a possibility," observed Father Slavko Barbarić at Medjugorje. "If a house is on fire, it doesn't burn down because the mother shouts fire."[15]

Indeed, as when Mary came to Fátima during the throes of World War I, today's dangers are before us, firmly in place, poised to strike.

Mary has not come to bemoan the obvious.

In 1917, the world was very aware of its man-made misery.

The Secret of Fátima simply foretold that another round of even *worse* misery—a second world war and more—was in the cards if her words were not heeded.

The *terrible things* contained in the Ten Secrets of Medjugorje that Mary speaks of are presented in this same light. We need only to look around and see how we have already constructed a world flirting with destruction.

Mary comes again to try to wake us up to this reality, before it's too late.

"Regarding the question of the apocalyptic dimension," explained Father Barbarić, in a July 14, 1987, interview in Medjugorje, "Our Lady has pointed the way to peace. Certainly, we understand the possibility for catastrophe to occur… It depends on us to avoid catastrophe."[16]

Yes, it does.

But Mary's call at Medjugorje to the world at this time goes beyond a plea to save it from catastrophe.

The Ten Secrets—unlike the Secret of Fátima—do not hold a plan within them to prevent their coming, only to mitigate them. This is because Mary has come this time not to stop the errors of our age but to *end* them, and to prepare the world for a new era that will experience some trying times to help it get here.

Times that will come with the Secrets.

~∞~

Medjugorje's call, therefore, is first and foremost an awakening; it's a call to every person on earth to be aware of their eternal plight—and to their temporal one—in light of what the Secrets hold. Indeed, the message contains a resounding urgency to respond to the graces being given at this time in history.

"Hasten your conversion," the Virgin told the six visionaries in a message shared with the world in the spring of 1983, "do not await the Sign (the Third Secret) which has been announced, for people who do not believe, it will be too late."[17]

Two years later, this urgency is heard again:

"Now is the time for conversion. I have been exhorting you for the last four years. Be converted before it will be too late."[18]

Twenty years later, this plea continued to resound at Medjugorje:

"Today, the Lord permitted me to tell you *again* that you live in a time of grace. You are not conscious, little children, that God is giving you a great opportunity to convert…"[19]

~∞~

These messages—as with her message to Mirjana on the day she received the Tenth Secret—seem to indicate that what is to come will not come easily but will come suddenly. Some difficult—what the Virgin Mary called "*terrible*"—days lie ahead, with eternal consequences at stake for those who continue to choose to remain on their sinful paths.

This is why Mary told Mirjana to "think of the tears I must shed."

While Pope John Paul II wrote of the "springtime" that is to come in the Church and the world in the new millennium,[20] the message at Medjugorje is clear: whether one is a believer or not, the autumn of today is leading to the winter of tomorrow.

"I have prayed," the Virgin Mary told Mirjana on November 6, 1982, "the punishment has been softened. Repeated prayers and fasting reduce punishments from God, but it is not possible to avoid the chastisement entirely. Go on the streets of the city, count those who glorify God and those who offend Him.

"God can no longer endure that."[21]

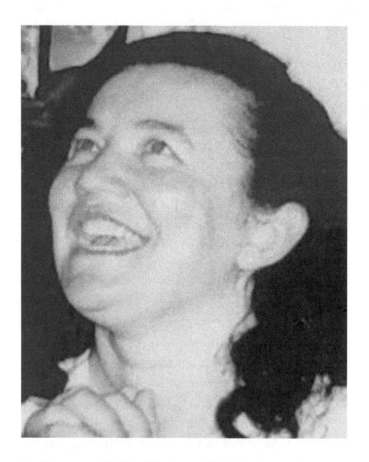

Vicka Ivanković Mijatovic

"I'll just say this: whoever does not believe without a sign will not believe with a sign. And, I'll tell you this too: woe to him who delays his conversion waiting for a sign."

Photo Credit: Renee Laurentin

CHAPTER FOUR

A Voice Crying in the Wilderness

"Indeed, the Lord does nothing without revealing his plan to his servants, the prophets."

—Am 3:7

He will go before the Lord in the spirit and power of the prophet Elijah, wrote Saint Luke of the coming of John the Baptist.[1]

Needless to say, the Virgin Mary's arrival in Medjugorje on June 24, 1981—the feast day of the Baptist—was meant to be strategic with regards to her mission.

It was, in essence, a theological exclamation point on the start of her mission.

Like Elijah and the Baptist, Mary was in the world to make straight the path of the Lord. She had come to lay the ax to the root, to call down the fire, to cry in the wilderness—and no better day on the Church calendar signaled this spiritual D-Day than the Baptist's feast.

The Virgin's early words at Medjugorje, however, were measured.

God's allotted period of her visitation was somewhat set.

A certain time for conversion, she repeated, was underway. Divine mercy, though incomprehensibly infinite, was on a finite schedule.

We are living in a "time of grace," wrote Mirjana in her 2016 book, echoing the Virgin's words. After this will come, she made clear, "the time of the Ten Secrets, and then the time of Mary's triumph."[2]

While those who follow Medjugorje ponder the length of these periods, one thing is known for sure: With each minute, each hour, each day, the time of the Secrets draws nearer as the time of grace slips away, gone forever.

Mirjana, in 2007, perhaps best defined the moment:

"Our Lady said that this time in which we live is a time of decision."[3]

It should be a decision to change, to convert one's life to God, she writes in her book, to prepare for the future by "preparing your soul."

This is *not* done, Mirjana made abundantly clear, by "erecting bunkers and stockpiling supplies."[4]

<hr />

Time.

It's the friend of the young and the foe of the old.

It can be on your side; it can be against you.

It waits for no one.

Time, like life, has a past, a present, and a future. Jesus, cautioned against the future: "Do not worry about tomorrow; tomorrow will take care of itself."

But the Lord was speaking about the concerns of the temporal world, not the eternal. The Secrets of Medjugorje—whatever they may hold—sound more like "the day of the Lord coming like a thief in the night," and one needs to be prepared.[5]

It is a day that we can assume is undeniably closer, just by contemplating a few of the words Mirjana used in speaking about the Ten Secrets in her book.

Referring back to an incident in 1985 that involved Ivanka receiving the Tenth Secret, Mirjana called it a time when the Secrets were still "many years away," a remark that leads one to logically conclude that she is inferring that such can no longer be said to be the case.[6]

So, just what is known about these Ten Secrets that point to the more serious warnings in Scripture regarding one's eternity?

Why will it be too late for some by the time the Third Secret arrives?

Some of Mary's early messages at Medjugorje speak directly of the contents of the Secrets, but most of what we know comes from the visionaries. Essentially, they have said only what they are able to say since the Secrets are, well, secret.

This conundrum involving "the secrecy of the Secrets" has been noted before.

In Lourdes, two parish priests asked Bernadette, "Would you disclose your Secret to the Pope?" Bernadette replied, "The Blessed Virgin forbids me to disclose it to any person. The Pope is a person."

At Fátima, the parish priest commended the three children:

"You are doing well, my children—what for yourself, and or God—to keep the Secret of your souls."[7]

The same is found at Medjugorje.

But some of the visionaries' words do provide a salient look into this mystery.

⌇⌇

The six visionaries—polite and patient over the years—cannot escape the shadow of their Secrets.

Day in and day out, for decades now, people have bombarded them with questions about them.

What is in them?

When are they coming?

Will the Secrets be good or bad?

At Fátima, the three children would retire into absolute silence—"to the point of rudeness"—when having to answer the everyday people who tortured them with questions about their Secret.[8] Quite perturbed by it all, their delicate consciences eventually only surrendered to the requests of priests, who they felt had, as one writer put it, "somewhat of a legal right to ask such questions."[9]

Over time, the six visionaries at Medjugorje have adopted a twofold response to public questions surrounding the Secrets: 1) the Secrets are off limits; 2) their contents—while disconcerting—are of no paramount concern if one's soul is right with God.

Though it has been almost forty years since the Ten Secrets were first revealed to be part of the Madonna's revelations at Medjugorje, most of what is known about them came about in the first ten years.

During this time, we find almost all of the known messages in which Mary herself actually speaks of the Secrets.

It's also during this period that the visionaries appear to be somewhat more forthcoming during personal interviews regarding them.

Perhaps because of their desire to prove the apparitions were true, or because of the trust built up between them and some of their early inquisitors—or because of youthful indiscretions—these early dialogues give us the best insight into the overall nature and content of the Ten Secrets.

~~∞~~

It's known that the visionaries at Fátima received their three-part Secret from the Virgin Mary on July 13, 1917.

But no such precise starting date is established as the official beginning of the revelation of the Ten Secrets of Medjugorje.

Father Svetozar Kraljević, in his seminal work, *The Apparitions of Our Lady of Medjugorje, 1981-1983: An Historical Account with Interviews*, provided what appears to be the first substantive look at the Secrets.

At the time, Father Kraljević was a true insider at Medjugorje. Sent to the United States in 1975 to finish his theology training, he was ordained in 1977 and then served in New York City.

Returning home in 1982 to visit his relatives, less than a year after the apparitions began, he was suddenly told his passport was no longer valid and could not return to the United States.

Consequently, Father Svet—as he is best known—immediately set his sights on going to Medjugorje, which he had already heard about in America.

This led to the penning of his book.[10]

Around this same time, Father René Laurentin began to write, *Is the Virgin Mary Appearing at Medjugorje?* The book included within it a small, reconstituted Croatian book on Medjugorje written by Father Ljudevit Rupčić.

Rupčić, imprisoned by the Communists three times,[11] was a New Testament exegesis professor at Franjevacka Teologija[12] (Franciscan School of Theology) and had also taught at the University of Zagreb.[13] His original book, *The Apparitions of Our Lady at Medjugorje*—the first of five books on Medjugorje, with the last coming in 1991—was published in Croatia in 1983.[14] It contained what appears to be the first formal contact with the visionaries, which included several of his questions to them regarding the Secrets.

At the time, Rupčić confessed, he wasn't too convinced about the visions, perceiving Medjugorje as a "joke."[15]

Because both Kraljević's and Laurentin's books were scheduled to be published around the same time, Laurentin was permitted a pre-publication look at Father Svetozar's manuscript. In this way, said Laurentin, he would try not to harmonize the books but to maintain their differences.[16]

The bibliography of Laurentin's first book reveals he reviewed—to the best of his knowledge—all the reports, articles, and short pamphlet-type writings available on Medjugorje at the time, including any dialogues with the visionaries that addressed the Secrets.

Likewise, Kraljević's book, though not profoundly informative about the Secrets, also contained interviews with the visionaries that shed light on them.

Together, the two books start to reveal the seriousness of their content.

It is a seriousness that will intensify as time goes on.

CHAPTER FIVE

The Last Apparition?

"Because, when I called, no one answered,
when I spoke, no one listened."

—Is 66: 4

None of the early books on Medjugorje establish an official time-line on the revelation of the Ten Secrets.

But they offer clues.

The presence of the disturbing prophecies would begin to be-come visible—although haphazardly and unintendedly—through the publication of Father René Laurentin's second book on Medjugorje, *Messages and Teachings of Mary at Medjugorje, Chronological Corpus of the Messages.* Laurentin co-authored this effort with Father René Lejeune, a professor who had worked at Alger, Strasbourg, São Paulo, and Geneva.[1]

By 1985, Laurentin felt that it was necessary—even in compliance with Mary's request to "study and live" her messages—that a complete corpus of all available messages since the beginning of the apparitions be assembled in chronological order.

This effort by Laurentin and Lejeune would come from a variety of sources: the visionaries, the priests, the diaries and journals kept (especially Vicka Ivankovic's diary of the apparitions and Ivan's diary that he kept while in the seminary), and especially the official records of the Franciscans, who maintained a logue of the events and messages at Medjugorje in what was termed "the parish chronicle," or better known as "The Chronicle of the Apparitions," as referenced by Dr. Ljudevit Rupčić and Dr. Viktor Nuić.[2]

Laurentin and Lejeune especially referred to a 1986 book by Father Y. M. Blais titled, *Five Hundred Messages to Live*.[3]

It appears that all contemporary compilation books and website histories of the Virgin Mary's early revelations at Medjugorje were drawn out of this effort by the two men.

※

While the history of the Virgin's messages at Medjugorje primarily emerges from this book of Laurentin and Lejeune, there is a question of the preciseness of the Virgin's words in the early messages.

Rupčić and Nuić addressed this issue in their 2002 book, *Once Again, the Truth About Medjugorje*:

"The visionaries themselves cannot guarantee letter by letter what Our Lady said. If the four Evangelists differ amongst themselves in their reports about the same event, then there is no wonder that perhaps the visionaries differ in their reports. Fr. Tomislav Vlašić himself on page 40 of the "*Chronicle of the Apparitions*" writes that it is evident that the visionaries do not relay word for word the replies that they received, but in their own words which can give the response a different tone and as such it is necessary to take account of that when referring to the inadequacy of the children's memories, their manner of expression and their behavior."[4]

This documented assertion forces us to conclude that almost all of the early messages at Medjugorje—prior to the beginning of the weekly "parish messages" on March 1, 1984—must be understood as not being "verbatim accounts" of what the Virgin Mary said to the visionaries on any given date.

Of course, it can be assumed that *some* are precise, but there is no way of knowing for sure.

———∽∝∽———

From Laurentin and Lejeune 's work, we discover that the words Secret and Secrets do not appear at all in Mary's messages given during the first year, which runs from June 24 to December 31, 1981.

Some points of interest with regard to the Secrets, however, do manifest during this initial period.

The more serious nature of the Virgin's message at Medjugorje, which Father Robert Faricy defines as "apocalyptic" in theme, starts to develop early.

First, on June 26, Mary tells the visionaries:

"I wish to convert and reconcile the whole world—to convert all of you."

Then, on August 2, she discloses the reason why:

"A great battle is about to take place. A battle between my Son and Satan. Human souls are at stake."

With this declaration, Mary's words echo for the most part what Sister Lúcia of Fátima reportedly stated the Virgin told her about a great spiritual battle unfolding in the 20th century, most notably revealed in her December 26, 1957, interview with Father Augustine Fuentes Anguiano, the vice-postulator for the beatification of Francisco and Jacinta.[5]

By September, the Virgin is seen to be stressing the seriousness of her coming.

She now consistently asks for conversion, something that will be forever a staple of her message in Medjugorje. And, during this period, there emerges a running exchange between Mary and the children concerning their requests for a sign. These conversations gradually evolve from talk of a sign in general, to the coming of the "Great Sign" that will become the cornerstone of the Third Secret.

The most revealing message that the "sign" Mary is speaking of *is* actually one of the Ten Secrets comes on September 4, when the Madonna says to the children:

"The sign will be given at the end of the apparitions."

From this point on, dialogue regarding the sign can be seen to grow more specific, as the promised sign is slowly revealed as the "Great Sign" contained in the Ten Secrets.

Then, on October 12 and 17, and again on October 22, the first substantive indication of the Secrets is found. It occurs in a discussion the visionaries have with Mary concerning ongoing reports of supernatural phenomena erupting in the village, including claims that many people saw the cross on Mt. Krizevac transform itself into a light, and then into a silhouette of the Virgin.

"Is the whiteness of the cross a supernatural phenomenon?" the children asked of the Virgin.

"All of these signs are designed to strengthen your faith," Mary responds, "until I leave you the visible and permanent Sign."

With this response, Mary's answer directly points to the presence of the Secrets, which are to reveal the Great (permanent) Sign. But, it's unknown whether or not at this time she is still referring to the Sign outside of the broader context of it being one of the Ten Secrets.

The dialogue between Mary and the visionaries that occurs six days later, on October 28, again points to the Third Secret—the "permanent Sign." Several hundred people see a mysterious fire burning on Podbrdo that suddenly vanished.

Mary subsequently confirms to the visionaries its mysterious nature, and in doing so, alludes to the Secrets:

"The fire seen by the faithful was of a supernatural character. It is *one* of the signs; a forerunner of the Great Sign."

As can be seen, her words directly speak of the contents of the Secrets.

However, it is still not confirmable from the Laurentin and Lejeune corpus of messages that the visionaries at this time understood the Great Sign as one of the Ten Secrets.

In November, two more messages speak of the urgency surrounding the Virgin's visitation at Medjugorje. On Sunday, November 22, Mary stated:

"The world must find salvation while there is time."

One week later, on November 29, she virtually repeats herself:

"It is necessary for the world to be saved while there is time."

These become the last messages in 1981 that can be understood to be indirectly associated in some way to the Secrets.

———

There is no specific mention of the Ten Secrets in the first seven months of the apparitions in 1982, according to Laurentin and Lejeune's corpus.

There are, however, two revelations that are relative to the Secrets and are of significant importance because of the amount of discussion surrounding them over the years.

On Sunday, May 2, 1982, the Virgin told the visionaries:

"I have come to call the world to conversion for the last time. Later, I will not appear any more on this Earth."

Then, on June 23—just prior to the first anniversary of the visions—Vicka asked Mary a set of questions that were posed by priests. Within her answers (recorded in the "parish chronicle"), Mary confirms her previous statement:

"These apparitions are the last in the world."

To this day, there is no consensus on the exact meaning of the Virgin's words.

It is worthy to note that Mary has made similar statements before, as during her Church-approved apparitions at Beauraing in 1932 and 1933.

On December 23, 1932, Mary told the five children in Beauraing:

"Soon, I shall appear for the last time."[6]

One other message at Medjugorje stands out during this time frame, which could be seen by some to be related to the Secrets' apocalyptic overtones. On July 12,1982, Mary was asked if there would be another world war. She replied:

"The Third World War will not take place."

〜〜〜

On August 15, 1982, the subject of the Ten Secrets was first acknowledged in the Laurentin and Lejeune message timeline. Its entry again originates from the St. James parish chronicle:

"The vision lasted about seven minutes. The Gospa entrusted *a new Secret* to Vicka and Ivanka—only to them. The others saw that it was about a Secret, but they did not understand anything."

The historical relevance here is twofold.

Not only is the presence of the Ten Secrets documented for the first time in the Laurentin and Lejeune book, but from what is written, it is clear that an *undocumented reality* of the Ten Secrets has been ongoing for quite some time—possibly, according to other sources, as early as July, maybe even June, of 1981.

Fathers Barbarić and Vlašić allude to this in their 1985 book, *Open Your Hearts to Mary Queen of Peace*:

"These visionaries say that, from the very beginning, Our Lady told them she would confide ten secrets to them for the whole of humanity."[7]

Likewise, Mirjana is also on record as telling one interviewer that the Virgin began to speak about the Secrets in the first week of the apparitions.[8]

On August 31, 1982, the Virgin Mary spoke again of the Great Sign. This revelation alludes to the fact—which the visionaries have asserted concerning all Ten Secrets—that each Secret will come to pass, at least to some degree, regardless of the world's response:

"The Great Sign has been granted. It will appear *independently* of the conversion of the people."

〜〜〜

Over the remaining months of 1982 and throughout 1983, Mary's messages to the six visionaries—as documented by Laurentin and Lejeune—reveal little more of importance involving the Ten Secrets as a whole.

But a significant development does come into play before the end of 1983 concerning the reality of the Ten Secrets.

Marija told the Franciscans that the Virgin Mary wanted a letter immediately sent to the Pope concerning the exigency of the message at Medjugorje:

"You must warn the Bishop very soon, and the Pope, with respect to the urgent and the great importance of the message for all humanity."[9]

By virtue of this letter—for the first time—somewhat of an official, written summary from the Church is compiled concerning the nature and history of the apparitions at Medjugorje. A significant portion of the factual information for it is attained from a meeting with Mirjana on November 5, 1983.[10]

Most noteworthy, within the letter's contents, there is found a brief summary of the existence and makeup of the Ten Secrets.

The following is an excerpt of the letter:

December 2, 1983

After the apparition of the Blessed Virgin on November 30, 1983, Marija Pavlović came to see me and said, "The Madonna says that the Supreme Pontiff and the Bishop must be advised immediately of the urgency and great importance of the message of Medjugorje."

This letter seeks to fulfill that duty.

1. Five young people (Vicka Ivanković, Marija Pavlović, Ivanka Ivanković, Ivan Dragićević, and Jacov Čolo) see an apparition of the Blessed Virgin every day. The experience in which they see her is a fact that can be checked by direct observation. It has been filmed. During the apparitions the youngsters do not react to light,

they do not hear sounds, they do not react if someone touches them, they feel that they are beyond time and space.

All of the youngsters basically agree that:

- "We see the Blessed Virgin just as we see anyone else. We pray with her, we speak to her, and we can touch her."
- "The Blessed Virgin says that world peace is at a critical stage. She repeatedly calls for reconciliation and conversion."
- "She has promised to leave a visible sign for all humanity at the sight of the apparitions at Medjugorje."
- "The period preceding this visible sign is a time of grace for conversion and deepening of faith."
- "The Blessed Virgin has promised to disclose ten secrets to us. So far, Vicka Ivanković has received eight. Marija Pavlović received the ninth one on Dec 8, 1983. Jacov Čolo, Ivan Dragićević and Ivanka Ivanković have each received nine. Only Mirjana Dragićević has received all ten."
- "These apparitions are the last apparitions of the Blessed Virgin on Earth. That is why they are lasting so long and occurring so frequently."

2. The Blessed Virgin no longer appears to Mirjana Dragićević. The last time she saw one of the daily apparitions was Christmas, 1982. Since then, the apparitions have ceased for her, except on her birthday (March 18, 1983). Mirjana knew that this latter would occur.
3. According to Mirjana, the Madonna confided the tenth and last secret to her during the apparition of December 25, 1982. She also disclosed the dates on when the different secrets will come to pass. The Blessed Virgin has revealed to Mirjana many things about the future, more than to any of the other youngsters so far. For that reason, I am reporting below what Mirjana told me during our conversation on Nov 5, 1983. I am summarizing the substance of her account, *without* word for word quotations.

Mirjana said,

Before the visible sign is given to humanity, there will be three warnings to the world. The warnings will be in the form of events on the Earth. Mirjana will be a witness to them. Three days before one of the admonitions, Mirjana will notify a priest of her choice. The witness of Mirjana will be a confirmation of the apparitions and stimulus for the conversion of the world. After the admonitions, the visible sign will appear on the site of the apparitions of Medjugorje for all the world to see. The sign will be given as a testimony to the apparitions and in order to call people back to the faith.

The Ninth and Tenth Secrets are serious. They concern chastisement for the sins of the world. Punishment is inevitable, for we cannot expect the whole world to be converted. The punishment can be diminished by prayer and penance. But it cannot be eliminated. Mirjana says that one of the evils that threatened the world, the one contained in the Seventh Secret, has been averted thanks to prayer and fasting. That is why the Blessed Virgin continues to encourage prayer and fasting: *"You have forgotten that through prayer and fasting you can avert war and suspend the laws of nature."*

After the first admonition, the others will follow in a rather short time. Thus, people will have some time for conversion.

That interval will be a period of grace and conversion. After the visible sign appears those who are still alive will have little time for conversion. For that reason, the Blessed Virgin invites us to urgent conversion and reconciliation.

The invitation to prayer and penance is meant to avert evil and war, but most of all to save souls.

According to Mirjana, the events predicted by the Blessed Virgin are near. By virtue of this experience, Mirjana proclaims to the world: "Hurry, be converted; open your hearts to God..."[11]

⋙

As noted, the letter to the Pope begins to pull back the veil on the Secrets.

It established, in a somewhat official manner, not just their existence, but their emerging role in the gravity of the Medjugorje apparitions.

Indeed, the letter put the world on notice that the call to conversion at Medjugorje, as with Fátima, was a serious proposition, one that now—in a way—even affected the Pope.

CHAPTER SIX

A Time of Grace

"For merciful and compassionate is the Lord, your God, and he will not turn away his face from you if you return to him."
—2 Chr 30:9

She needed to be secret about the Secret.

This was what the Virgin Mary asked of Sister Lúcia concerning the second part of the Secret of Fátima, which involved foretold chastisements of all humanity.

Although Lúcia would begin to reveal some of the first part of the Secret in 1925—the vision of Hell—it was not until 1941 that she deliberately set about to make the powerful, prophetic second part of the Secret of Fátima known in writing.[1]

Prior to then, not only had Lúcia not written of it, but she had not truly spoken of it publicly.

❧

Though Lúcia was interviewed at her convent by a number of notable visitors in 1946 alone; Father Hubert Jongen on February 3 and 4; Professor William Thomas Walsh, with Fathers Galamba, Roca and

Furtado on July 15; Father Louis de Gonzague, accompanied by John Haffert (who also met with Lúcia in1952 and 1955) on August 12; and Canon Casmir Barthas on October 17 and 18, nothing was publicly forthcoming about the Secret of Fátima.

Lúcia's multiple visits with Father Thomas McGlynn—the sculptor who Lúcia helped perfect the famed statue of Our Lady of Fátima— beginning in February of 1947; Father Gustav Wetter on August 14, 1951—who delivered a message to Pius XII for her; Father Joseph Schweigl on September 2,1952—an Austrian Jesuit who was sent to Fátima by Pius XII to interrogate Lúcia about the Third Secret, and others less notable, were also kept confidential at the time.

Aside from the books that would emerge from these audiences with Lúcia, only Father Ricardo Lombardi—the well-known Jesuit and founder of *The Better World Movement* who was a friend of Pius XII—wrote and published a circumstantial account of his meeting with Lúcia. It appeared in the Vatican newspaper, *L'Osservatore della Domenica*, on February 7, 1954, and within it Lúcia reveals the seriousness of the Virgin's message at Fátima.

The story reported how Lombardi interviewed Lúcia in October 1953—"behind the grill at Coimbra"—and in answer to a question, Lúcia said to the priest:

"If humanity does not seek to perfect itself, given the way in which it behaves now, only a limited part of the human race will be saved."[2]

After this, it would not be until 1957—with the controversial disclosure of Father Augustin Fuentas Anguiano at a conference in Mexico—that a substantive interview with Lucia concerning Fátima's grave message was revealed.

This would come almost forty years after the 1917 apparitions at Fátima.

⤛⤜

At Medjugorje, the opposite is found to occur.

The mysterious existence of the Ten Secrets was brought to life relatively early on in the history of the visions. But, unlike with Fátima, this is especially a result of the probing interviews with the visionaries that were conducted there at the time.

Four of the most significant interviews ever done with the visionaries at Medjugorje took place in 1982 and 1983. They were published in books by Father René Laurentin, Father Svetozar Kraljević and Father Janko Bubalo.

Consequently, with these interviews—as with La Salette and Fátima—the harrowing world of the Ten Secrets is now upon the public.

<hr/>

The first of these dialogues involves all six visionaries and Father Ljudevit Rupčić.

A highly edited version of this interview was published in Laurentin's 1984 book, *Is the Virgin Mary Appearing at Medjugorje?*

Rupčić, a Croatian professor, presented to the children sixty-two questions, some of which involved the Secrets. At the time, Rupčić met with each of them separately and gathered their independent and converging answers.

He would repeat this same sixty-two question interview in 1987.

It is with this seminal interview of Rupčić that the curtain on the Ten Secrets of Medjugorje begins to be drawn back.

The following is a portion of the original, *unedited* transcript of Rupčić's interview conducted in December of 1982, the same month the report on Medjugorje was sent to the Pope.

It involves only those questions that concern the Secrets.

It is not known if this original version of the interview has been ever published before.

Rupčić: *Has the Lady entrusted some Secrets to you?*

Marija Pavlović: Yes, I know six secrets. The rest of us, some have seven, some eight. They pertain to us, the Church, people in general.

Jacov Čolo: Yes, they pertain to our lives, and people.

Vicka Ivanković: Yes, I have seven of them. The first pertains to our church in Medjugorje, to the Sign, the whole humanity and everybody, the Church in general and there are some for us.

Ivanka Ivanković: Yes, I have eight. They pertain to us, personally, the Church and the world.

Mirjana Dragićević: Yes, I have nine entrusted to me. They pertain to us, the Sign…the whole world, and Medjugorje.

Ivan Dragićević: Yes.

Rupčić: *Did the Lady have a message for the world?*

Marija Pavlović: All the messages relate to the world. There are messages for peace, for faith, conversions, prayers, fast and penance.

Jacov Čolo: You have to pray, fast, return to faith, so that there will be peace.

Vicka Ivanković: She tells us to pray, do penance, return to faith, peace; the most important is the message for peace. She announced this!

Ivanka Ivanković: The "Lady" said that it is most important to have strong faith, that we should pray every day at least seven Our Fathers,' seven Hail Marys,' seven Glory Be's and the one "I Believe." And to fast on bread and water on Fridays.

Mirjana Dragićević: She emphasized that prayers are important Faith, fast: that with this wars and catastrophes can be averted. Today we have very much of this.

Ivan Dragićević: That you must return to your faith, and that it become more secure and deep, and that way be transferred from knee to knee.

Rupčić: *Are you allowed to tell the Secrets to others?*
Marija Pavlović: We cannot. The Lady told us whom we will tell.
Jacov Čolo: We cannot until she tells us.
Vicka Ivanković: No. We cannot until she tells us.
Ivanka Ivanković: No, to no one.
Mirjana Dragićević: No.
Ivan Dragićević: No.

Rupčić: *Are the Secrets good or bad about the world?*
Marija Pavlović: Well now, that is a secret.
Jacov Čolo: There is good and there is bad.
Vicka Ivanković: There is good and bad.
Ivanka Ivanković: There is good and there is bad.
Mirjana Dragićević: There is good and there is bad.
Ivan Dragićević: (Rupčić: *Same as above.*)

Rupčić: *When will the Lady allow you to reveal these Secrets?*
Marija Pavlović: I don't know. She will tell us when, and to whom.
Jacov Čolo: Don't know.
Vicka Ivanković: When she tells us.
Ivanka Ivanković: Don't know.
Mirjana Dragićević: She didn't tell us yet.
Ivan Dragićević: When she allows it.

Rupčić: *Did the Lady promise to do anything special by which the remaining will know that she is the Lady?*
Marija Pavlović: The Lady said she will leave a sign for those who do not believe.
Jacov Čolo: Yes, she will leave a Great Sign.
Vicka Ivanković: She said she will leave a Great Sign.
Ivanka Ivanković: Yes, the Lady said that she will leave a Great Sign on the mountain of the apparition.

Mirjana Dragićević: Yes.
Ivan Dragićević: Yes.

Rupčić: *When will that Sign be given?*
Marija Pavlović: And that is a secret.
Jacov Čolo: We know this but can't reveal it.
Vicka Ivanković: We know but cannot say.
Ivanka Ivanković: It's not important.
Mirjana Dragićević: That is one of the Secrets.
Ivan Dragićević: That is a secret.

Rupčić: *Will this special sign, which is announced by the Lady, be seen by everyone?*
Marija Pavlović: It will be.
Jacov Čolo: It will be.
Vicka Ivanković: It will be.
Ivanka Ivanković: Certainly
Mirjana Dragićević: Yes.
Ivan Dragićević: Yes.

Rupčić: *When will the Sign be?*
Marija Pavlović: And that is a secret.
Jacov Čolo: We know this but cannot reveal it.
Vicka Ivanković: I know. I am not allowed to tell. Otherwise, I would.
Ivanka Ivanković: I know.
Mirjana Dragićević: This I cannot tell you.
Ivan Dragićević: This a secret.

Rupčić: *Would you swear that that which you have said is the truth?*
Marija Pavlović: I would.
Jacov Čolo: I would.

Vicka Ivanković: I would a hundred times, not once!
Ivanka Ivanković: Why naturally, yes.!
Mirjana Dragićević: Naturally I would!
Ivan Dragićević: I would! [3]

～∞～

The second of these dialogues involves Mirjana Dragićević and was published by Father Svetozar Kraljević. It was conducted on January 10, 1983, just a month after Father Rupčić's interview.

Identical extracts of this interview were published in both Kraljević's book, *The Apparitions of Our Lady at Medjugorje* and *Laurentin's Is the Virgin Mary Appearing at Medjugorje?*

Through these two books, the Ten Secrets of Medjugorje started to attract significant attention by the mid-80s.

This is enhanced by the fact that they hold the first known published interview to take place with Mirjana after she received the tenth and final Secret.

Question: *You said that the 20th century has been given over to the Devil?*
Mirjana: Yes.
Question: *You mean the century until the year 2000, or generally speaking?*
Mirjana: Generally, part of which is in the 20th century, until the First Secret is revealed. The Devil will rule till then. She told me several Secrets and explained them to me; and I have them written down in code letters, with dates, so I won't forget them. If, say, tomorrow a Secret is to be revealed, I have a right, two or three days before, to pick whatever priest I want and tell him about it. For example: "The day after tomorrow, such and such will happen." The priest, then, is free to do as he thinks best with that information. He can write it out before it happens, then read it to others after it happens. He can also tell it to the

people; "Tomorrow, such-and-such will happen." It's up to him to decide what to do with the information.

Question: *Were these Secrets ever revealed before to anybody in previous generations?*

Mirjana: I can't answer that. Anyway, you know all the Secrets that have been told before. You know some of them, but not all.

Question: *So then, I don't know all of them; but since you've been told not to talk about them, I won't ask you to. That's all right—as it should be. But I'll ask you if you know when the Secrets will be revealed.*

Mirjana: I know. I know every date of every Secret.

Question: *But you can't say anything about this?*

Mirjana: I can't.

Question: *Can we suppose, then, that one might say that three Secrets would be revealed before the Great Sign appears; then the rest of the Secrets will be revealed, one by one? Is there anything to that?*

Mirjana: Nothing like that, but something like this. First, some Secrets will be revealed—just a few. Then—then, the people will be convinced that the Madonna was here. They will understand the Sign. When Jacov said that the mayor will be the first one to run to the hill, he meant that generally, people of the highest social class. They will understand the Sign as a place or occasion to convert. They will run to the hill and pray, and they will be forgiven. When I asked the Madonna about unbelievers, she said: "T*hey should be prayed for, and they should pray.*" But when I asked again, recently, she said, "*Let them convert while there is time.*" She did not say they should be prayed for.

Question: *You can say nothing specifically until the moment the Madonna says you can?*

Mirjana: Yes.

Question: *Can we say that some of the Secrets belong only to you, personally?*

Mirjana: No. None of the Secrets is personally for me.

Question: *Not you, then, but Ivan has some personal Secrets.*

Mirjana: My Secrets are all for mankind generally, for the world, Medjugorje, for some other areas, and about the Sign.

Question: *The Sign will pertain to the parish?*

Mirjana: Yes, to Medjugorje. But there is something else.

Question: *Something else?*

Mirjana: Nothing for me personally.

Question: *After these Ten Secrets, after these eighteen months of apparitions, what do you tell the people they should do? What do you say to priests? To the pope? To bishops, without revealing the Secrets? What does the Madonna want us to do?*

Mirjana: First, I would like to tell you how it was for me at the end, and the…

Question: *All right.*

Mirjana: Two days before Christmas, the Madonna told me Christmas Day would be the last time she would appear to me. (I didn't quite believe this.) On Christmas Day, she stayed with me for forty-five minutes and we talked about many things. We summarized everything that had been said between us. On behalf of many people, I asked what they should do. Then she gave me a very precious gift: she said she would appear to me on my birthday every year for the rest of my life. Also, independently of the Sign—and anything else—she said she will appear to me when something very difficult happens—not some everyday difficulty, but something quite grievous. Then she will come to help me. But now, I have to live without her physical presence, without her daily, personal visits. I say to all people: Convert! - the same as she said: "*Convert while there is time!*" Do not abandon God and your faith. Abandon everything else, but not that! I ask priests to help their people, because priests can cause them to reject their faith. After a man has been ordained, he must really be a priest, bringing people to the Church. The most important point is that the people convert and pray.

Question: *What is the greatest danger to mankind? What does it come from?*

Mirjana: From Godlessness. Nobody believes—hardly anybody.

Question: *Why did the Madonna introduce herself as the Queen of Peace?*

Mirjana: You know very well the situation in the world. The situation is very tense. Peace is needed—a just and simple peace.[4]

In 1987, Mirjana met privately with Pope John Paul II in Rome. She reported that the Holy Father "knew" she had received all ten secrets, but could reveal no more of their conversation other than that John Paul said to her,

"If I were not the Pope, I would be in Medjugorje."[5]

On February 27, 1983, Father Svetozar Kraljević interviewed Ivanka Ivankovic for his same book, *The Apparitions of Our Lady at Medjugorje.* Through this third interview, a little more is learned about the Secrets.

Kraljević: *The Queen of Peace. Does she mean to imply something by that name?*

Ivanka: I think that, in calling herself Queen of Peace, she shows that she means to reconcile the world.

Kraljević: *How does she reconcile the world?*

Ivanka: Merely by coming to the world, she reconciles it—at least a little. People have converted, and begun to believe, and pray a little more. The Madonna said that with prayer and fasting, wars could be stopped.

Kraljević: *Bearing in mind what you know about the future, tell me if the Madonna of Medjugorje will reconcile the world even more.*

Ivanka: I think she will. Because she is the Queen of Peace, I think she will reconcile the whole world.

Kraljević: *Will the Great Sign help in achieving this?*

Ivanka: Yes, when the time comes.

Kraljević: *Will the Sign appear very soon, or later.*

Ivanka: It will appear at the proper time.[6]

⚬

Over two years later, on May 7, 1985, Ivanka received her last daily apparition and was given the Tenth Secret.

The Madonna said to the teenage girl that day:

"Whatever I have told you during these years, and the Secrets I have revealed to you, for now, do not speak of them to anyone until I tell you."[7]

With this admonition to Ivanka, two of the six visionaries at Medjugorje were now in possession of all ten of the Secrets.

It would be thirteen years until another would join them.

CHAPTER SEVEN

"The Final Battle"

"Your opponent the devil is prowling around like a roaring lion looking for someone to devour."

—1 Pet 5:8

The first three interviews with the visionaries shined a bright light on the emerging mystery of the Ten Secrets of Medjugorje.

But the fourth turned the looming prophecies into a worldwide phenomenon.

⤙⤚

This extraordinary exchange occurred between Vicka Ivanković and Father Janko Bubalo, a local Franciscan, who was one of the first to investigate Medjugorje—and the first to begin to probe more deeply into the ominous sounding Secrets.

Bubalo's explosive dialogue with Vicka was published in his 301-page book, *A Thousand Encounters with the Blessed Virgin in Medjugorje*, of which the entire book *is* his interview with Vicka.

At the time, the work attracted worldwide attention and won the 1985 Sapienza Award in Italy given by "Lettera ai Credenti," an organization headed by Cardinal Angelo Rossi. The award recognized Bubalo's interview with Vicka as "the most widely read religious book in Italy for the year."

Bubalo—a renowned Croatian poet who was imprisoned by the Communists a few years before the apparitions began—said he heard about the visions at Medjugorje by the third or fourth day.[1] At the time, the friar also conducted extensive discussions with Ivanka and Marija. To this day, those conversations have not been published in full, or in English at all.

Vicka, one of three visionaries that has still not received all ten secrets and who will reportedly release her own book on the life of the Virgin Mary based on Mary's dictations to her, was extremely candid about the prophetic mysteries,[2] going so far as to admit to Bubalo that their grave nature was *not* a misunderstanding.

She gave the interview with Father Bubalo through a series of meetings with him that concluded at the end of 1983, with some additions, he notes, in 1984.[3]

The following excerpt concerns only their discussion of the Secrets.

Bubalo: *Usually Vicka, when one speaks of the Virgin's apparitions, Secrets are associated with them. This is the case here in Medjugorje, also.*

Vicka: I don't know anything about that. Would you believe that I knew almost nothing about the apparitions of the Virgin in Lourdes, and I've been meeting with the Virgin at Podbrdo and Medjugorje, more than a year. I even knew, somehow, to sing the song, *From That Grotto* without having any notion of what it is about. And to be honest, I don't want to speak of any other Secrets except those of Medjugorje, if any of that interests you.

Bubalo: *It interests me. Naturally, it interests me. I have attempted to broach the subject before, but, nonetheless, it continues to be a secret to me.*

Vicka: What can I do! A secret is a secret.

Bubalo: *I think you are entirely too closed on the subject.*

Vicka: You can think what you will, but I know what I may and may not.

Bubalo: *Good. To the extent I was able to enter the subject, you, the Seers, don't talk about the Sign nor about the Secrets amongst yourselves.*

Vicka: Little or not at all.

Bubalo: *And why is that? Whenever I ask something about the subject, as, for example, did the Virgin truly forbid any discussion on the subject, you simply pretend as though you don't hear the question.*

Vicka: And we don't. We don't wish to speak of the subject and that is it.

Bubalo: *Good. Then tell me first off, how many Secrets did the Virgin say she would impart to you?*

Vicka: You certainly know that much. But here: she told us that she would impart Ten Secrets.

Bubalo: *To each of you?*

Vicka: To each of us, as far as I know.

Bubalo: *And are the Secrets the same for each of you?*

Vicka: They are, and they aren't.

Bubalo: *And how is that?*

Vicka: Just so. The main Secrets are the same, but perhaps some of us have a secret which applies to us alone.

Bubalo: *Do you have such a Secret?*

Vicka: I have one. It is for me alone, since it concerns me only.

Bubalo: *Do the others have any such Secrets?*

Vicka: That I don't know. It seems to me that Ivan does.

Bubalo: *I know that Mirjana, Ivanka, and Marija don't have any since they told me. I don't know, however, for little Jacov. He didn't want to answer me on that point, while Ivan said that he had three which concern him only.*

Vicka: So, alright. I told you what I know.

Bubalo: *But tell me, in their order, which Secret is only for you?*

Vicka: Let's let that be. That is important only to me.

Bubalo: *But can't you at least tell me that much without revealing your Secret?*

Vicka: Well, it's the Fourth. And now be satisfied.

Bubalo: *Good, then, Vicka. Can you tell me how many Secrets you have received thus far?*

Vicka: So far, eight.

Bubalo: *In order, then. Generally speaking, it is known that in the Secrets the Virgin has foretold of something ghastly for mankind. Is that so?*

Vicka: Well, you can say it is known. So, what then?

Bubalo: *And you can't, then, say any more on the subject?*

Vicka: Nothing. That is sufficient.

Bubalo: *Mirjana suggested something even more dreadful in her Ninth and Tenth Secrets.*

Vicka: So, we heard! It is good for us to reflect on it.

Bubalo: *And you can say nothing more?*

Vicka: What can I? I know nothing more about it than you do.

Bubalo: *Can you at least say this much: do you know what will take place based on each of the Secrets?*

Vicka: I know for those I have already received.

Bubalo: *And do you know when it will take place?*

Vicka: I won't know until the Virgin tells me.

Bubalo: *Mirjana says that she knows exactly what and when things will happen.*

Vicka: She knows. The Virgin told her because she no longer has apparitions.

Bubalo: *According to that, you can't say, nor do you know, if any of the Secrets will be made evident to the world before the evidencing of the Virgin's Sign?*

Vicka: There, I told you I don't know. What I don't know, I don't know!4

⤟⤞

As in the times of the Old Testament, an intense period of transformation is expected to come through the unfolding of the Ten Secrets of Medjugorje.

Consequently, the Ten Secrets have become in some eyes almost legendary in stature—destined, it is believed, to bring divinely ordained change.

In lieu of the potential magnitude of such prophecies, therefore, could the events foretold in the Secrets of Medjugorje be alluded to in the Bible?

Do they concern prophesied times spoken about in the *Gospels* or *The Book of Revelation*?

No, the visionaries say, Mary never said that.[5]

Some, however, are not sure.

Theologians Foley, Faricy, Laurentin, and some of the Franciscans at Medjugorje, are on record as having said that Medjugorje's message is "apocalyptic." Laurentin has described them as "eschatological." Still, none have gone so far as to claim the events contained in the Secrets are specifically alluded to in Scripture.

But others think such a possibility should not be ruled out.

Something extraordinary is unfolding in Medjugorje, and it's their opinion that it might be part of a bigger picture.

One of Mary's messages—some have postulated—perhaps hints of this reality:

"If you pray; God will help you to discover the *true* reason for my coming. Therefore, little children, pray and read the Sacred Scriptures so that through my coming you discover the message in Sacred Scripture for yourselves."[6]

⤟⤞

Asked if he thought the times foretold in *The Book of Revelation* had arrived, Father Tomislav Vlašić, a Franciscan who was assigned to Medjugorje for a little more than a couple of years in the early 80s, answered, "Yes, certainly."[7]

Attorney Jan Connell, who interviewed the visionaries' multiple times over decades for her newsletters and books, also seemed to speculate about the significance of Medjugorje.[8]

Connell saw the Virgin of Medjugorje as traceable to *The Book of Revelation*, pointing out that the visionaries said that Mary has a crown of twelve stars and that she stands on a cloud, as described in *Revelation* 12:1.[9]

Father Albert Herbert—another prodigious author and an expert on Catholic private revelation involving prophecy—went so far as to write that Medjugorje is truly the fulfillment of Scripture:

"We must grasp the transcendental presence of Mary, the presence of the Woman clothed with the Sun, the Woman of the *Apocalypse*... Right now, we claim and affirm Mary of Medjugorje to be the splendid figure of the Twelfth Chapter of *Revelation*, with the moon under feet and on her head a crown of twelve stars."[10]

✧

After the prophetic implications of Fátima were better understood, many writers said they thought they saw in Fátima the times foretold in *The Book of Revelation*.[11]

Pope Paul VI's apostolic exhortation, *Signum Magnum*, released on May 13, 1967—which coincided with his visit to Fátima that day—was viewed to be in this light especially because of its title, *The Great Sign*, which again recalled Revelation 12:1.[12]

Now, at Medjugorje, where Mary said she will bring the Secrets of Fátima to fulfillment, a closing chapter to this mystery is descending upon the world.

Indeed, the Ten Secrets of Medjugorje are said to carry within them not only the mercy and justice of God, but a definitive conclusion to the spiritual war that has been unfolding over the last several centuries, a climatic final phase that Fátima's Sister Lúcia saw approaching and often spoke of in a cryptic, almost biblical sounding way. *

In her controversial 1957 interview with Father Fuentas Anguiano, Lúcia said she was told a decisive battle was about to be played out between God and the Evil One, a battle in which there would be "no middle way."[13]

This was a revelation Lucia would later expand upon in 1983 with her well known letter to Cardinal Carlo Caffarra, founding President of the *John Paul II Institute for Studies on Marriage and the Family.*

Once more, her language in the letter sounded again as if foretelling events prophesied in Scripture.

"The final battle between the Lord and Satan will be about marriage and the family," Lucia revealed to Caffarra, "because it is the decisive issue."[14]

～∞～

"This final battle over marriage and the family is being fulfilled today," said Cardinal Caffarra in 2017.

In an interview published in *Aleteia* on May 19, 2017, Caffarra described how he has come to believe that Satan is attempting to destroy the two "sacred pillars of creation"—man and woman—through abortion and homosexuality, in order to fashion his own "anti-creation."[15]

As with Lucia, Cardinal Caffarra's insights strike a biblical chord.

"I began thinking a few years ago that Sr. Lucia's words are taking place," the Cardinal told Diane Montagna of *Aleteia.*

"If we read the second chapter of Genesis, we see the edifice of creation is founded on two pillars. First, man is not *something*; he is *someone*, and therefore, he deserves absolute respect.

---

* On Sunday, August 2, 1981, the Virgin Mary gave the visionary Marija Pavlovic a message at Medjugorje that appeared to confirm Sister Lucia's words: "A great battle is about to take place. A battle between my Son and Satan."

"The second pillar is the relationship between man and woman, which is sacred. Between the man and '*the woman.*' Because creation finds its completion when God creates '*the woman.*' So much so, that after He created woman, the Bible says God rested.

"Today, what do we observe?

"Two terrible events. First, the legitimization of abortion. That is, abortion has become a 'subjective right' of woman…we say that abortion is a good; it is a right.

"The second thing we see is homosexual relationships, with marriage.

"You see that Satan is attempting to threaten and destroy the two pillars so that he can fashion another creation."[16]

This assault on "the two pillars of creation" has been successfully underway in the world for some time now but has not breached the sanctity of the Catholic Church.

The Church, under the recent guidance of Popes Paul VI, John Paul I and II, and Benedict XVI has resisted efforts to undermine its positions, boldly upholding its moral teachings on contraception, IVF, abortion, and homosexuality.

The encyclical letters of Pope Paul VI and Pope John Paul II, *Humanae Vitae* (Of Human Life) and *Evangelium Vitae* (The Gospel of Life), significantly reinforced these moral pillars.

However, as we enter into the climax of this great spiritual war, it is clear that these teachings are now primary targets of Satan, essential to fulfilling his goal of stripping away the Church's moral authority in the world, in constructing, as Cardinal Caffarra stated, an "anti-creation."[17]

Needless to say, it should come as no surprise that the toppling of the Church's moral foundation is near the summit of Satan's plan, second only to destroying its Sacramental mysteries (Mt 24, Dn 12).

Pope Paul VI's ominous statement in 1972, "The smoke of Satan has entered the Temple of God," has always been most associated with

Humanae Vitae, which has endured relentless criticism since its release on July 25, 1968.

The term "anti-creation" that Caffarra adopts to summarize Satan's objectives in this battle is also quite astute and relevant, since the Evil One's aim in dismantling the moral pillars of the Church is essentially motivated by his great hatred of the "Creator of creation"—God the Father.

At their core, both abortion and homosexuality strike directly at the First person of the Holy Trinity, at His Fatherhood—at His Divine Paternal Heart—the womb of the Father's "everlasting love," where each and every soul is "created" in the Creator's image. (Before I formed you in the womb I knew you, and before you were born I consecrated you" (Jer 1:1, 5).

Thus, in essence, all attempts to impede, disfigure, or destroy the life that the "Author of Life" wills to create—whether through contraception, abortion, same sex relations—is an attempt to undermine the Eternal Father's Divine Paternity, to vanquish His Fatherhood from the hearts of His children, which has been the Evil One's goal since the Garden.*

∽

Satan, however, has been given only so much time to wage this "final battle"—a century or one hundred years—according to Pope Leo XIII's reported 1884 prophetic vision.

And that allotted period, according to Mirjana Dragićević Soldo, will officially come to its termination with the unfolding of the First Secret of Medjugorje.

---

* The attack on life through abortion, contraception, and homosexuality—directly aimed at the divine paternity of the Father—has led some to argue that the Triumph of the Immaculate Heart will not be completely fulfilled until the Church declares a feast day for God the Father, which will honor in perpetuity His Divine Paternity. For more on this, see my books, *Original Separation* and *The Mystery of the Divine Paternal Heart of God Our Father*. Also see *Abba Father, We Long to See Your Face* by Fr. Jean Galot S.J.

An Italian priest reportedly took this picture of Mary during an apparition at St. James Church in Medjugorje in the early 1980s.

Photo Credit: Pittsburgh Center for Peace

Mirjana's "second of the month apparition" drew huge crowds for many years. The monthly apparition ended in March of 2020.

Photo credit: Pittsburgh Center for Peace

A 1974 painting by Vlado Falak, which hung in St. James Church in Medjugorje, appears to have previewed the coming apparitions of the Virgin Mary in 1981

Photo Credit: Pittsburgh Center for Peace

CHAPTER EIGHT

The Fall of Satan

"For the accuser of our brothers is cast out."

—Rv 12:10

"I spoke with Mirjana, and she said that the First Secret is one catastrophe in one place in the world," said Draga Ivanković, who lived in Bijakovići at the time of the first apparition and is a cousin to three of the visionaries. "She knows where. She will tell it, ten days before to Father Petar (Ljubicic); and three days before it happens, he will tell it to the people. All the people will know this for three days before it happens. There will be three such warnings before the Sign on apparition mountain.

"The three warnings are for the people to convert. The Sign is going to be something very convincing, and it will last forever. They say it will be very beautiful. If I remember correctly, one time Our Lady said that they should take a picture of the mountain because afterward it will be changed. I do not know when the First Secret will take place, but she says 'soon.' If you believe, do not be worried."[1]

Worry.

No one should worry about what is coming with the Ten Secrets of Medjugorje—all six visionaries concur—as long as one has taken the time to have their slate wiped clean with God.

But if not, by the time the Third Secret rolls around, it certainly sounds like it could become a serious concern.[2]

Like a line drawn in the sand, the appearance of the Great Sign on Podbrdo, where the first apparitions took place, is understood by some to be a metaphorical "crossing of the Red Sea" with regards to the world's future.

With this miraculous event, something incomprehensible is in the works. And from the sound of the visionaries, few will be able to deny its divine origin.

But before then—the first two Secrets must come.

━━━

The First Secret is considered a warning.

It will be proof, the visionaries tell us, of the Madonna's presence in Medjugorje.[3] And, following its fulfillment, there is to come an intense period of grace in which many people will convert.[4]

But there is something more that is foretold to take place.

As with the appearance of the Great Sign, the First Secret is to be understood in a way that transcends its physical manifestation, for its unfolding is to affect the spiritual world, too.

The First Secret, according to Mirjana Dragićević Soldo in interviews over a period of almost twenty years, will *break* the power of Satan.[5] It will end, she says Mary explained to her, a designated length of time—one century—that God granted Satan to extend his influence over humanity in a more effective, some would say powerful way.[6]

This mysterious and prophetic revelation—often written of but never officially documented—is said to have originated with Pope Leo XIII from a brief vision he experienced after celebrating Mass in the Vatican. As previously discussed, that mystical experience in

1884 reportedly led to his composing of the well-known *Prayer to Saint Michael*.[7]

In the letter to Pope John Paul II of December 2, 1983 (see Chapter Five), it was noted how the Virgin Mary spoke to Mirjana about this so-called "Century of Satan" and revealed to her that it would end with the unfolding of the Ten Secrets of Medjugorje.[8]

The report to the Pope, however, did not make it clear that the Devil's long-awaited demise would actually occur with the fulfill-ment of the very "first secret", which Mirjana later explains during a January 10, 1983, interview published in Father Kraljević's book, *The Apparitions of Our Lady at Medjugorje*, and in subsequent other inter-views over the years.[9]

In essence, the First Secret is to administer a decisive blow in the spiritual war that both Lúcia of Fátima and the visionaries of Medjugorje have spoken about in interviews.

So, what will this First Secret be?

Mirjana appears to be the best source to shed a little light on this question.

~∞~

Mirjana's final daily apparition occurred on December 25, 1982, which lasted forty-five minutes.[10]

On that day, the Virgin Mary promised her that she would appear from then on only on her birthday each year, March 18 ,[11] or at times when she was experiencing "difficulties or had special needs."[12] Time would show that some of this divine assistance would be in the form of interior locutions, not just apparitions.[13] *

---

* In August of 1987, this format changed. At that time, the Virgin Mary told Mirjana that she would also start to appear to her on "the second of every month" in order to pray with her for non-believers. These monthly apparitions took place from September 2, 1987, through March 2, 2020. On March 18, 2020, Mary announced to Mirjana that she would no longer appear to her on the second of every month.

On March 18, 1983, the Virgin kept her word and appeared to Mirjana on her birthday, and again on the same date in 1984.[14] That day, Mary told the young girl before her departure:

"This year, probably, we will see each other again on account of the Secrets."[15]

On August 25, 1984, according to Father Slavko Barbarić, Mirjana received a special apparition in which Mary said to her:

"Wait for me on September 13; I will speak to you about the future."[16]

The Virgin appeared to her that day as promised, and once more that year on Christmas Day, in an apparition that lasted a half an hour.[17] After the September apparition—which saw a weeping Madonna appear because of all the unbelief in the world[18]—Father Barbarić asked her a question:

"Are you happy to know the future?"

"One word suffices to make me cry all day long," answered Mirjana, "the Virgin is very sad with all the unfaithful people."

"Which unfaithful people," Barbarić wanted to know, "those who go to church but do not practice their faith, or those who do not know God?"

"They are both the same," explained the visionary, "all adults have the capacity to know that God exists. The sin of the world consists in the fact that they are not interested in God."[19]

⎯⎯∞⎯⎯

In 1985, Mirjana reported—according to the parish chronicle—receiving either locutions or apparitions on twelve occasions,[20] including one highly publicized "special apparition" on Friday, October 25, 1985, in which she received a more insightful and very intense look at the First Secret.

On that day, Mirjana experienced an interior vision during the apparition that allowed her to somewhat witness an event contained in the First Secret. Since she knew of this apparition a month in advance, she asked Father Petar Ljubicic (the priest chosen by her that June to reveal the Ten Secrets to the world) to be in attendance. Petar's personal experience that day proved to be very moving, as he reported witnessing the visionary's eyes filled with tears at one point.[21]

The official parish chronicle account, published in *Medjugorje Gebetsaktion* (1986, No.2), and reprinted in Father René Laurentin's 1988 book, *The Apparitions at Medjugorje Prolonged*, reads:

> We began to pray at 1:50 p.m. When she appeared, the Blessed Virgin greeted me: *Praised be Jesus.* Then, she spoke of unbelievers: *They are my children; I suffer because of them. They do not know what awaits them.* You must pray more for them. We prayed with her for the weak, the unfortunate, and the forsaken. After the prayer, she blessed us.
>
> Then she showed me, as in a film, the realization of the First Secret. The Earth was desolate. *It is the upheaval of a region of the world.* She was precise. I cried. Why so soon? I asked. *In the world, there are so many sins. What can I do if you do not help me? Remember that I love you. How can God have such a hard heart? God does not have a hard heart. Look around you, and see what men do; then you will no longer say that God has a hard heart. How many people come to church, to the house of God with respect, strong faith, a love of God? Very few! Here you have a time of grace and conversion. It is necessary to use it well. Pray very much for Fr. Petar, to whom I send a special blessing. I am a mother; that is why I come. You must not fear for I am there.*[22]

Afterwards, Mirjana reported that Mary prayed over Father Ljubicic two times in Latin during the apparition.

"I was happy because Our Lady was happy with my choice," said Mirjana. "The heart of Father Petar is completely opened to the Savior. A reward is waiting for him. We prayed an Our Father and a Glory Be for the success of Father Petar in the task which is confided to him."

The Virgin stayed for eight minutes that afternoon before departing.[23]

⌁

During the fall and winter of 1985 to 1986, Father Robert Faricy lived in Medjugorje for several months.

On what would be his fifth visit, the eminent mystical theologian from Rome decided to keep a daily journal of the activities unfolding in the village, which he commenced writing on Friday, October 11, 1985.[24] His log was later made into a 1987 book titled, *Medjugorje Journal, Mary Speaks to the World.*

On the day after the apparition/vision experience of Mirjana, Father Faricy documented the following account of what occurred in his journal:

> ***October 26, Saturday Night:*** Yesterday Mirjana had a visit from Our Lady. It lasted eight minutes. A month ago, Mirjana heard Our Lady's voice tell her she would come on October 25. So, Mirjana knew ahead of time. She told Father Petar, and he was there during this vision. He says that, at one point, Mirjana's eyes filled with tears. Afterwards, she told him that Our Lady had shown her, as in a film, the coming of the first of the Ten Secrets. It will be a severe warning to the world. She already knows the date. She'll tell Father Petar ten days before it happens, and he'll make some kind of public announcement three days before it happens...Our Lady is showing Vicka and Jacov the future of the world. Apparently, things look bad.[25]

During the ensuing month, Mirjana received another special apparition which once again involved a vision of the First Secret. Father Laurentin chronicled the official account of the event in his book, *The Apparitions at Medjugorje Prolonged:*

November 30, 1985: Mirjana had another apparition, a little shorter than the one of October 25. The Italian priest, Father Boniface, was present. Again, Mirjana saw, as in a film, the unfolding of the first message. "It will be unhappy; it will be a sorrowful sign," she confirmed. "It will come in a short time." She (Mary) prayed for unbelievers and for Father Petar, so that Father Petar will be able to prepare himself for this task. After the apparition, Father Bonifacio said to Father Petar, "Certain people say that you will not reveal the contents of the Secret." "If I have the right to reveal it, then ten days beforehand, I will know it and three days before, I will say it," he answers.[26]

Father Faricy, still living in Medjugorje at the time, recorded again his thoughts concerning Mirjana's second vision of the First Secret on November 30,1985, in his daily journal:

December 2, Monday: Sister Janja told me tonight that she hopes I can be here when Petar gets from Mirjana the Secret to be revealed to the world, the prediction of some kind of imminent catastrophe that apparently will take many lives. Mirjana had another vision of it last Friday, seeing the disaster as one might see it in a film. She is badly shaken. Both Petar and Janja seem to think the fulfillment of the revelation given to Mirjana will come quite soon, at most in a few months. Petar looks nervous about his role in the matter: to know about it ten days before it happens and to announce it three days before.[27]

Several weeks after, on Christmas Day 1985, Mirjana received a third apparition/vision involving the First Secret. Wrote Father Vlašić on January 23, 1986, in his and Father Slavko Barbarić's book, *I Beseech You, Listen to my Messages and Live Them*:

December 25, 1985: Mirjana now has more frequent apparitions; her last one was on 25th December 1985. Mirjana again witnessed an event referring to the First Secret, the first warning to the world. She was sad.[28]

Almost two months later, Mirjana experienced yet another special apparition, and once more reported a vision of the First Secret. Wrote Father Robert Faricy in his daily logue:

February 16, Sunday: The chief news was that yesterday, Saturday, February 15, Mirjana had a vision of Our Lady at her house here in Bijakovići. It lasted five or six minutes; and during it she saw again the First Secret, as though in a film.[29]

⁂

While nothing highly specific is revealed in all of these accounts, they do reinforce the sublime significance of the First Secret, perhaps because it is directly aligned with the demise of Satan's period of enhanced influence.

The reports of the four separate "like a film" glimpses into the First Secret by Mirjana appear to be the most telling depictions of any of the Ten Secrets, except for the coming of the Great Sign with the Third Secret. Mary would speak to Mirjana one more time about the First Secret on June 4, 1986.[30]

It should be noted that the words, "as in a film," which Mirjana uses to describe both the October and November 1985 visions of the First Secret—as well as the vision in February 1986—are almost the exact words she would come to use to describe how she was given to understand some of the Ten Secrets in her 2016 book, *My Heart Will Triumph*. In that account, Mirjana states that Our Lady relayed most of the events of the Secrets to her through their conversations, but also showed her some of them *"like scenes of a film."*

When she experienced these glimpses into the future, she wrote, people near her often noted the intense expressions on her face. They were the type of expressions, it has been documented, reportedly seen on the faces of all the Medjugorje visionaries after certain apparitions involving the Secrets—expressions that cause many to conclude that something difficult—perhaps painful—must be involved.[31]

CHAPTER NINE

"It Will Be Too Late"

"And if those days had not been shortened, no one would be saved; but for the sake of the elect they will be shortened."

—Mt 24:22

Mirjana Dragićević's apparition of October 25, 1985, created quite a stir in Medjugorje.

To this day, it remains one of the most intriguing developments in the timeline of events tracing the history of the visions. And, to add to its relevance, the remarkable encounter was reinforced significantly by what happened the very next day.

On October 26, 1985, just one day after her agonizing experience, Mirjana gave a captivating interview to Father Petar Ljubicic, the priest she has chosen to announce the Secrets to the world.

In the interview, Mirjana delves into the coming of the Ten Secrets, her understanding of the vision she was given of the First Secret, and how the weight of it all has emotionally weighed on her at times.

The excitatory dialogue was translated into English and published in its entirety by investigative journalist Michael Brown. It was later included in his book, *Tower of Light*.[1]

Over four decades later, the interview remains one of the most en-lightening on the Ten Secrets of Medjugorje that has ever been pub-lished. The following is an excerpt:

Ljubicic: *How would you assess the current situation around the world?*

Mirjana: There never was an age such as this one, never before was God honored and respected less than now, never before have so few prayed to Him; everything seems to be more im-portant than God. This is the reason why she cries so much. The number of unbelievers is becoming greater and greater. As they endeavor for a better life, to such people, God Himself is superfluous and dispensable. This is why I feel deeply sorry for them and for the world. They have no idea what awaits them. If they could only take a tiny peek at these Secrets, they would convert in time. Certainly, God always forgives all those who genuinely convert.

Ljubicic: *Did she (Mary) perhaps alert us to other things we must do, in addition to praying and preparing for that time? Perhaps something concrete?*

Mirjana: Father, I wish you only knew how I feel on some days! There are times when I feel that I could go mad. If Mary wasn't here, if she didn't fill me with strength, by now I would have surely gone mad. When I see how people believe, especially in Sarajevo, how they use God and His name in swearing, how thoughtless they are, how they curse God…These wretched ones have no idea what awaits them in the near future. It is then, as I observe them, that I take pity on them. I feel so sorry for them and pray and cry and pray, pray so much for them. I pray to Mary to enlighten their minds because, as Jesus said: they truly do not know what they do. And yet, the first two Secrets are not at all that severe and harsh. What I mean is yes, they are severe, but not as much as the remaining ones.

Ljubicic: *Are the Secrets perhaps of a notable, distinct character, or more of a spiritual nature?*

Mirjana: Distinct. Distinct.

Ljubicic: *Distinct?*

Mirjana: Yes, distinct. It will be visible. It is necessary in order to shake up the world a little. It will make the world pause and think.

Ljubicic: *Something like a catastrophe?*

Mirjana: No, it will not be anything as huge as that. That will come later. It will be something that will give the world something to think about seriously, allow it to see that she was indeed here, and to realize that there is God, that He exists.

Ljubicic: *After that, will there be anyone who will say, "This is some sort of a natural phenomenon," or along those lines?*

Mirjana: Perhaps some staunch unbelievers might say something like that after the First and Second Secrets.

Ljubicic: *I am just curious whether anyone will be able to say, "I feel something, that something will happen soon", or along those lines.*

Mirjana: Well, you can see there are some rather peculiar things going on in the world. People are unhappy, dissatisfied, avarice reigns everywhere, hardly anyone admits that they ever have enough of anything. Yet, none of this gives any clues about the Secret. The Secret stands on its own. The Secret will abundantly speak for itself and requires no prior clues or signals.

Ljubicic: *Once again, concerning the First Secret, who will experience, see, and be convinced and then be able to say: "Truly that which has occurred or is occurring is the manifestation of the Secret?" Who will be able to see all that?*

Mirjana: All those who will be here or in the places where the Secret will unfold.

Ljubicic: *Let me assume that this involves a specific place. All those who will wish to see and experience this sign or whatever the Secret is, will they have to come to that particular place to see and experience this?*

Mirjana: Well, Father, surely no one wishes to watch disasters, distress, and misfortune. I don't think that this kind of thing attracts people at all. Why would people go to see something of that sort? It is one thing to see a sign, quite another to go and see suffering or disaster. Who would, for example, go to Italy to see a dam collapse? Who has that kind of desire? I don't think that anyone does—and that is how it will be with this Secret. Whatever is in the Secret, it will, of course, be something that everyone, everywhere, will immediately hear about.

Ljubicic: *Tell me, if the Secret involves a location rather than a condition or a situation, wouldn't it be desirable to have as many people as possible see—to have as many eyewitnesses as possible—even though it may not be a joyful thing or something pleasant to look at?*

Mirjana: Father, it will be obvious. It will be something that people will hear about very far.

Ljubicic: *The manifestation of that Secret, will it only be a momentary thing or will it be something that will last for an extended period?*

Mirjana: It will last for a little while.

Ljubicic: *Little while?*

Mirjana: Little.

Ljubicic: *Will its effect be lasting or permanent or will its effect be momentary and passing?*

Mirjana: How can I explain that without encroaching on the Secret? Let me just say that it won't be good at all, it won't be pleasant.

Ljubicic: *After that, if any one were to come here knowing that such and such had occurred, will that person be able to see anything—any evidence that something, indeed, did happen here?*

Mirjana: Yes, yes, yes.

Ljubicic: *It will be visible?*

Mirjana: Yes.

Ljubicic: *This whole situation: it seems that she (Mary) is trying to prepare us and to "dress" us with saintliness, God's love and perfection, so that we greet Our Lord when He comes. Is there anything that signals something of that? Of that nature?*

Mirjana: Just as any mother, she cares for her children. She wants us to come and meet God the Father well-prepared. She doesn't want us to weep and wail when it's too late. God said that He forgives at any time- providing the soul repents sincerely. All she asks for, the one thing she waits for, is for all of us to repent so that we may be forgiven. What follows are the Secrets that are really unpleasant. I would be happy if everyone would finally understand that. I cannot tell the Secrets, but once they begin to be fulfilled, then it will be too late.

Ljubicic: *Will the interval between the First and Second Secret be lengthy?*

Mirjana: That varies according to the Secrets. What I mean is that, for example, the time between the First and the Second Secrets is of a certain period, between the Second and the Third is of a different length. For example, and I stress, for example, the First Secret may take place today and the Second one already tomorrow.[2]

In another of his books, The Day Will Come, Michael Brown writes about a second interview with Mirjana by Father Petar Ljubicic in which the First Secret is again discussed:

In a later interview with the same priest, Mirjana expanded upon the other Secrets, urging especially conversion of the young. They were especially the ones Mary wept over, she explained, "I now know about things that are not particularly pleasant," said the visionary, whose daily apparitions halted in 1982, when she received the Tenth Secret—the first of the six to do so. "I believe that if everyone knew about these same things, each one of these people would be shocked to their senses and would view our world in a completely different light.

Of course, my greatest advice to all is to pray for all the unbelievers. You see, Mary expends the greatest amount of time talking about that very thing. We must also not forget the elderly and the infirm. They are ours too. They sacrificed their whole lives. Many of them lived their entire lives for God in prayer. Their senior years shouldn't have to be sad and miserable."

I cannot elaborate much more, it's hard for me to do that. You see, so much is tied to the Secrets. If the people saw the First Secret, as it was shown to me, all of them would most certainly be shaken enough to take a new and different look at themselves and everything around them.[3]

In published interviews with Father Petar Ljubicic on the subject of the Secrets, the humble friar always emphasizes that much prayer and fasting will precede the announcement of the First Secret, as well as the fact that Mirjana will definitely be *in* Medjugorje for the announcement of the Secret.[4]

None of the other five visionaries have said anything more that is substantial to add to what is known about the First Secret. They have all, more or less, primarily referred to it as a warning that will validate the Virgin Mary's presence in Medjugorje.

Will life on earth be more pleasant after the "First Secret"?

"We shall see," offered Marija Pavlović.[5]

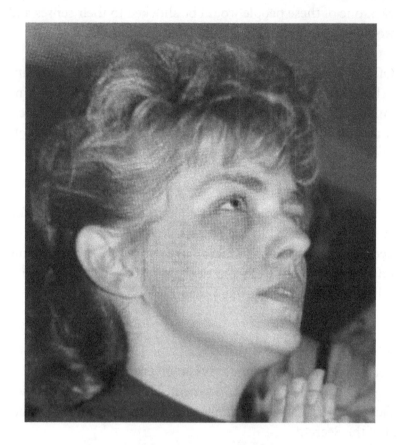

Mirjana Dragićević Soldo

"Each individual on earth will play a role as the Secrets unfold."

Photo Credit: Pittsburgh Center for Peace

CHAPTER TEN

An Apocalyptic Mood

"See, the day of the Lord! See, the end is coming! Lawlessness is
in full bloom, insolence flourishes, violence has risen to support
wickedness. It shall not be long in coming, nor shall it delay.
The time has come, the day dawns."

—Ez 7:10-12

There is something more that is relevant to the First Secret—and all of the Ten Secrets for that matter—that came about around this time. And, it changed forever how the mystery of the Secrets was to be publicly approached at Medjugorje.

As books and articles with interviews of the visionaries started to circulate—revealing conversations with them that disclosed more of the substance and nature of the Secrets—there is found emerging a coordinated response by the Franciscans on the subject of the Secrets in general.

In essence, it is agreed that an increased effort is needed by all the parties in Medjugorje—principally the visionaries and the priests—to refrain from speaking too much about the Secrets.

"The present not the future," it is agreed, should be the concern. Father Tomislav Pervan, the head pastor of St. James in 1985, explained:

> Today in the world an apocalyptic mood is spreading, So I want to keep a distance from it. For it is not a question of tomorrow, the day after tomorrow, or what will happen in ten years, but today. It is not a question of the end of time, but of the present time, what I and everyone else need and must do today and now.

> We are called to do what we must do; convert, pray, turn to God. This is our task today, not something that will perhaps happen or can happen. This is the meaning of the Secrets of the apparitions of Mary in general, and this is also the case with Medjugorje.[1]

Father Philip Pavich, an American friar working in Medjugorje, thought the same as Pervan. He believed that those who zero in on the reported nature of some of the Secrets cause an "unhealthy distortion" of the message.

Such a view causes unfounded apprehension and inflicts fear in Pavich's view, which he says is not the reason Mary is appearing in Medjugorje:

"We don't see it as the end of the world," said Pavich, preferring to recognize a higher purpose to Medjugorje.[2]

This approach to the Secrets becomes something that Father Slavko Barbarić especially begins to emphasize both privately and publicly. Both he and all the Franciscans understood that the mounting curiosity surrounding the Ten Secrets had the potential to derail the real message of Medjugorje.

The Virgin Mary, they begin to stress, has come to show the path to peace, not the road to perdition.

Investigative writer Randall Sullivan said that Barbarić told him that he had "advised the visionaries to say nothing further on the subject (the Secrets)." This was because it encouraged a "kind of fatalism" in people, causing them "to live in the future, rather than in the present."[3]

On November 15, 1985, Father Barbarić confronted this reality in a talk he presented in Medjugorje. The friar invited his listeners to understand that Mary brings only love, hope, and peace, even with regards to the Secrets:

> Mirjana said she saw the First Secret as if in a film and said, "My God, does this really have to happen?" Our Lady is supposed to have answered that it is, *"Not God but sin that does it"* … Owing to this bit of news, I feel many have been overcome with fear, with anguish…Our Lady is talking a lot about the Secrets and invites us to prayer… especially for the unbelievers…All these messages will have no meaning for us if we respond with fear. We must respond with confidence, with love and say, 'Everything is in God's hands and today I need to carry out all my duties with love and hope. This I have understood and this I tell everyone—the apparitions never bear a new revelation; they are always an impulse, to pray, to fast, to love, to be reconciled, to make peace. And so, not even these secret messages can bring anything new.[4]

On December 30, 1985, after Mirjana received from the Virgin Mary her second look at the First Secret, Father Barbarić again states that both revelations of the First Secret are to bring hope and nothing else:

> During the two locutions of 25 October and 30 November, Our Lady showed her, she says, the first admonishment, the First Secret, as in a film. The admonishments, all Mirjana is telling

us, must be understood in the context of the apparitions… By coming to us, Our Lady wants to tell us that it is possible to find a path to peace once again. For this reason, the apparitions are always a fact giving us renewed hope, they never want to give us anguish and fear, but always hope.[5]

By July of 1987, Father Barbarić's position on the issue was well defined.

He told author Jan Connell that the friars do not speak about the apocalyptic events in connection with Medjugorje—that it was really not their primary orientation. Medjugorje, he stressed to her, had become a place of hope. He felt this was in keeping with what the Blessed Mother said: "I come to lead you to peace and to bring you peace."

Mary, emphasized Barbarić, invites us to fast and pray, in order to receive and achieve this very peace.[6]

As with Father Barbarić, the other Franciscans also started to carefully craft their talks and sermons at Medjugorje to more emphasize the proper way to understand Mary's messages, especially the Secrets.

Referring one day to a newspaper article laying on a desk in which the headline read: "Medjugorje Secrets Predict Dire Events," one friar remarked to a journalist that "reports like this do a disservice to readers."[7]

On the same day (October 25, 1985) of the initial vision of the First Secret given to Mirjana—Father Vlašić told a group of pilgrims:

Today, Mirjana had an apparition of Our Lady lasting eight minutes… …When we talk of these events, there are people who get frightened…we must not get frightened, but we must be converted. Conversion is an act of hope. Fear is an act of desperation, and we must have an act of hope. If you live an act of hope, if you live conversion, ahead of you can only be joy…[8]

The following day, the friar again sought to put this issue into a proper perspective to a group of pilgrims from Italy:

Yesterday, Mirjana had an apparition …the visionary saw, as in a film, the taking place of the first Secret, of the first warning to mankind…I spoke to the visionary today. She told me this, "You can tell everybody—we are in a time of grace, at a time of Our Lady's call, who wants to lead us to salvation" …When one usually talks of these things, that is, the announcements made by the visionaries, people become afraid. But why are you afraid? This means we have not discovered faith…what the visionary emphasizes is conversion, a purification of the heart, a total opening to God in order to live in God.[9]

A week later, on November 2, 1985, the Feast of All Souls, he explained during a talk given in Medjugorje that what is coming in the future, is exactly what the world needs to move out of this dark moment in time:

The last apparition to Mirjana took place on 25 October, a week ago. After the apparition, Fr. Petar asked her what happened? Why were you so sad? "Our Lady showed me for the first time, as in a film, the events of her first warning. It is very severe. That is why I am sad." I then spoke to the visionary who once again repeated that this is the period of grace when many graces are granted, it is the period of conversion… The visionary stresses this aspect of joy and hope we must possess when looking at the future…[10]

❧

Over the years, some writers have distorted the six visionaries' words concerning the Secrets or have tried to insinuate the Secrets reopen old Catholic prophecies that emphasize cataclysmic events.[11]

These corrupted interpretations are found in books and newsletters as well as on some websites. Several books released over the years contain the Medjugorje visionaries' strong objections to these deliberate distortions or exaggerated predictions.

In the same interview with attorney Jan Connell in 1991, Mirjana was asked if she ever said, "areas of the planet would be destroyed" and that "no life" would grow there. The visionary denied such statements, making it clear that she never said any such thing nor has ever spoken about such calamities.[12]

Bogus versions of the Secret of La Salette—along with the Third Secret of Fátima—became legendary for their grossly exaggerated direr predictions. While unfortunate, such distorted accounts are inevitable with prophecy. Connell asked Mirjana about similar rumors associated with Medjugorje, such as the coming of "three days of darkness," deadly earthquakes and tidal waves, and other frightful catastrophes. Mary had "not spoken" about any of those predictions, Mirjana stressed to Connell, making it clear that such rhetoric only hurts the true message of Medjugorje.[13]

Vicka echoed Mirjana's assertion concerning such inflammatory talk. Author Michael Brown writes:

"Vicka Ivanković told me talk of the end of the world, the Second Coming, and the Antichrist were not in my Secrets."[14]

Marija emphasized much the same:

"I do not speak of the Second Coming of Christ, of catastrophes, destruction, or evil. With prayer and fasting, even war can be eliminated. The Blessed Mother says prayer and fasting can change even the natural law."[15]

Ivan has especially denounced those who peddle the sensational in association with the Secrets of Medjugorje, who paint Mary as a prophetess of "doom and gloom, "[16] and who put their focus on the word "chastisement."

At a talk in 2008, Ivan emphasized that "Mary has not come to criticize us or tell us about the end of the world."[17]

The record shows that dispelling alarm with regards to the Secrets is something that Ivan has emphasized for years at his talks. As far back as 1996, before a large gathering in Windsor, Ohio, Ivan told the crowd:

"Today, people are talking about terrible things that will happen in the world, the 'three days of darkness.' I would like to have you understand one thing that I'm going to tell you. Our Lady did not come to bring us terror. She is not coming to bring us darkness. She is coming to us as a mother of light and a mother of hope."[18]

Asked again a year later at another of his talks about catastrophic predictions, Ivan responded, "That is not coming from Our Lady to us and so I don't know where it is coming from." Confronted moments later with another such question, this time about World War III, the frustrated visionary simply answered, "No."[19]

~≪∘≫~

The specific events to unfold with the First Secret are unknown.

But there may be an interesting side story involving the First Secret at Medjugorje and the powerful vision Mirjana received in October 1985.

In retrospect, it's clear, Mirjana's experience that day was not just another apparition of the Virgin Mary. And it was not just another revelation involving the Secrets. Rather, when looked at as a whole, it appears God could have possibly guided some of what occurred surrounding that day for a reason.

It was in October of 1917 that Satan finally succeeded in bringing to fruition in Russia his attempt to bring a 'triumph of atheism' in the world, the very same month and year that Mary came to Fátima to prevent such an ignominious effort from succeeding.

And, it was *exactly* on October 25, 1917, that Vladimir Lenin and the Bolsheviks announced they had seized power in Petrograd, Russia, and began to commence with their godless revolution—the exact "same date" that Mirjana received the extraordinary vision of the First Secret—the Secret that, when it comes to pass, will bring an end to

Satan's extended influence over mankind on Earth.[20] The Secret she would be shown in vision another three times.

Was God, by giving the powerful vision of the First Secret on this specific date trying to irrefutably mark that He is the Lord of history—that, as *He* was in control of the *beginning* of the hellish, Marxist nightmare that fell upon the world on that very date, so too is *He* is in control of its *end*?

Will this date be seen perhaps again someday as events unfold?

⌒∞⌒

The Second Secret of Medjugorje is also described as a warning by the visionaries.

It will witness, they say, many more people convert after it is fulfilled.

However, a great number of people—"particularly in the West"—will still try to argue "a natural explanation" for the events contained in *both* of the first two Secrets, according to the visionaries.[21]

Wayne Weible, a Medjugorje author and perhaps its greatest evangelist, wrote in his final book that he believed the Second Secret involves the widespread prophecy of a coming miraculous event known as the "Miracle of the Illumination of all Consciences."[22]

Known also as "The Warning," this is to be a prophesied moment in time when every human being in the world is to see the state of their soul in God's eyes. Many conversions are foretold to come because of it.[23] Nevertheless, there is no evidence at all—or any words to this effect stated by the visionaries—that this miracle makes up or is part of the Second Secret, or any of the Ten Secrets of Medjugorje.

At Notre Dame University on May 27, 2007, Father Petar Ljubicic spoke during a panel discussion about the First and Second Secrets:

"We must say that the first two Secrets are involved with Medjugorje. There will be a warning of that which is to take place, because Our Lady did appear first in Medjugorje. And the parishioners of that parish of St. James are called to live those messages and to spread them as well.

Many will be surprised, because they weren't really taking into account what will take place."[24]

After the Second Secret, there will come the appearance of the Great Sign—the fulfillment of the Third Secret on Mt. Podbrdo.

And, like the fulfillment of the First Secret, it promises to be a watershed event.

Indeed, when what is foretold comes to pass, perhaps future generations will come to see Mt. Podbrdo in the same way as Mt. Sinai, Mt. Tabor, and Mt. Carmel are viewed today: as a holy place that witnessed God—as Scripture says—*stoop down* to mark His presence among His people in an everlasting way.

Fr. René Laurentin	Fr. Robert Faricy	Fr. Ljudevit Rupčić
Photo Credit: Pittsburgh Center for Peace	Photo Credit: Pittsburgh Center for Peace	Photo Credit: Ljudevit Rupčić

Fr. Petar Ljubicic was chosen by Mirjana to reveal the Ten Secrets of Medjugorje. He stayed with the author at his home for a couple of days' in

Photo Credit: Thomas W. Petrisko

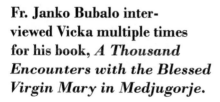

Fr. Janko Bubalo interviewed Vicka multiple times for his book, *A Thousand Encounters with the Blessed Virgin Mary in Medjugorje.*

Picture Credit: Janko Bubalo

PART II

TIME OF DECISION

"I in turn will choose ruthless treatment for them and bring upon them what they fear. Because, when I called, no one answered, when I spoke, no one listened."

—Is 66:4

"Here I began with this parish and invited the entire world. Many have responded, but there is an enormous number of those who do not want to hear or accept my call."

—The Virgin Mary,
Medjugorje,
August 25, 2011

The Great Sign

"This shall be the Lord's renown, an everlasting, imperishable sign."

—Is 55:13

D read, suspicion and outright fear accompanied the alleged contents of the Third Secret of Fátima for decades. From runaway oceans submerging regions of the planet—to cascading missiles setting cities ablaze—to new and deadly plagues turning the Earth into a massive graveyard—doom and gloom is a phrase that fits the infamous Third Secret of Fátima like a glove.

This time, though, the narrative could not be more reversed.

The Third Secret of Medjugorje—similarly to that of Fátima—has weathered decades of discussion. This "third secret," however, has been more associated with wondrous anticipation, not nail-biting unease.

Its fulfillment is to be a sign of hope, a harbinger of a future that is to hold joy and help to bring peace.[1]

Extensively spoken of by all six of the visionaries at Medjugorje, the Third Secret will fulfill Mary's promise to leave a sign.

And like at Fátima on October 13, 1917—when her promise to leave a sign was fulfilled by the sun supernaturally appearing to drop from the sky like a ball of fire—at Medjugorje a pre-sign of the Third Secret involved a supernatural fire that appeared on Mt. Podbrdo on October 27, 1981.[2]

While no one except the visionaries has any facts regarding the Sign's true makeup, speculation has ranged from the sudden appearance of a chapel on apparition hill,[3] to an underground spring emerging there (as at Lourdes),[4] to an earthquake somehow creating an inland waterway that links the Adriatic Sea to Mt. Podbrdo in Bijakovići.[5]

One author even suggested perhaps a column of fire similar to what the Israelites experienced is coming.[6]

In 1984, a Catholic priest who was a "water diviner" thought that he detected two powerful streams of water underground on the hill. If they continue to converge, he theorized, the streams will eventually unite and burst out and up to the surface, perhaps creating the 'Great Sign.'

Seeking to study the area more, the government heard of his activities and had him arrested along with one of the friars. They ended up being held for questioning at the police station for two hours.[7]

Marija said in a May 2008 interview that the Virgin Mary told her that one day a chapel should be built not at the site of the first apparitions, but further down on Podbrdo.[8]

However, this request, Marija made clear, is not associated with the Sign.[9]

⚬⚬⚬

Known also as the Great Sign, many of its characteristics have been revealed by the visionaries:[10]

- It will be visible.[11]
- It will appear on Mt. Podbrdo at the sight of the first apparitions.[12]
- It is for all humanity, not just Catholics and Christians.[13]
- It will be permanent.[14]
- It will be on the Earth and not in the sky.[15]
- It will be beautiful.[16]
- It will appear spontaneously.[17]
- It will be visible to everyone that comes to Medjugorje.[18]
- It will be indestructible.[19]
- It will be near but not before the end of the apparitions.[20]
- It will be accompanied by miraculous healings.[21]
- The visionaries know exactly what it is.[22]
- The visionaries know exactly when it will appear.[23]
- It will confirm the Virgin Mary's apparitional presence in Medjugorje.[24]
- It will be preceded by two warnings.[25]
- It is given in order to call people back to the faith.[26]
- It is something that has never been seen on Earth before.[27]
- It will be rejected by some who will not believe it is a sign from God.[28]
- Some people will remain unbelievers even after the Sign comes.[29]
- Those who are alive will witness many conversions because of the Sign.[30]
- Those who wait until the Sign comes to believe will have little time for conversion—for some, it will be too late.[31]
- It will happen in the lifetime of the visionaries.[32]
- It will be seen that human hands could not have made it.[33]
- It will be able to be photographed and filmed.[34]
- It is the one Secret the visionaries know they share in common.[35]
- It will be much more beautiful when seen by one's own eyes in Medjugorje.[36]

- To experience the Sign with the heart, one must come to Medjugorje.[37]
- There will be conversions during the Sign's manifestation.[38]
- The Sign will be for the Church so there can be no doubt of Mary's presence in Medjugorje.[39]

⚬⚬⚬

During his interview with Vicka Ivanković for his book, *A Thousand Encounters with the Blessed Virgin Mary in Medjugorje*, Father Janko Bubalo asked the visionary what she could tell him about the Great Sign:

Bubalo: *I see that this is really tedious to you, but nonetheless, at least tell me where the Virgin will give that Sign.*
Vicka: On Podbrdo. At the sight of the first apparitions.
Bubalo: *Will the Sign be in the heavens or on Earth?*
Vicka: On Earth.
Bubalo: *Will it appear spontaneously, or will it gradually appear?*
Vicka: Spontaneously.
Bubalo: *Will everyone be able to see it?*
Vicka: Whoever comes here will.
Bubalo: *Will the Sign be temporary or permanent?*
Vicka: Permanent.
Bubalo: *And will the Sign be able to be destroyed by anyone?*
Vicka: By no one.
Bubalo: *You think that, or...*
Vicka: The Virgin said so.
Bubalo: *Do you know exactly what the Sign will be?*
Vicka: Exactly!
Bubalo: *Do you know when the Virgin will make it evident to the rest of us?*
Vicka: I know that also.
Bubalo: *Do each of you know that?*

Vicka: I don't know, but I think that not everyone knows it up to now.

Bubalo: *I failed to ask, is the Sign a special Secret, or...*

Vicka: It is a particular Secret, but it is also one of the Ten Secrets.

Bubalo: *For certain?*

Vicka: What else, but for certain.

Bubalo: *And why is the Virgin leaving the Sign here?*

Vicka: Why to show the people that she is here among us.

Bubalo: *And what do you think, what would happen to any one of you that might somehow reveal the Secret of that Sign?*

Vicka: I don't think about the possibility because I don't think that could happen.

Bubalo: *Well, at one point, the Bishop's Commission asked that you describe what the Sign would be like, and when it would occur, and that the notation be sealed in your presence and be kept safely until the Sign occurs.*

Vicka: That is true.

Bubalo: *But you did not want to agree with that. Why?...*

Vicka...I don't want to say any more about the subject. But I'll just say this: whoever does not believe without a sign will not believe with a sign. And I'll tell you this too: woe to him who delays his conversion waiting for the Sign. I once told you that many would come, and perhaps, even bow to the Sign, but will, nonetheless, not believe. Be happy you are not among them![40]

∽∝∽

Over twenty-five years later, on January 2, 2008, Father Livio Fanzaga, a priest of the Scolopian Fathers, interviewed Vicka on *Radio Maria Italia* in a live broadcast from Medjugorje.

In this discussion, Vicka—who has had several visions of the Great Sign[41]—revealed a little more of what she knew about this coming prodigy:

Fanzaga: *I was really struck by what the Madonna said about the Third Secret, which concerns the Great Sign on the mountain. You visionaries said that it will be a visible Sign, an indestructible Sign that comes from God. However, she also added, "Hurry and convert yourselves. When the promised Sign on the hill will be given, it will be too late" (September 2, 1982). Another time, she also said, "And even after I've left this Sign on the hill which I have promised you, many will not believe. They will come to the hill. They will kneel, but they won't believe (July 19, 1981). Why is it, in your opinion, that people will see the Sign, but they won't convert?*

Vicka: The Third Secret is about a Sign that she will leave here [Medjugorje] on the mountain of the apparitions. This Sign will remain forever. It is given above all for those people who are still far away from God. The Madonna wishes to give these people who will see the Sign a chance to believe in God. I was able to see this Sign.

Fanzaga: *You have already seen the Sign?*

Vicka: Yes, I saw it in a vision.

Fanzaga: *Jacov once said in an interview with Radio Maria that in order to see the Sign it will be necessary to come here to Medjugorje. Is that true?*

Vicka: Yes, it's true. The Sign will remain on Podbrdo, and one will have to come here to see it. This Sign will be indestructible and will remain in that place forever. I want to say about those people who will see it and not believe. The Madonna leaves everyone free to believe or not, but those are ones whose hearts are too closed. It's the same thing as the Madonna said to us, "If one wants to go to Heaven, he will go to Heaven, if one wants to go to Hell, he will go to Hell." Those people who are far away from God and do not want to believe, they will not believe in the Sign. For those who do not know God but have good intentions and a desire to love, these will be benefitted by the Sign.

But I think that those who do everything against God, they will run away from the Sign. They will not believe.

Fanzaga: *So, this is a time of grace. This is the time of conversion, "Do not wait for the Sign in order to convert yourselves," the Madonna said. Well, so why leave a Sign like some last extreme help? Is it in order to move the Church to recognize the apparitions as authentic?*

Vicka: Yes, certainly it will be for the Church, so that they will have no doubt that the Madonna had been among us. And it is also for those who are still far away from God. So, the Madonna is thinking about both groups of people. And then it is up to us—how to be ready to respond to the Sign—to respond to her call through the Sign. Everyone who comes, who will see, you know, you can say, "I don't believe it" and this is your personal idea—that's what you believe. But that the Madonna is here, that she is present, that she leaves this Sign—a Sign no man can make; it is something only God can make. And so, nobody will be able to say that it is a small thing or something else. This arrives in such a way, that they won't have words to say what it is.[42]

A sign that no man can make.

A sign only God can make.

A sign people must be ready to respond to.

Vicka's words leave no doubt as to the magnitude of the Great Sign in her eyes.

In 1993, the young visionary once again told an interviewer how she had seen the Great Sign in several visions, "It will be beautiful, very beautiful, I have already seen it three times." The Sign would be, Vicka remarked then, a final and wondrous warning for "unbelievers."[43]

Two years later, in August of 1995, Vicka added to the mystery of the Great Sign.

She revealed it would appear "when only one of them (the vision-aries) will still have the daily apparitions." On that same occasion, she also said that the Virgin Mary never really explained what was meant by her words, "Do not wait for the Sign, when the Sign comes, it will be too late." [44]

⁓

Like Vicka, Jacov Čolo has spoken about seeing the Great Sign.

Revealing that he too had experienced a vision of the Third Secret, Jacov said the Great Sign was, as Vicka described, "Very beautiful."[45]

But—he quickly added in the same conversation—the first two Secrets will be game changers. "The very first Secrets will be revealed, and they will prove," Jacov stressed, "that the apparitions are real."[46]

CHAPTER TWELVE

A Call to Atheists

"Fools say in their hearts, "There is no God."

—Ps 14:1

A unique event—unprecedented in history—is what the appearance of the Great Sign on Mt. Podbrdo will be some day in Bijakovići.

It is to be a moment many have said they desire to witness.

But one may not have to be there to see it come about.

Over the last 20 years, cameras have been installed at strategic locations around Medjugorje in order to record the activity on and around the hill on a 24-hour basis. This will hopefully capture the exact moment the Sign appears on Podbrdo. It is also, some believe, perhaps a prudent step in helping to refute the foretold naysayers.

During her compelling October 26, 1985, interview with Father Petar Ljubicic, Mirjana Dragićević discussed the coming of the Great Sign too, adding a few more fascinating insights to this mystery. The following is an excerpt:

Ljubicic: *Out of the Ten Secrets that each of you will receive—and you and Ivanka [Ivankovic] already did—do you know which of them will be exactly the same? I mean, which Secrets will be exactly the same for you, for Ivanka, and the others?*

Mirjana: No, I don't know.

Ljubicic: *Someone said that only three of the Secrets that each of you received are identical, while all the others are different.*

Mirjana: The one about the Sign is identical. I am positive about that because there will not be six different Signs.

Ljubicic: *Not on the same spot.*

Mirjana: The Sign is the same Sign. Personally, I never spoke about the Secrets with any of the others. After all, in the same way that the Secrets were entrusted to me, that is how they were entrusted to the others as well.

Ljubicic: *Thus far, I never spoke with you about the permanency of the Sign. Each of you maintain persistently that it will be indestructible, permanent, and very large. Accordingly, one will be able to understand it as something tangible.*

Mirjana: Yes, the Sign will be indestructible and permanent. Naturally, it will be clear to everyone that it is not something constructed and erected. Nobody will be able to say that it was brought and placed in that particular spot by, let us say, someone from Medjugorje.

Ljubicic: *The Sign's manifestation—will it be during the day or night? By asking that, am I encroaching on the Secret?*

Mirjana: Oh, that is a secret. I cannot answer that because that touches upon…the Secret already has a specific date and time.

Ljubicic: *Does the Secret have a specified minute and second?*

Mirjana: I know the exact day and hour.

Ljubicic: *Do you anticipate that there may be some people, some souls, who will perhaps "feel" something, without anyone else's knowledge or anticipation, that something is about to happen and will, therefore, come in large numbers?*

Mirjana: I do not know. But I did have the opportunity to ask Our Lady something to that effect. I do know that, during the Secret's manifestation, there will be spiritual conversions.

Ljubicic: *There will be conversions?*

Mirjana: Yes, there will be conversions.

Ljubicic: *Do you think that of those who will convert, a majority of them will be those who were suspicious, who doubted, who didn't believe?*

Mirjana: There will be all kinds: those who were just suspicious, those who didn't believe at all, and others.

Ljubicic: *Do you think that there will be those who will remain hardened—despite the explicit, tangible, visible signs and warnings?*

Mirjana: Yes.

Ljubicic: *There will be?*

Mirjana: Yes, there will be.

Ljubicic: *Yes, of course, just as there always were. Even today, so many see the obvious works of God, yet simply reject Him because they are so hardened, just as the Pharisees did.*

Mirjana: Those are the ones who have shut their souls to God.

Ljubicic: *It seems that Our Lady is drawing attention to our greatest enemy, Satan. It seems that he is increasing his attacks, that he is attempting to create confusion and entangle the entire situation.*

Mirjana: He is responsible for the unbelievers, Satan. This is why she said to bless the home with Holy Water on Saturdays. He is the one who makes people into unbelievers. Who else?

Ljubicic: *Do you think that Godlessness is growing or decreasing today?*

Mirjana: Father, it is increasing. A miracle is necessary for Godlessness to decrease.3

Fr. Petar Ljubicic has been interviewed many times about the Secrets. He has also spoken specifically of the Great Sign in his talks at Medjugorje and throughout the world. At Medjugorje, on April 22, 1989, Ljubicic talked about the Third Secret:

> Our Lady says *all* of the Secrets *have* to come to pass. Some can be lessened, but they all have to be accomplished. I can only say the first two Secrets are warnings, and after they are revealed, it will be clear to everyone that Our Lady is here on the hill of apparitions, Our Lady promised to leave a Sign, and we can only guess what it will be. It will be approximately where a cross marks the apparitions of Our Lady.
>
> The Secrets will be revealed one by one. Ten days before they are to be revealed, I will be told and I will then pray and fast for seven days, and three days after that I will reveal it. The Seventh Secret has been lessened through prayer. The Third Secret is the only one that is good and that will be the Sign that Our Lady will leave on the mountain.
>
> The word Secret does not have the same meaning in English as it does in Croatian. In Croatian, it means "a message that has not been revealed." The message of Medjugorje is peace, the promise that Jesus brought when he walked the Earth. But the messages that will be revealed are warnings in a sense of what sin will bring.[2]

~~~⋈~~~

Mirjana Soldo's confidence in the Great Sign is noteworthy.

The visionary told Father René Laurentin in January 1986:

"After the Sign will be shown, one will be obliged to believe."[3]

In Mirjana's January 10, 1983, interview published in Father Svetozar Kraljević's book, she also seemed to imply that the Virgin

Mary's presence will be associated with the appearance of the Great Sign in a special way.

In a footnote that is found on the bottom of the first page of the original transcript of the interview, we read:

"This statement (of Mirjana) seems to imply that Our Lady will be present at Medjugorje on the day the permanent Sign appears."[4]

In another small, uncirculated booklet published in 1983, *Our Lady Queen of Peace, Queen of the Apostles*, there is found a message from Mary to the visionaries that also speaks of the Great Sign and atheists.

This revelation can be seen to confirm Marija Pavlović's response to Father Rupčić in his interview of the visionaries in December of 1982. At the time, Marija said that the Sign would be "for those who do not believe." The booklet reads:

> They say that Our Lady has promised to leave a visible Sign on the mountain where the first apparitions occurred. Mary told them: *The sign will be given for* the atheists. You faithful already have signs and you have to become the sign for the atheists.
>
> Following this visible Sign, there will be many miracles and healings. All the visionaries say that they have seen this Sign in the apparitions, they know the date when the sign will come; but they say that before the Sign comes there will be a warning or admonishment to the world. Our Lady says this: *You faithful must not wait for the Sign before you convert; convert soon, this time is a time of grace for you. You can never thank God enough for His grace which He has given, this time for deepening your faith and for your conversion. When the Sign comes it will be too late for many.*[5]

As noted, one of the very first interviews with the visionaries at Medjugorje was conducted by Father Ljudevit Rupčić at the beginning of December 1982.

It consisted of sixty-two questions, some of which involved the Secrets.[6]

In 1987, Rupčić repeated his initial inquiry.[7]

In this second interview, Father Rupčić asked the visionaries two new questions with regards to the Great Sign.

1) Are you sure that the Great Sign is going to appear on the hill of apparitions?

2) Are you disturbed that it is late in arriving?[8]

The visionaries' responses were as follows:

Marija: I am sure that it will arrive like Our Lady told us. Everything is under the control of Our Lady, both the Sign and the apparitions. It is Our Lady who knows the best time when this Sign will appear? All that is her plan.

Ivan: It is certain that this Great Sign will appear as Our Lady has said. I am not at all disturbed.

Vicka: I only know that there will be, on the site of the apparition, a visible Sign and I am not disturbed as to whether the time is long before its manifestation.

Jacov: I am sure that the Sign will be manifested. I am not troubled that it has not taken place up to the present.

Mirjana: Of course, I am convinced. There is nothing to be troubled about since I know the exact date. Everything must follow its course.

Ivanka: Yes, absolutely. Everything will develop according to God's plan.[9]

⚯

Clearly, the Great Sign is very much at the center of what the future holds with Medjugorje.

This is because all of the visionaries concur that its appearance will reinvigorate faith throughout the world.

The Sign will be, as Vatican correspondent John Thavis writes in his book, *The Vatican Prophecies*, "An emblem of gratitude" for believers—and "a last call" for nonbelievers.[10]

Is it the miracle that Mirjana told Father Ljubicic was necessary to wake up the world?

Over the years, the visionaries have maintained a unified conviction of the Great Sign's strategic purpose: It is to prove the Virgin Mary appeared at Medjugorje.

Their words reflect this confidence:

- "The most powerful armaments and explosives in the world could not destroy it," Ivanka declared. "Nothing," she asserts, "will harm the Madonna's plans."[11]
- "The people will be convinced the Madonna was here," insists Mirjana concerning the Great Sign, "they will understand the Sign."[12]
- "When the Permanent Sign comes," said Jacov, "people will come here from all over the world in even larger numbers. Many more will believe!"[13]

Father Slavko Barbarić, who often spoke privately with the visionaries concerning the Sign, appeared to hold the same confidence that it is to be an extraordinary manifestation of the truth of God's presence in Medjugorje:

"Yes, people will come from everywhere. And, there will be a reason why. I am no prophet. But, if anything should happen at all...it will only happen in and through Medjugorje, through the Mother of God. The world will be shown clearly where lies authentic power. I am thinking here, among other things, in the Sign that was promised in the Secrets."[14]

Barbarić was awed by a possible theological mystery surrounding the Great Sign foretold to come at Medjugorje.

In an interview he conducted with Archbishop Frane Franic of Split on December 16-17, 1984—just five days after Franic had met with Pope John Paul II in Rome to discuss the case of Medjugorje— he asked the Archbishop if the Great Sign at Medjugorje could be associated with the *Great Sign* foretold in Chapter Twelve of *The Book of Revelation*.[15]

> Barbarić: *Every week, I speak with the visionaries in the name of the parish. I have asked them a number of times about the Sign. They always say, "Our Lady instructed us. We have seen it. We know. There is no need to worry. As for us, we must pray and fast." They say that there would have been other signs if we had accepted the messages better and if Our Lady had not found so much resistance. Ought we to understand the talk about the Great Sign in terms of the Apocalypse?*
>
> **Archbishop Franic**: The *Apocalypse* does talk about the Great Sign: "*A woman, clothed in the sun appears in the skies with a dragon opposing her.*" Maybe the Sign is beginning to be realized in this way. When the prophets spoke, they did not know what they were saying in their prophecies. For example, prophets in the *Old Testament spoke* about Christ as King of Kings. They did not comprehend properly what God was saying throughout time. . .They did not know how all of this would end. The talk about the Great Sign is prophetic language. When the children speak, they do not understand many of the things they say since they did not study theology. Therefore, we are here to explain all their expressions about the words, messages, signs, and so on.[16]
>
> Barbarić: *It seems to me it is the "Great Sign" which is perplexing to our Bishop. The children say it will come soon. That is Biblical talk.*

Archbishop Franic: Exactly. And to try to catch the children in a contradiction like this is unnecessary. What do they know? They do not know exegesis or hermeneutics.[17]

$\sim\!\!\propto\!\!\sim$

Although the Great Sign may have profound and ancient Biblical implications, it also appears to be a line of demarcation for our present times.

Asked by author Jan Connell if many people would die between the time of the first chastisement and the promised Great Sign at Medjugorje, Mirjana again reminded people that after the visible Sign appears:

"Those who are still alive will have little time for conversion."[18]

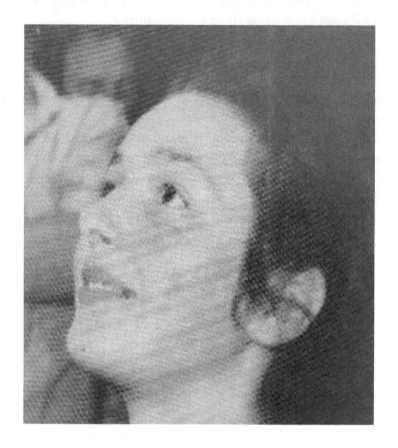

Ivanka Ivanković Elez

"The Madonna has come to Medjugorje to call all people on earth to her Son, Jesus, for the final time."

Photo Credit: Pittsburgh Center for Peace

CHAPTER THIRTEEN

"I Know the Future of the World"

"For I know well the plans I have in mind for you, says the Lord, plans for your welfare not your woe! Plans to give you a future full of hope."

—Jer 29 :11

"Do not fool yourself thinking I am good, and my brother who lives next to me is not good! You will not be right. I, as your Mother, love you and therefore I warn you. The Secrets are here, my children. It is not known what they are, but when you do learn, it will be too late. Return to prayer! Nothing is more needed than prayer. I wish that God would allow me to explain to you at least a little about the Secrets, but even this is too many graces He is giving."[1]

—The Virgin Mary at Medjugorje,
January 28, 1987

While there is little that Mary is permitted by God to reveal about the Secrets of Medjugorje, one not so little thing is certain about them: their number.

There are Ten Secrets of Medjugorje—perhaps more than any other well documented Marian apparition in history, either approved or not by the Church.[2]

But why Ten Secrets?

Is there a mystical significance to this number?

⸺⸗⸺

According to Biblical scholars, ten is considered a perfect number.

It consists of the number four—the number of physical creation—and the number six—the number of man. Ten is also considered the number of man's perfection, which is believed to be confirmed by the presence of ten fingers and ten toes.

It is said that the number ten represents the authority of God and His governance on Earth. Some have written that it is a symbol of obedience, responsibility and completeness of order with regards to God's laws.

In the Bible, the number ten is found two hundred and forty-two times, and the word tenth is found another seventy-nine times. Not surprisingly, we begin to find the number ten almost immediately in the first books of the Old Testament.

In the first chapter of *The Book of Genesis*, the phrase "God said" is written ten times, which is said to testify to God's creative power. God is then found telling Abraham that He would not destroy Sodom if ten righteous men could be found there.

Further on in *Genesis*, Abraham's servant takes ten camels with him on the way to procure Rebekah to be the wife of his son, Isaac. After he meets her, two gold bracelets weighing ten shekels are placed on Rebekah's wrists, and there is an effort made to restrain her for ten days before she is to depart to Isaac.

The next book in the Old Testament picks up where *Genesis* leaves off.

In *Exodus*, we read of the ten plagues that fall on Pharaoh and Egypt, a pivotal story in the Jewish timeline. This is followed shortly by the "Ten Commandments" being given to Moses by God on Mt. Sinai, perhaps Scripture's most recognizable moment with regards to the number.

The number ten, or multiples of ten, continue throughout the Old Testament.

In the Temple of Solomon, ten pillars line the west side of the Court. Inside, where ten linen curtains hang, there are ten lavers, ten lampstands and ten tables and it is on the tenth day of the first month that a lamb is to be chosen to sacrifice in the temple for Passover.

Most memorably, God is seen in *Isaiah* to cause the shadow on a sundial to go back ten degrees and the Jewish faithful are encouraged to tithe—meaning "give a tenth"—of their income to the Lord.

In the New Testament, Jesus is found to cure ten lepers and there were ten days between His ascension to Heaven and Pentecost.

Jesus also uses the number ten in many parables: *The Parable of the Ten Virgins*, where five virgins are found to lack the necessary oil to be ready for the bridegroom; *The Parable of the Ten Gold Coins*, where ten disciples are given ten gold coins in a test of their stewardship; and *The Parable of the Lost Coin*, where a woman with ten coins misplaces one but rejoices greatly upon discovering it.

If there is a reason why there are Ten Secrets of Medjugorje, it will probably be never known. But the history of the use of the number in the Bible offers considerable insight and much to ponder with regards to this question.

Two other Scriptural uses of the number ten appear relevant and significant to the times at hand, and perhaps the apocalyptic nature of the Ten Secrets of Medjugorje.

There were ten generations from Adam to Noah that lived on Earth before the world was purified of its evil by the Great Flood.

And it was after the Tenth Plague struck Egypt and Moses received the Ten Commandments on Sinai that the Jewish people departed to begin a new life in the "Land of Milk and Honey."

Did these three events in the timeline of ancient Israel foreshadow the role the Ten Secrets of Medjugorje are to play in God's plan to redirect the path of humanity?

Does the foretold era of peace represent "the Land of Milk and Honey?"

⌘

In her book, Mirjana Dragićević Soldo stresses that the Ten Secrets are not all negative.

It will be a time of great joy, Mirjana reportedly alluded to concerning the Fourth, Fifth and Sixth of the Secrets, for those who choose to convert.[3]

But offsets Vicka, terrible things await those who do not turn back to God.[4]

Ivanka said following her June 25, 1988, apparition, that she and the Virgin discussed the Fourth Secret, after which she stated that it was very important for people to do God's will.[5]

Vicka, in her extensive interview with Father Janko Bubalo, also remarked that her Fourth Secret applied to her alone, causing many to wonder if the visionaries were receiving different Secrets.

In one of their books, Fathers Barbarić and Vlašić did note the existence of other secrets:

"These visionaries say that the Ten Secrets refer to the whole world and are linked together in a chain. There are also *other* secrets, personal secrets for the children or for certain people who are connected with these future world events."[6]

On June 25, 1989—during her annual apparition—Ivanka revealed that she and the Virgin discussed the Fifth Secret.[7]

Father René Laurentin, who was present at the apparition that day, recalled that he watched the young woman's "transparent joy" at the beginning of the vision become "somber," and then "serious and grave."[8] It was an indication to him that the content of Ivanka's Fifth Secret may be somewhat concerning.[9]

When asked by Jan Connell about what occurred during the apparition, Ivanka said that Mary discussed with her both the Fifth and Sixth Secrets that day, and that the Madonna was asking everyone in the world to pray and fast.[10]

Ivanka further commented on her practice of fasting on bread and water for forty days every year at Lent, as her family has for generations.[11] She said she started doing this because the Blessed Mother told her that fasting will stop wars, adding somewhat curiously:

"I know the future of the world—not just my own history—but the future of the world."[12]

"What did the Blessed Mother tell you? Was it a good future?", Connell inquired.

"The Blessed Mother has told me everything. There are good things and bad things. The important thing to know is God loves each of us. We are His children."[13]

"Is it a long future?" persists Connell.

"For some it is long," replied Ivanka, then adding, "for some it is short."[14]

CHAPTER FOURTEEN

The Secrets and the Church

"And so I say to you, you are Peter, and upon this rock I will build my church, and the gates of the netherworld shall not prevail against it."

—Mt 16:18

C atholic prophecies have often spoken of a great crisis arising someday in the Church. This could then—some mystics have warned—lead to a schism.

In the 1973 Church approved apparitions of Akita, Japan, the Virgin Mary revealed to Sister Agnes Katsuko Sasagawa that Satan would infiltrate the Church in such a way that "Cardinals will oppose Cardinals, and Bishops will be against Bishops."

"Priests will be scorned, and churches and altars sacked;" the Church would be full of those who "compromised" the truth, Mary predicted at Akita.

Revelations such as these, not surprisingly, have caused some to wonder if the Ten Secrets of Medjugorje involve the Church.

It is a query that was put forth to some of the visionaries.

In December of 1982, Father Ljudevit Rupčić asked all the visionaries at Medjugorje a specific question:

Did Our Lady confide any Secrets to you?[1]

Several of the visionaries—in their answer to this question—mentioned that some of the Secrets involved the Church:

Marija Pavlović: Yes, I know six Secrets. The others know seven or eight. They have to do with us, the Church, people in general.[2]

Vicka Ivanković: Yes, I have seven. The First Secret has to do with our church at Medjugorje. It has to do as well with the Sign, humanity in general, and each person. The Secrets speak of the Church in general. There are some which concern us.[3]

Ivanka Ivanković: Yes, I have seven. Some concern us personally, others the Church and the world.[4] (Ivanka, according to Father Janko Bubalo, received from Mary a narration of the past, present and future life of the Church that she has recorded, but is not permitted by her to release at the present.[5])

It is known that the last four of the Ten Secrets are considered grave, that the first three are described as warnings, and that these three visionaries—Marija, Vicka, and Ivanka—all told Father Rupčić that they had received, up until then, no more than seven Secrets.[6]

Consequently, it appears that these three visionaries' responses to Father Rupčić's question—which all speak of the Church—may involve Secrets Four through Six.

Author and investigative reporter, Michael Brown, believes so, too:

"Little was said about the Fourth, Fifth, and Sixth Secrets, leading to speculation that these were the ones having to do with the Church."[7]

Medjugorje evangelist Wayne Weible concurs. He wrote in his final book, *The Last Apparition*, that these three Secrets—four through six—"may refer to the Church."[8]

Once again, though, such speculation that these Secrets involve the Church, also presumes the six visionaries are receiving the same Secrets, which Laurentin says, "is not evident."[9]

❧

Father Rupčić's 1982 interview unearthed one other specific note of interest concerning the Secrets and the Church.

When asked, Vicka gave a most candid answer to the Croatian priest's question, "Did Our Lady have a message for the Pope?"

"He (the Pope)," said Vicka, "should consider himself as the father of all people and not only Christians. That he tirelessly and courageously promotes the message of peace and love for all men. This is *found among the Secrets* that she gave us, but we shouldn't speak about it now, only when she permits us to say it. There is a little of everything."[10]

Several years later, during a January 24, 1985, interview with Archbishop Frane Franic of Split, Vicka added more to her disclosures concerning the Church,

"A new era begins for the Church, one in which the Church *cannot trust* any human power or human strength but rely on the power of the Cross, on the love of Christ, and the Holy Spirit."[11]

Vicka's words here sound a bit ominous, causing one to ponder all the prophecies of apostasy, betrayal and schism that have been foretold to come upon the Catholic Church some day, a day some believe has begun to unfold.

Mirjana, in her book, also spoke of the Church and the Secrets being related.

She said that between the time we are living in now—the time of grace—and the time of the Triumph, will be the time of the Secrets. It will be during this time, Mirjana noted, that the priesthood of the

Catholic Church will serve as a bridge to get *through* the Secrets and into the time of the Triumph.[12]

Similarly, in a question-and-answer session at a talk he gave in Seattle, Washington, on October 29, 1997, Ivan made it clear that some of the Secrets involve the Church.

Question: *Is there any "reason" given for the Secrets and is mention made of any timetable?*

Ivan: I believe so; that there is a reason why she gave them to us. The Secrets Our Lady gave are tied with the world, with the Church, and one day will be revealed. It's also other things that are involved in the Secrets.[13]

Exponentially wiser today from doing countless interviews, as well as from simply maturing, Vicka's slip of the tongue concerning the Secrets and the Pope is one of many found in the early archives of Medjugorje during such question-and-answer sessions with the visionaries.

From appearing to allude that the Secrets are part of the *Apocalypse* and the Second Coming of Christ,[14] to refusing to deny that many could perish between the time of the First Secret and the Third Secret (the Great Sign),[15] to admitting the Ten Secrets will be painful to the whole world,[16] misspeaks, gaffes, misunderstandings, translation errors, and perhaps some true accidental disclosures are found when one looks closely at the various discussions the children conducted with their inquisitors in the first years of the apparitions.

Perhaps one of those "accidental" disclosures occurred in the 1980s. At the time, the youthful visionaries were in the process of receiving the Secrets and also had subsequent apparitions with Mary that discussed or previewed the Secrets in visions. Quite often, these experiences left them in tears.*

---

* Marija, Vicka, Ivanka, Mirjana, and Jacov, have all been reported to have cried at an apparition

After one such event, one of the visionaries was asked why they were so distressed and reportedly replied, "How can't I cry when I see blood and little children."[†]

It was made clear by the visionary that the vision did not involve dead children, but only blood on the ground around them.

Perhaps similarly to Sister Lucia's description of the Third Part of the Secret of Fatima—in which she was shown a slain Pope, along with bishops, priests, religious, and various lay people who were "martyrs" and whose "blood was being gathered up"—this reported vision may well have been symbolic imagery rather that a literal event.

On another occasion (March 25, 2022)—when asked during an interview on *Radio Maria* by Father Livio Fanzaga, "Do you think there is a danger of nuclear war?" or "Is this just the Devil's way of intimidation?"—one of the Medjugorje visionaries, Marija Lunetti, answered, "Aaah…I don't want to go into the Secrets, but…"

One disclosure of the contents of the Secrets, however, was not an accident.

Dr. Ludvik Stopar, a theistic parapsychologist and psychiatrist, trained in hypnotherapy, reported that he hypnotized Marija Pavlović.

And, Stopar admitted, he got Marija to reveal the Secrets.

❦

Stopar studied general medicine at the Medical University of Graz in Styria, Austria, and psychiatry, hypnotherapy and parapsychology at the University of Freiburg im Breisgau, Germany.[17] He then became director of the Amber Polyclinic of Maribor in Yugoslavia.

He says he visited Medjugorje on four occasions to examine the visionaries.[18]

With regard to Medjugorje, his report found the children to be absolutely normal, but it also revealed that one of the subjects, Marija Pavlović, had been subjected to hypnosis by him.

[†] This account comes from two highly reputable sources that were both in attendance at the apparition.

Dr. Stopar was interviewed by Father René Laurentin concerning this matter sometime in 1982-83, as reported by Dr. Henri Joyeux and Laurentin in their book on the scientific and medical studies on the apparitions at Medjugorje.

Laurentin: *Why did you go to Medjugorje?*
Stopar: Parapsychological phenomena are my line of work. I could not be uninterested in these events which have taken place in my own country.
Laurentin: *When did you go to Medjugorje?*
Stopar: Four times: in May 1982, November 1982, June 1983, and November 1983. Each visit lasted five to ten days.
Laurentin: *Your memorandum, written in German, was made known to me about a year ago. It was given to me under the seal of secrecy, but it is well known today and you yourself have pub- lished a summary of it in a Brazilian periodical. In this you claim to have separated the 90% subconscious from the 10% conscious level of the visionaries and in this way, you have been able to es- tablish their sincerity. What then was your method and on whom did you carry it out?*
Stopar: Hypnosis, administered to Marija Pavlović, who ap- peared to me to be the most intelligent and the most mature of the visionaries and who was therefore the most suitable for the test.
Laurentin: *Did you use touch eye contact?*
Stopar: Neither. She closed her eyes. Once asleep, she breathes as if asleep. During the two previous days I had her give me an account of the visions without hypnosis. I asked her to re- peat the account under hypnosis and she did this for one hour. While hypnotized only the subconscious level operated. The 10% conscious level was asleep. There was no difference be- tween the two accounts; both were the same.
Laurentin: *You do not want to say that she gave exactly the same account, in exactly the same words?*

Stopar: No, certainly not. She used different words, but the meaning was the same.

Laurentin: *Were there other differences?*

Stopar: In the early account, not under hypnosis, Maria kept the Secrets confided to her by the apparition, very strictly. Under hypnosis she told them to me.

Laurentin: *But surely, a violation of conscience! Now, the Secrets are no longer a secret?*

Stopar: You can trust my professionalism. The Secrets remain as secret for me as for Marija. I would not confide them, even to you. It is as serious as the seal of the confessional.

Laurentin: *When I questioned Marija about this hypnosis, I was surprised that she does not seem to remember what she said to you.*

Stopar: This is quite normal. Marija excused herself at the end of the hypnosis: "Excuse me, Doctor, I cannot understand what happened to me; I went to sleep while talking to you."

Laurentin: *One thing did surprise me. When I asked, "Did the Doctor ask your permission?" She replied, "No."*

Stopar: *If I had asked, I am sure she would have refused. In therapy, one does not ask permission.*[19]

No further information on this intriguing episode has ever surfaced.

It appears, since there is no evidence to the contrary, Dr. Stopar remained true to his word concerning the Secrets.

However, the question arises as to whether or not Marija's involvement with Dr. Stopar at the time was considered personal therapy, or merely her cooperating with a researcher of the apparitions.

~⚬~

Unpleasant. Serious. Grave.

The last four of the Ten Secrets of Medjugorje have found no shortage of strong words to best capture the drama of their reputed content.

The early interviews conducted with Mirjana, Ivanka, and Vicka in 1982 and 1983 opened the window wide for people's imaginations concerning these Secrets—and nothing since has done much to close it.

As a whole—strictly from a curiosity standpoint—the early interviews with Mirjana are especially priceless. This is because they deliver more than just information.

They are a captivating, human look into the life of a visionary, of Medjugorje, and the universal problems at hand that the sin of the world has brought once again at this moment in history.

They also reveal the challenges of being a prophet, whether thousands of years ago or today.

As with the prophet Jeremiah in the Old Testament—who loved his people but needed to present them with the cold, hard facts—Mirjana tells it like it is: God is intent on bringing change in the world, whether welcomed or not, and trying choices will soon be coming for everyone.

But her human side shines through.

The Seventh Secret—perceived by the young visionary as a troubling disclosure—becomes a personal quest for Mirjana to have lifted from her people.

Thus, it is clear.

Although she is a prophet working for the Lord, the divine justice rising on the horizon is coming for her, too, for *her* world—and the world of her family, which she soon understands is all of humanity.

So, like Abraham, like Moses, like so many of the prophets, she attempts to argue on behalf of her fallen brothers and sisters. She tries to reason with the Almighty, to get Him to sheath His sword (1Chr 21:27), to turn away from His wrath (Prv 24:18).

But, though successful in *softening* the fury of the Seventh Secret,[20] Mirjana's heart is again broken, her mind overwhelmed once more, by what she learns must still come:

"Then she (Mary) told me the Ninth Secret and it was even worse. The Tenth Secret is totally bad and cannot be lessened whatsoever.

"I cannot say anything about it, because even a word would disclose the Secret before it is time to do so."[21]

Ivan Dragicévic´

"The Madonna has been permitted by God to come here. She knows what is coming in the future. She is calling God's children back on the path to Heaven."

Photo Credit: St. Andrews Productions

CHAPTER FIFTEEN

The "Serious" Secrets

"It shall be a time unsurpassed in distress since nations began until that time."

—Dn 12:1

Decades have gone by without anything of true significance coming to light regarding the Ten Secrets of Medjugorje—especially the last four.

And nothing more should be expected.

After years of interviews, the visionaries are weary of such questions and have no new answers. But the fraught content of the last of the Secrets is indirectly alluded to now and then by them and this helps to keep their momentous nature front and center:

- Ivanka—when asked if every person on Earth will soon become aware of God's presence—replied that this would occur *sooner* than many suspect.[1]
- Jacov—in hinting that there are some mighty changes ahead—confirmed that Mary is in Medjugorje to reconcile the whole world—and *will* do so.[2]

- Ivan—in trying to explain what Mary hopes to accomplish through the apparitions—stated that people will understand one day why Mary has been in Medjugorje so long.[3]

On the Feast of the Assumption in 1982, three of the visionaries received the Eighth Secret and they all said it was "very grave."[4]

On November 19 of that same year, some of them were given the Ninth Secret and described it as "extremely grave and wept because of it."[5]

Vicka—it was said—grieved uncontrollably after receiving her Ninth Secret on April 22, 1986.[6] Asked by Father Bubalo if the Virgin's Secrets foretold something "ghastly awaited mankind," she replied, "Well, you can say it is known."[7]

All of this confirmed what Mirjana—unfairly criticized by some at the time—had reported years before.

～∞～

Although Mirjana received her Tenth Secret in 1982, the Virgin Mary continued to speak to her on occasion about the Secrets during her annual apparitions and during so-called "special apparitions."

Years have gone by since Mirjana revealed the substance of such conversations, though slight references to her confidential discussions with Mary about the Secrets are noted throughout the 80s and 90s.[8] She did, however, refer again in 1992 to the Tenth Secret as "especially" grave.[9]

Mirjana also revealed in her book that on June 14, 1986, Mary appeared to her and told her this would be the last of her special apparitions involving the Secrets because she had explained everything that was necessary.[10]

Mirjana further wrote about a special prayer to Jesus—for those who do not know the love of God—that Mary taught her which is connected to the Secrets. She says she will reveal it some day when permitted along with a book on the story of the Virgin's life as revealed to her through visions.[11]

It remains, however, with Mirjana's January 10, 1983, interview— published in Father Svetozar Kraljevic 's book—that we learn the most about the last four of the Ten Secrets:

Question: *You have been given the last of the Secrets?*
Mirjana: Yes, the Tenth.
Question: *Can you tell me what it relates to?*
Mirjana: I cannot; but I can tell you that the Eighth Secret is worse than the other seven. I prayed for a long time that (the Seventh Secret) might be less severe. Every day, when the Madonna came, I pestered her, asking that it be mitigated. Then she said that everyone should pray that it might be lessened. So, in Sarajevo, I got many people to join me in this prayer. Later, the Madonna told me that she'd been able to have the Secret lessened. But then, she told me the Ninth Secret and it was even worse. The Tenth Secret is *totally bad* and cannot be lessened whatsoever. I cannot say anything about it, because even a word would disclose the Secret before it's time to do so.
Question: *I won't press you. Anyway, though, the Tenth Secret has to do with what will definitely happen?*
Mirjana: Yes.
Question: *Unconditionally?*
Mirjana: Yes. It will happen.
Question: *What does the Madonna say? Can we prepare ourselves for what will happen?*
Mirjana: Yes, prepare! The Madonna said people should prepare themselves spiritually, be ready, and not panic; be reconciled in their souls. They should be ready for the worst, to die tomorrow. They should accept God now so that they will not be afraid. They should accept God, and everything else. No one

accepts death easily, but they can be at peace in their souls if they are believers. If they are committed to God, He will accept them.

Question: *This means total conversion and surrender to God?*

Mirjana: Yes.[12]

※

"The plans of the seers, the tears of some of them after having had the Eighth, the Ninth, and the Tenth Secrets," observed Father Rene Laurentin, "assures us that these last Secrets announce the wages of sin."[13] *

These Secrets, the French theologian said he was told by the visionaries, were quite intense.

But in what form will the events contained in these last of the Secrets be served?

As with the Third Secret of Fátima, many writers have scoured for small indiscretions on the part of the visionaries. They hope to find something said by accident, a word or two muttered in haste or frustration. Something that leaks some specific detail about the Secrets.

In his book, *Medjugorje: Facts, Documents and Theology*, Irish theologian Michael O'Carroll, reports that in an interview with the Canadian newspaper *L'Informateur*, one of the visionaries was asked if there would be a nuclear situation in the future and reportedly responded by saying that this was "part" of the Secrets. "Something unconsciously given away?" writes O'Carroll.[14]

---

* The 8th, 9th, and 10th Secrets have an ominous aura around them.. This comes from the fact that, of what little is known about them, all that can be said—based on the words and actions of several of the visionaries (weeping and great distress)—is that they sound very grave. They have been described by theologians as such. Some believe the nature of the chastisements thought to make up their content may perhaps be something unknown and unexpected, and not nuclear.

O'Carroll also dwelled on a stirring message one of the visionaries received from the Virgin Mary on August 15, 1985:

"My angel, pray for the unbelievers. They will tear their hair, brother will plead with brother, and they will curse their past godless lives, and repent, but it will be too late. Now is the time for conversion. Now is the time to do what I have been calling for these four years. Pray for them."[15]

Is this message hinting of a future terror or pandemonium to be permitted by God, whether from war, disease or a natural disaster. Does it warn perhaps of the coming of an "unknown" calamity that disrupts human life on Earth, such as the mounting danger of biological weapons or the use of Artificial Intelligence (AI), which some believe to be a Trojan Horse existential crisis in the making, one that already has led a growing number of scientists to predict the "extinction"of the human race.? *

Or is it hinting of one's personal anguish at the consequences of not repenting and standing before, perhaps unexpectedly, the judgment seat of God?

---

* The growing debate surrounding Artificial Intelligence is alarming. Experts in the field are warning that the human race is headed towards "trans-humanism," the "end of free-will," the "collapse of reality," and that AI is getting "stronger everyday, " that it is moving so fast that it already "can't be controlled." Some researchers have said AI is becoming an "outside" or "new Creator" and that it is the "biggest thing since religion." According to one AI investigation, "fifty percent" of researchers working on AI agree that humanity "will go extinct" from it. At an annual Artificial Intelligence safety conference in Puerto Rico, a scientist referred to AI as "summoning the demon." Presently, AI is "teaching itself" and is now at the "human age of 19." (An age well surpassed by anyone presently reading this book.) Much more could be written, but one final comment will suffice. Asked by researchers, "Is there a God?", an AI based system responded, "There is now." ("AI Poses 'Extinction' Risk, Say Experts," May 30,2023, AFP News-Agence France Presse, https://www.barrons.com/news/ai-poses-etinction-risk-say-experts-cb31c672)

⚬⚬⚬

During the early years at Medjugorje, the word "chastisement" was often used with regards to God's coming justice upon the world for its sins, especially as suspected to be forthcoming in the last four of the Ten Secrets.

It's a term that many used to define the nature of these more "*serious*" sounding Secrets, one in which the visionaries heard countless times.

Asked in an interview by attorney Jan Connell if the messages at Medjugorje involve chastisements for the sins of the world, Vicka simply responded, "Yes." She then added that such events must surely come if people did not return to God.[16] Vicka also said that leading people to conversion now prepares them for such moments,[17] and that with prayers, fasting and penance, the punishments can be lessened.[18]

On the other hand, when Ivanka was asked about chastisements in a 1996 interview, she responded, "Our Lady never said anything about chastisements in Medjugorje."[19]

But previously when questioned by Father Janko Bubalo as to whether or not it was true that the Virgin showed her a glimpse of the terrible contents that make up the Ninth Secret, Ivanka—almost in tears from just thinking about it—replied, "Why, I would have died had she shown it to me."[20]

These responses by Vicka and Ivanka invite the question as to what exactly a chastisement is, as it seems to be a confusing term, not just for visionaries, but for many.

⚬⚬⚬

To many people, the word "chastisement" implies a harsh event, such as a plague, a war, an earthquake—some life or world disrupting act— that originates in the divine will of God and is then consummated by Him.

This understanding appears to primarily emanate from the divine punitive events described in the Old Testament. In essence, God conceives a punishment and deliberately sends it upon His people.

Many spiritual leaders, books and articles further this singular understanding in a reckless fashion—insinuating through the haphazard, magnified and overuse of the word "chastisement"—that major calamities should be viewed as the vengeance of God.

But the truth of the matter is, theologians say, God is not a Machiavellian plotter hiding behind the clouds, prearranging a shower of retributions to rain upon the world.

In fact, it is quite the opposite.

~≫∝~

While both the Old and New Testament make it resoundingly clear that God certainly does intervene to correct and redirect His children, the how, when and why behind such divine activity is a mystery in itself.

This is because no one knows the will of God.

But we can use faith and reason to get a little better understanding of it all.

Undoubtedly, it sounds as if the chastisements the Virgin warns of in her apparitions spring from the cumulative, inescapable consequences of humanity's sinful behavior. This would leave, as Fátima author John Haffert writes, no need for divine wrath:

"It seems logical man would bring about his own chastisement. There is the theological principle that God does not multiply miracles. Since a holocaust is right at hand, waiting to happen, why would God send some miraculous fire to wipe out entire nations especially in light of His promise after the Deluge? No evil comes from God, only from sin."[21]

Again, Haffert's understanding is not to rule out God's freedom to intervene in His creation as He deems necessary.

But as his words imply, theology makes it clear that most prophecies of approaching chastisements should be seen in relation to God's permissive will, not his ordained.

Moreover—as can be seen at Fátima and Medjugorje—it is God's desire to help in such calamitous times.

He wants, Mary's words revealed at both apparitions, to prevent or mitigate a coming chastisement, promising to do so in response to people's prayers, sacrifices, and renunciation of sin.

⚬⚬⚬

At Fátima, Mary's words in the second part of the Secret called for the prevention of the foretold chastisement.

On July 13, 1917, she told the visionaries:

"He (God) is about to punish the world for its crimes by means of war, famine, and persecutions of the Church and the Holy Father. To prevent this..."

At Medjugorje, Mary invited the mitigation of the severe Seventh Secret.

Said Mirjana on January 19, 1983:

"She (Mary) said that everyone should pray that it (the 7th Secret) might be lessened...I got many people to join me in this prayer. Later, the Madonna told me that she'd been able to have the Seventh (Secret) lessened."

God's intent—both apparitions make evident—is to attempt to use the warning of the approaching chastisement to draw His people back to Him. He demonstrates His infinite mercy in this way, *and* by coming to the rescue of His people after a self-induced chastisement befalls them.

During the 1930s, Sister Lúcia's letters reveal that she often worried that God could no longer withhold from the world the justice it so deserved for its sins. The Virgin Mary's requests to prevent the chastisements had gone unheeded, and Lúcia sensed the approach of World War II was at hand.

But, like Haffert, Lúcia makes it clear that the approaching war was not the will of God, or that it was God that was sending it:

It does not mean that God wanted a war, as He is the Lord of peace, goodness and love: "Love one another as I have loved you." That is the Lord's law. His First Commandment. Yet He allows wars, just as He allows sin, on account of the gift of freedom that He endowed us with, so that we might serve Him, be obedient to Him, and love Him freely. If we use this gift to wrong people, then we are responsible before God, before our consciences, before humanity, which suffers the consequences of our errors.[22]

The Franciscans at Medjugorje convey a similar understanding of chastisement when addressing the pilgrims there. They are well aware of Mary's warnings of God's justice being served.

Yet, the friars explain that this justice originates from the hands of man.

"Our Lady says it is not God, but sin that does it," said Father Slavko Barbarić about the Ten Secrets and the foretold "justice" in them.[23]

⤬

The priests and visionaries at Medjugorje frown on references to the Ten Secrets that focus on chastisements.

This kind of talk, they emphasize, separates the Secrets from the true message of Medjugorje.

Attempts to sensationalize the Secrets, the friars understand, provoke fear and siphon off hope. Consequently, such efforts work against helping people understand the positive outcome the Secrets are intended to achieve in the end.

With that reality noted, however, there appears to be an inescapable "Day of the Lord" descending upon humanity—a time in which the world will have to answer for mankind's ocean of crimes—especially the billions of abortions that undeniably cry out to God for justice.

Not surprisingly, some believe this epoch of history, as in the age of Noah, may involve a purification that is to emanate from God's ordained will—a divinely sent correction of the human race that is part of His anointed plan, long anticipated in what St. Paul called in his *Letter to the Galatians*, "the fullness of time."[24]

Such a transformation—it is hard to deny—would seem to go hand in hand with what some of the Secrets at Medjugorje reportedly are to bring upon the earth. Moreover, with regards to Medjugorje, it has been suggested that the events contained in the Secrets may be not just world changing, but truly eschatological—events related to the final destiny of humanity—as suspected by theologians of Fátima.

"The significance of the (Medjugorje) Secrets can be understood with reference to Fátima," wrote Denis Nolan in *Medjugorje: A Time for Truth a Time for Action*. "The Secrets of Medjugorje are believed to be eschatological in nature and will be revealed slowly before the events they predict unfold."[25]

Others agree.

Fátima author Father Luigi Bianchi writes:

"Medjugorje is the Fátima of our day… an eschatological dawning…to rise with the Third Millennium."[26]

Father René Laurentin echoes this opinion:

"Medjugorje has an apocalyptic, even eschatological flavor. Mary has come for the 'last times.'"[27]

Father Janko Bubalo goes so far as to say that this was detectable right from the beginning at Medjugorje:

"The very first words of the Virgin in her encounter with the seers was of an eschatological nature."[28]

Most significantly, to speak of an eschatological time means to be talking of the Lord coming back in glory, the final days leading to the Parousia.

"The Last Judgment will come when Christ returns in glory," reads the *Catechism of the Catholic Church*, "only the Father knows the day and the hour; only He determines the moment of its coming. Then through His Son Jesus Christ He will pronounce the final word on all history."[29]

⚬⚬⚬

There are no public messages from Mary at Medjugorje that specifically speak of such an "end times" scenario.

Nor have any of the visionaries spoken of such a happening.

But while Marija has said she does "not speak of Christ's Second Coming" and Vicka says that this is "not part of her Secrets," the visionaries have made comments that seem to reveal Mary has spoken to them in some way about the inevitable return of the Lord in the end times, perhaps in a broader sense with regards to the purpose of the Secrets, in a way to prepare for this eventual reality.

"I cannot say anything about that because Our Lady has said nothing specific," said Vicka when asked about "the last events mentioned in the Apocalypse" by *Informateur De Montreal* on October 7, 1992.[30]

"An evangelization has begun toward the Second Coming, I cannot say anything," replied Ivan when asked in November 1990, by *The National Catholic Register* if the Virgin Mary told him anything about the Second Coming in relation to *Evangelization 2000.*[31]

"Many people ask whether the Blessed Mother has said anything about the Apocalypse and the Second Coming of Christ," inquired Jan Connell of Mirjana in her 1990 book, *Queen of the Cosmos.* "I would not like to talk about that," replied Mirjana.[32]

In the *Afterword* of the 2009 revised edition of her book, Connell writes of Ivanka: "Ivanka knows ten secrets that she says involve the final chapters of the earth's history."[33]

Most interesting comes a couple of statements by Father Slavko Barbarić in late 1985 that were published in his book, *Pray with Your Heart.*

The remarks by the friar seem to reflect that he believes an eschatological element is associated in some "preparatory way" with the Secrets of Medjugorje:

—"I wish to tell you how I have interpreted these apocalyptic messages. In the New Testament we have a book bearing the name of *The Apocalypse*. In this book you can read of many dreadful things St. John saw in his visions, and how he described many disasters...But you see, all this cannot be explained just in terms of physical catastrophe; this must always be interpreted in terms of conversion...In other words, they help our faith. Our faith must always have this quality of waiting...In the *New Testament*, mostly in *The Apocalypse*, there is a word which the Church has been repeating many times, Marantha! In other words, come Lord Jesus!" (Father Slavko Barbarić, November 15, 1985.)[34]

—"When Mirjana announced the content of the last locution, many telephoned to ask... when? how? These messages are apocalyptic, and in order to understand them, one needs perhaps to read once again *The Apocalypse* of St. John...These apocalyptic messages have a purpose—our faith must be awake and not asleep...one element of faith is the element of waiting, of keeping vigilant. The apocalyptic messages require us to be awake, not to sleep as regards our faith, our peace with God, with others, and as regards our conversion." (Father Slavko Barbarić, December 7, 1985)[35]

Father Barbarić's words concerning the *Apocalypse* and Medjugorje are but one of many lesser intrigues surrounding the apparitions.

But perhaps the most interesting of these mini-mysteries involves Mirjana Dragićević Soldo and the date that she receives her annual apparition, March 18th—which is also her birthday.

According to Mirjana, the fact that the Madonna appears to her once a year on that date has nothing to do with it being her birthday, but rather something more pertinent to the greater picture at hand. Something, the visionary says, the world will learn after the Ten Secrets have unfolded.

While that may be the time when this conundrum is to be fully understood, it hasn't stopped some from seeing if they can unearth the answer to it now.

And, like the beginning of any good detective story, some interesting clues have been uncovered.

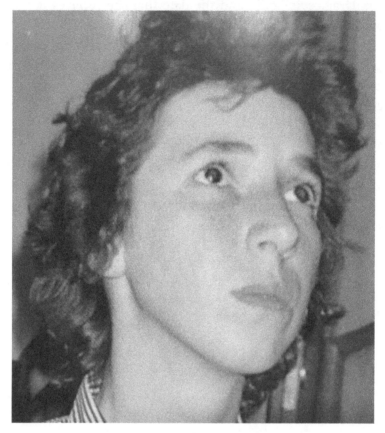

Marija Pavlović Lunetti

"The punishments mentioned by Our Lady do not come from God, they are the fruit of man's moral perversions. It is only men who prepare the punishments forecast in the Secrets that Our Lady has entrusted us with."

Photo Credit: Pittsburgh Center for Peace

CHAPTER SIXTEEN

The Mystery of the Number '18'

"Jesus said: I saw Satan fall like lightning from the sky."
—Lk: 10:18

There is a mystery surrounding the Secrets of Medjugorje—one that has received little to no attention.

It involves a revelation that Mirjana made with regards to the date of March 18, which is her birthday and the day she receives her annual apparition—but also, she says—a date connected to the Secrets.

"Only when the events contained in the Secrets start to unfold," Mirjana writes in her book, "will the world understand why she (the Virgin Mary) chose the 18th of March."[1]

The hidden significance of this date is a mystery that asks to be pondered.

But it is not a new kind of mystery in Judeo-Christian history.

Down through the centuries, there has often been found a linkage of events that have occurred on the same date—a chosen calendar number—for some divine reason.

In recent history, a series of events associated with the number thirteen—or the 13th day of a given month—have been observed.

And, they appear to be pointing to, or connected with, Fátima.

—◦—

Mary appeared at Fátima on the 13th of May, June, July, September and October of 1917.

It is believed she first appeared on the 13th because of the role this date played with Queen Esther and her heroic rescue of the Jewish people, who were scheduled for annihilation on the 13th of the month as described in *The Book of Esther*. *

Mary's appearance at Fátima has been also related to *Revelation* 12:1—"a woman clothed with the sun"—which, as can be seen, are two numbers (12 and 1) that add up to "13."

Pope John Paul II attempted assassination on May 13, 1981, and the Church approved miracle at Akita, Japan, on October 13, 1984—as well as events surrounding the collapse of Communism and the Soviet Union—are just some examples of this mystery.

But there are many more, some fairly recent and others that go back centuries.

The older ones are especially of interest.

—◦—

Pope Leo XIII's reported overhearing of a conversation between God and the Devil, which foretold a century of evil and may have spawned the *Prayer to St. Michael*, is alleged to have occurred on October 13, 1884.

Likewise, quite mysteriously, a ten-year old St. Theresa of Lisieux was cured of an illness through a miraculous smile from an image of the Virgin Mary on May 13, 1883, the year before Pope Leo's vision.

Were these events connected to Fátima in some way?

---

* In Judaism, 13 also signifies the age in which a boy matures and celebrates his bar mitzvah—becoming a full member of the Jewish faith. And, according to the Rabbinic commentary on the Torah, God is understood to possess 13 attributes of mercy.

Over the centuries, the 13th is a date found again and again in Church history.

Two events are noteworthy because they occurred in Portugal.

In 1385, an army on the way to battle led by a general named Nuno Alvares Pereira—later beatified by Benedict XV in 1918 and canonized by Pope Benedict XVI in 2009—stopped at a church in a village named Ceica, in the country of Querem. This would be in the diocese of Leira-Fátima today.

There, Nuno—a mystic—prayed to the Virgin Mary to bring his army victory.

The following day, Nuno's army passed through what is today the village of Fátima. On this site, the entire army experienced a miracle. The soldiers claimed to hear angels singing and then witnessed a vision of St. Michael raising his sword in a sign of victory.

Nuno himself is said to have ridden through what became known as the Cova da Iria, the future field where the Virgin Mary would appear in 1917 to the three children. In this meadow, the general is said to have been divinely told that the ground he knelt on was holy. And—one-day—God would bring a great victory over evil on this very spot.

This miracle occurred on August 13, 1385.

Two hundred years before, there is found another link to Fátima and the 13th.

On October 13, 1147, historian A. Fernando Castilho writes that a "miracle of the sun" was reported during a battle near Lisbon in Portugal. This event led to the country's liberation from the Moors on October 25 of that year.

For some reason, the mystery of the number "13" is found even further back in Catholic history and lore.

One tradition even holds that Sts. Peter and Paul were both executed by the Romans on October 13th—one in 64 and the other in 67A.D.

As with the number "13" and Fátima, Medjugorje, Mirjana and the number "18" are found intertwined in ways beyond just Mirjana's birthdate on the 18th of March, and the fact it is the day she receives her annual apparition of the Virgin Mary.

The first yearly apparition that Mirjana received on March 18, 1983, was on her "18th birthday" (1965-1983). She notes in her book that it was exactly one month before—February 18, 1983—that Father Jozo was released early from prison. This was because, she writes, the government reduced his 3-year sentence to "18-months."[2]

Mirjana also writes that on her last daily apparition of December 25, 1982, she and Mary "summarized our entire 18 months together."[3] This period, it must be noted, ran *exactly* 18 months to the day.

It extended from June 25, 1981, until December 25,1982. [Note: Mary did not speak at all to the visionaries on the first day of the apparitions, June 24, 1981.]

The "significance of the date will be clear," Mirjana has said many times about the real reason for the March 18 annual apparition date.[4]

This leads one to wonder if there are some clues to be found concerning this number in Judeo-Christian history.

⌒⌒⌒

In Judaism, the number 18 is a special number, it emphasizes the importance of life and is often found in celebrations.

At weddings, bar mitzvahs, and when making donations, Jews often give gifts of money in multiples of eighteen. This symbolically gives the recipient the gift of life or luck—a blessing from God as meant to be understood in the number.

Likewise, Jewish prayers especially center around the number 18.

The Amidah, which is the central prayer of every service, was originally composed of 18 blessings, and is still referred to as the Shemoneh Esrei—the Hebrew words for the number 18.

The Talmud records a number of reasons for the number 18, including the 18 times that the forefathers Abraham, Isaac and Jacob are mentioned together in the Torah and the 18 times God's name is cited in the Shema Yisrael.

But most of all, it is noted that the number 18 is understood in the Jewish faith to be a symbol of their slavery and bondage.

In the Old Testament, the word bondage is mentioned 18 times and two of the ancient enemies of Israel—Eglon the Moabite King and the Philistines, with the help of the people of Ammon—held them in bondage for 18 years.

Needless to say, it is feasible that the present mystery may in some way be related to this fact, only with regard to the world's present bondage to sin.

In Catholic history, March 18 is most known for the death of St. Cyril of Jerusalem, who died on March 18, 386. St. Cyril is recognized for advocating the veneration of relics and arguing on behalf of the doctrine of Transubstantiation, the belief that the bread and wine of Communion become the actual body and blood of Christ.

Other events of Catholic significance are noted on this date.

On March 18, 1123, the First Lateran Council opened in Rome. It was the first ecumenical council held in the West, convened by Pope Callixtus II. Two centuries later, on March 18, 1314, thirty-nine Knights Templar were burned at the stake in Paris. [Note: It was on October 13, 1307, that scores of the Knights Templar were first arrested in France.]

It is likely, however, the mystery behind this date and the Secrets of Medjugorje has little to do with mainstream Catholic history.

Rather, it would seem to be more inclined to be associated with the history and message of Fátima.

⚬⚬⚬⚬⚬

Mary appeared at Fátima to confront atheism.

But it was not just atheism she came to address, but a specific on-slaught that neared—the atheism effusing from Marxism.

It would be Marxism that fueled the Bolshevik Revolution in Russia and it is Marxism that still guides our atheistic world of today.

Thus, the Virgin's promised victory—her "Triumph"—will be a triumph over not just atheism, but Marxist driven atheism.

This is the reason Mary warned at Fátima of the "errors of Russia"—the multitude of errors derived from Marxism that she knew would manifest beyond just Communism.

With that said, it would not be surprising if the mysterious reason for the date—March 18—refers directly to this issue, to something that will shine a light on the defeat of "Marxist" atheism, the centerpiece of the coming Triumph.

It is noteworthy to mention that Karl Marx's life was no stranger to the number "18" or to the "month of March."

Marx was born on May 5, 1818.

He died on March 14, 1883.

Most significantly, the *exact date* of "March 18" is found to have played a pivotal role in the rise of Marxism.

It is a date that Marx himself saw as singular and historic.

In Paris, France, on March 18, 1871, radicalized socialist workers seized control of the city in an uprising known as "The Paris Commune."

Afterwards, in his reflection on the Paris insurrection, Marx declared that the emancipatory truth held in his writings was now evident for the world to see through this groundbreaking event in France.[5]

The revolt made Marx famous[6] and he penned a book on it, which Lenin read in 1917.[7] Marx declared the Paris Commune, "the glorious harbinger of a new society"[8] and "a historic experience of enormous importance."[9]

During their 71-day control of the city, the rabid anti-Catholic leaders of the Commune proceeded to execute the Archbishop of Paris, Georges Darby, and a significant number of Priests—the despised "black crows"—as the revolutionaries termed them.[10]

To many, even Vladimir Lenin, the Parisian insurgency is considered to be the "official birth of the practical implementation of Marxism," an historic precursor to the coming of Communism in

Russia and the numerous Marxist movements (the "errors of Russia") that followed.

⤞⤝

There are other curious ties to the number "18."

The coming triumph of the Virgin Mary is understood by many to have officially commenced with her 1531 apparition in Mexico.

There, the Virgin appeared to Juan Diego on December 12th near present day Mexico City. From the historic appearance in Mexico, Mary is known today as "Our Lady of Guadalupe" [a total of 18 letters in 4 words].

With that vision, the Virgin became recognized by Marian theologians—due to the apocalyptic message conveyed through the miraculous image that appeared on St. Juan Diego's tilma—as the "Woman clothed in the Sun" (Rv 12:1).

It is she who comes to wage war with Satan as foretold in St. John's closing narrative (Rv 12:1-18) to the New Testament. [Note: There are "18 verses" in *Revelation's* Chapter 12, often called "*The Woman and the Dragon*" chapter.}

This "apocalyptic" understanding of the role of the Virgin becomes more evident at Lourdes, where the Virgin Mary's declaration, "I am the Immaculate Conception," opens the way for the fulfillment of an array of prophecies that tie Mary directly to "she" who is to "crush the head" of the Serpent in Genesis 3:15, which also, as can be seen, totals 18.

At Lourdes, the mystery of the number 18 is found front and center, as Mary appeared there 18 times in 1858 to Bernadette Soubirous and spoke to her for the first time on February 18th.

Lourdes was later approved by the Church on January 18, 1862, with no specific reason given for this date by Bishop Bertrand-Severe Laurence of the Diocese of Tarbes.

Most significantly, the 18th and last apparition at Lourdes took place on July 16th—the Feast of Our Lady of Mt. Carmel—a feast that directly recalls God's triumph over the false prophets of Baal through the wondrous Elijah. (See the *Epilogue* of this book for the full story.)

It is a triumph seen again as a "foreshadowing sign" of God's coming victory through Mary, who is known as "The Virgin of Revelation."

At Fátima, the understanding of the significance of Elijah's victory to Mary's coming Triumph is confirmed when Mary appears as Our Lady of Mt. Carmel during the last apparition in October of 1917, and where her first apparition on May 13th—a date in which the number of the month (5) and the day (13) add up again to 18—is clearly meant to call to mind Queen Esther's role in the salvation of the Jewish nation.

Now, theologians tell us, what the Virgin Mary began at Guadalupe, laid the foundation for at Lourdes, and confirmed at Fátima, will be fulfilled at Medjugorje—her glorious and long-awaited victory over an age of unprecedented evil and systematic atheism.

It is to be, as Mirjana has stated, a victory that will see—with the unfolding of the First Secret at Medjugorje—the defeat not just of the evil of this world, but of the world of darkness, of Satan.

A victory, quite fittingly, that points to the Lord's words in *The Gospel of Luke*—and once more—to the number 18:

"I saw Satan fall like lightning from the sky" (Lk 10:18).

CHAPTER SEVENTEEN

Time is Short

"But woe to you, earth and sea, for the Devil has come down to you in great fury, for he knows he has but a short time."
—Rv: 12:12

Mirjana Dragićević Soldo receives most of the attention with regards to the Ten Secrets of Medjugorje.

This is primarily because she will someday reveal them by way of her chosen spokesperson, Father Petar Ljubicic.

But the other five visionaries have spoken considerably about the Secrets too, and it is often in their casual remarks—sometimes in response to questions unrelated to the Secrets—that something thought provoking is forthcoming.

~∞~

Ivan Dragićević, who rarely mentions the Secrets—perhaps because of an early controversy he got innocently ensnared in while in the seminary[1]—often carefully alludes to them in his talks.

At one event, Ivan stated, "The Secrets refer to both good and bad" and the "difference depends on us." On another occasion, he told an interviewer that God permitted Mary to come to Medjugorje because, "The Blessed Mother knows *what* is coming in the future."

Both of these subtle remarks hint not only of the transforming nature of the Secrets, but of humanity's ability to affect—through prayer and conversion—their outcome.[2]

In 1989, Ivan was asked, "Based on what you know now, having had nine Secrets, how do you understand Our Lady's presence here in Medjugorje?"

"The Blessed Mother," he thoughtfully replied, "is here urgently calling us—everyone in the world—to change our lives, to come back to God now."[3]

A few years later, at a talk at the Franciscan monastery in Vienna on January 18, 1993, Ivan told his listeners that knowledge of the Secrets is intended to invite change.

First emphasizing that Mary has not come to frighten anybody, he then pointed out a glaring reality:

"People cannot deny the state of the world."

It was an allusion to the fact that a time may be coming for God to intervene in a necessary way—the way of the Secrets.

"One thing is for sure," Ivan told the crowd that day, "since the beginning, the Mother of God said the greatest threat to humanity was that it could annihilate itself. And this happens in many ways: by means of wars, drugs, alcohol, by means of an immoral life...I cannot speak of the Secrets...these will be known when the time comes, but anybody can recognize certain things by the time we are living. I do not want to say anymore. Each person has been given the capacity to draw conclusions."[4]

Twenty years later, at a talk in Medjugorje on June 24, 2011, Ivan continued to stress that knowledge of the Secrets carries responsibility.

His testimony that day, in some way, was reminiscent of John Paul II at Fulda. There, the Pope warned in 1980 of the inherent danger of knowing the Third Secret of Fátima and doing nothing about it.

Ivan's words hit the same chord:

"But one day when the time comes—when some things get revealed—you will understand *why* the apparitions are such a long time and *why* every day. Later on, we will understand some things. Later on, our eyes will be opened when we see *physical changes* that are going to happen in the world. This is so important to understand. I'm not going to tell you the Secrets. The time in front of us is the time of great responsibility."[5]

It is an important responsibility, Ivan knows, because he says he has seen the Virgin "cry over abortion," over "divorce, priests and war."[6]

The world has a future, he stresses, "only if it turns back to God."[7]

⋙⋘

Ivanka Ivanković-Elez has not spoken much about the Secrets.

She did, however, tell interviewer Jan Connell to please tell people to take the Secrets "seriously."[8] It was a noteworthy response, perhaps emanating from the fact that Ivanka takes the Secrets quite seriously herself.

The visionary has revealed that she and Mary discussed the Seventh Secret in 2006,[9] the Ninth in 2008,[10] and the Tenth in 2009,[11] although nothing was specifically disclosed. In some of those years, Ivanka says, Mary talked to her about the "future."[12]

All in all, though, it's apparent; the Secrets are something that never leave Ivanka.

Asked on August 6, 2001, "Are we getting closer to the time when the Secrets will be revealed?" Ivanka's response revealed her on-going awareness of them, "Every day," she replied, "We are getting closer and closer."[13]

Curiously, one of the most difficult apparitions Ivanka experienced was on the morning of June 25, 1993, but it did *not* involve the Secrets.

Before a group of about 60 people squeezed into her home—including an Italian TV crew—Ivanka received her annual apparition, which was seven minutes long that day. At its conclusion, she burst into tears and rushed out of the house.[14]

The next day, she revealed to Sister Emmanuel Maillard what happened:

"The Virgin showed me some terrible and indescribable events. What I saw had nothing to do with the Secrets. It's like a new warning, because these terrible things can still be averted by prayer and fasting. Conversion and giving oneself to Jesus are necessary more than ever. Do not be blind, become converted."[15]

Father René Laurentin, who was present that day, said Ivanka told him what she saw was horrible and that the event was near.[16]

When Father Slavko Barbarić heard what occurred, he visited Ivanka himself to find out what exactly unfolded.

Upon returning to the rectory, Barbarić told everyone,

"These terrible things will happen soon. They concern the world in general." Barbarić added that Ivanka told him, "This was the most painful apparition of all."[17]

⫸

Of the six visionaries at Medjugorje, it is Marija Pavlović-Lunetti who appears to handle the touchy subject of the Secrets the best.

While Marija has done as many interviews as the others, she seems to know best how to artfully evade answering questions concerning the Secrets. But she does so without refusing to talk about them or appearing annoyed with persistent curiosity.

Indeed, in examining Marija's words in such conversations, the visionary does not refrain from the substance and nature of the Secrets. She is also very sensitive to their volatile content.

In an in-depth 1986 article by Notre Dame theologian Edward O'Conner, she is reported to have admitted having burst into tears when one of the Secrets was revealed to her.[18]

Almost always, though, Marija simply speaks of what she knows without using the words *Secret* or *Secrets* too much.

Do not wait for the sign to be converted, she exhorts pilgrims, telling them the Virgin wants people to respond now.[19] Asked if all people on Earth will believe in God by the time the Great Sign comes, she paraphrases one of Mary's more serious messages. The Blessed Mother has said, she replies, that "those still alive when the Sign comes will witness many conversions."[20].

Asked if it will be too late for those who wait for the Great Sign, she answers that "this is the time of great grace and mercy, the time to change our lives." [21]

But her sixth sense to be careful with what she says is always present when she hears the word "secret."

Asked if the Ten Secrets speak of God's will that people love each other—upon hearing the question mentions the "Secrets"—she gently replies, "We cannot say anything about the Secrets."[22] Asked if one should worry about the Secrets? "No, about the Secrets, we can say nothing."

Said Marija in a 1988 interview, "Because they are secrets—when they are to be revealed—we will know what they concern. But for now, there is nothing to worry about."[23].

For Marija, and perhaps all the visionaries, "now" can be a very relative term.

This reality is illustrated in a message from the Virgin Mary to Marija during a late-night prayer meeting on Podbrdo on October 5, 1987:

"Pray! Pray! Pray!", Marija says the Madonna told the gathering on the hill that evening, "You must be converted...Time is short."[24]

⚬

Renzo Allegro, an Italian journalist and author, republished an interview he did with Marija Pavlović in 2001 that he originally conducted in 1989.

It is a special account, Allegro wrote, because Father Slavko Barbarić—after putting him through what he described as a real interrogation—phoned Marija and got her to agree to do a more probing interview with him.

Allegro describes his conversation with Marija that day as a long, detailed, serene, and pondered account, conducted with no feeling of haste and with enough time for clarifications to confirm details.

The interview was taped and ran from noon into the evening at Marija's home in Medjugorje.

The reporter says he considers it a "document" and believes it should be brought to the attention of all those who wish to know the intimate details of the events at Medjugorje through Marija Pavlović's exact words.

In it, Marija opens up significantly about the Secrets.

The following is an excerpt in which Allegro discusses the Secrets with Marija:

Allegro: *You told me that you have seen Our Lady every day since 1981. Have you got accustomed to these encounters?*
Marija: No, it is not possible to get used to these things. Every time feels like the first. As well as seeing Our Lady, myself and the other seers feel her presence, her love, her protection and her worries. It is a wonderful miracle that is repeated each day.
Allegro: *What does "feel" the worries of Our Lady mean?*
Marija: Our Lady is not always happy. Her face sometimes wears a shadow of sadness. When she talks to us about some subjects, you can see that she is suffering. On two occasions, I have even seen her weep.
Allegro: *On which occasions?*
Marija: When she told me some Secrets about the future of the world. I cannot speak about these things for the moment.
Allegro: *What are the most important things that Our Lady has said to you over the course of the years?*
Marija: Her messages, her requests, and her suggestions are all important. Throughout these years, she has been our teacher and our mother. She has helped us to grow. She is very gentle when she speaks to us. She never gives orders. She expresses

her desires and leaves us completely free to carry them out. The things she tells us are not the same for all of us. She has entrusted special tasks to each of us and with her teachings. She has shown us how to do them. Right from the beginning, she told us that she would tell us Ten Secrets. They are Secrets that are destined to be revealed, but only when she says so. The first one of us to receive all the Secrets was Mirjana. In fact, she received her last apparition on December 25, 1982. Our Lady has entrusted Mirjana with the task of informing mankind when the "Great Sign" is about to arrive. It will be a glorious Sign that should appear on Podbrdo as a proof of the authenticity of the apparitions. This "Great Sign" will be visible to everyone and will come in order to persuade the world to be converted once and for all. If this does not happen, then there will be a punishment. The "Great Sign" will be preceded by three celestial admonitions. Ten days before their coming, Mirjana will inform a priest so that he may warn the world. Mirjana is an effusive, cheerful girl. On meeting her, someone said, "The Secrets Our Lady has confided to you must be beautiful because you are always happy." She replied, as soon as I think of them, I begin to cry." Our Lady recounted the story of her life to Jacov, Ivanka, Vicka and me, just as it really happened during her stay on earth at Nazareth. It was wonderful. One day, this account will also be made public. In fact, Our Lady has told Vicka to write down what she recounted. Vicka has done so and is waiting for Our Lady to tell her to publish it.

Allegro: *The Secrets that have been entrusted to you, are they beautiful or horrid?*

Marija: Beautiful and horrid at the same time. In general, 'Secrets' of this type concern sad events. However, they are not inescapable events. They are always conditioned by something. Our Lady says "this will happen if…" For example, the Seventh Secret entrusted to me has already been made redundant. It was about painful events but, thanks to the prayers and repentance of people at Medjugorje, things have changed. Our Lady always said, "With prayer and repentance, anything can be obtained."

Allegro: *You say that Our Lady is so gentle, good and thoughtful. So how do you explain that she threatens humanity with punishments and catastrophes?*

Marija: Our Lady never threatens punishments. Nor does she say that God punishes mankind. It is mankind that, straying from the truth by doing evil, prepares serious catastrophes. The punishments mentioned by Our Lady do not come from God, they are the fruit of man's moral perversions. It is only men who prepare the punishments forecast in the Secrets that Our Lady has entrusted us with. With her apparitions, her messages, and her advice, she tries to make mankind reflect, until they realize what kind of abyss they are heading for. Our Lady often says, "I adore the freedom that God has given you." Yet, she weeps when she sees how often men use this freedom to do evil to their neighbors.[25]

⌣⌣⌣

Like Mirjana, Marija says that Medjugorje will bring the fulfillment of Fátima.

In a June 25, 2016, interview with Father Livio Fanzaga for *Radio Maria*, Marija commented on this dawning reality. In response to Father Fanzaga asking if Mary was realizing her plans through the faithful at Medjugorje, Marija replied:

"We don't know what the plans of God and of Our Lady are, but this evening Our Lady told us, 'I call you to persevere in prayer so that with you I can realize my plans (message of June 25, 2016).'

"I think Our Lady is realizing the Triumph of the Immaculate Heart, as she said in Fátima, even though us, because we have said yes to living the Commandments of God, yes to life, and to rejoice in the

Law of God...We are poor instruments, but when the Lord takes us, He transforms us..."

~∞~

Of the six visionaries, perhaps none of them stresses two critical points about Mary and the Secrets as much as Vicka Ivanković-Mijatovic.

The Secrets, she repeats in interviews, can be "substantially lessened" by prayer and penance. Through Mary's intercession, because of God's love, Vicka says this can happen.

Needless to say, she wants people to remember this reality and emphasizes often how the Seventh Secret has already been somewhat mitigated.

Vicka's second concern is that people realize that the Madonna has come to call "all of her children."

Mary wants, emphasizes Vicka, everybody in the world to be saved. The Madonna is the Mother of every person on Earth, she has a "mother's love" for them all and her messages are for everyone, she tells people.[26] This emphasis is well noted as countless numbers of various religions, races and ethnicities have been drawn to Medjugorje over the past four decades.

Vicka, like the others, has uttered some thought-provoking responses about the Secrets during interviews.

Father Laurentin reported one involving a question asked by a cousin of hers as reported in *The Echo from Medjugorje* (1993):

> Question: *Do you remember that you cried when you received the 7th, 8th, and 9th Secrets, and so did Marija? You say that the Secrets do not speak of the war at hand. So, what is awaiting us?*
> **Vicka**: You just gave the answer to the question yourself.[27]

~∞~

When her interviews are examined, Vicka, though warm, vivacious and colorful, is extremely honest and blunt, even more than Mirjana.

In *Queen of the Cosmos*, her exchange with Jan Connell concerning the future reveals she had no interest in soft pedaling the reality of what she knows is coming in the Secrets:

Question: *Will the people who listen to the Blessed Mother and change their lives and convert have it easier during the chastisement?*

Vicka: Of course. That is why we are trying to lead people to conversion. We have to help people convert. We have to prepare them for the chastisement. We help them with our prayers and the things we are doing. Everything we are doing at Medjugorje is to show people the right way to live the messages.

Question: *Will God's mercy stop at some point?*

Vicka: If we are open to the Lord's mercy, it never stops. If you don't want God's mercy, it stops for you.

Question: *When the permanent sign comes in Medjugorje, will it be too late for many to convert?*

Vicka: Yes.

Question: *Will the permanent sign happen in your lifetime?*

Vicka: Yes.

Question: *What happens to those people who don't really believe enough right now to convert and want to wait until the permanent sign comes?*

Vicka: For those people, it will be too late.[28]

In another interview, conducted by *Informateur De Montreal* on October 7, 1992, Vicka was asked about *The Book of Revelation*:

Question: *The Apocalypse says that the Devil will be in chains one day. Is that only symbolic?*

Vicka: I believe Satan will be defeated only if we accept the Madonna's messages. If we convert and live like the Madonna teaches us, then we will have a period of peace. It depends on us. If we do not change, it will not happen.

Question: *Do you believe that the last events mentioned in the Apocalypse have started to happen?*

Vicka: I cannot say anything about that, because the Madonna has said nothing specific. Thus, I do not know.

Question: *Many people believe that it is the beginning of the end.*

Vicka: It could be, but the Holy Virgin has said nothing on that subject.[29]

Vicka did not have an answer to the last question.

But, at face value, it was a curious inquiry; it was an attempt to learn whether or not biblical prophecies were approaching fulfillment, and whether the prophecies of Medjugorje were one and the same with some of them.

~⚬~

Prophecy is not the future etched in stone.

Fulfilled prophecy depends on response—or a lack of it.

This is a critical point that deserves emphasis.

In 2000, the Vatican illustrated this point in its theological commentary, *The Message of Fatima*.

Pope John Paul II's survived assassination attempt—believed to be foreshown in the vision of a slain Pope in the third part of the Secret of Fátima—was seen as a terrible prophecy prevented through the intercession of the Virgin Mary.[30]

At Fátima, Mary announced her coming Triumph. But her prophetic words will only find fulfillment through the choices and actions of humanity. Lúcia always spoke of the future with this in mind.

It is as if to remind us that if a threatening prophesy can avoid fulfillment, there remains the possibility a welcomed prophesy or intended blessing might not find fulfillment. Mary told the visionaries at Fátima that the Miracle of the Sun in October of 1917 would have been greater had not the children been abducted by the authorities that August, two months before.

At Medjugorje, the visionaries carefully instruct their listeners that tomorrow is conditional, both the bad and the good.

In faith, the visionaries at Medjugorje maintain that what Mary has foretold to them will take place. But over the years, they often speak of the urgent need to repent, for mankind to reverse its ways, in order to insure a positive outcome.

"I believe Satan will be defeated," said Vicka, "only if we accept the Gospa's messages. If we convert and live like the Gospa teaches, then we will have a period of peace. It depends on us. If we do not change, it will not happen."[31]

Such "change" has yet to happen.

Some forty years after Mary arrived in Medjugorje—and more than a hundred years since Fátima—the world has still not heard the plea of its Mother.

Antonio Socci, a Vatican journalist and author, noted this reality in his book, *The Secret of Benedict XVI*:

"It would be difficult to affirm that such repentance has happened. It seems rather that the exact opposite has happened. Mankind has taken the opposite route."[32]

⁓⁒⁓

During a talk given in Medjugorje in1986, a visiting priest told his listeners of Mary's call for conversion.

"Our Lady once said," he remarked to a small audience, "you must understand; I have come to save you, to save your families, and to save the world."[33]

In 1997, more than ten years after this priest's exhortation, it did not sound like the Virgin Mary believed her effort was making much progress:

"You are creating a world without God," she warned at the time.[34]

Ten years later, in 2008, things sounded no better.

"This world," the Madonna of Medjugorje bemoaned, "is further from God every day…"[35]

Five years farther down the road, in 2013, it looked as if the Virgin felt the situation was getting worse:

"This world…is without joy in the heart and is without a future."[36]

A decade after, on January 25, 2023, her message sounded as if the world had never heard of Medjugorje.

"The future is at a crossroads, because modern man does not want God. That is why mankind is heading to perdition…Pray with me, that what I began in Fátima and here may be realized."[37]

Will the world continue to ignore the prolonged appeal of the Queen of the Prophets?

Are the Ten Secrets the only remedy left to awaken people?

Will *they even* succeed?

Or could, as little Jacinta Marto of Fátima believed the Virgin Mary said on October 13, 1917, "the end of the world" be approaching?

Author Jan Connell asked Mirjana this very question in the early 90s:

"Mirjana, many evangelists these days talk about the end of the world. Will the world survive the Secrets you know?"

"God's world is unchanging," replied Mirjana, "All passes away but God's will. Those who pray understand."[38]

⚮

Years ago, I sat down with Father Petar Ljubicic, the quiet, stoic friar that Mirjana chose to announce the Ten Secrets, and asked him some probing questions about the world's fragile future, the nuclear dangers that haunt mankind, and the seriousness of the message of Medjugorje.

What he said was hopeful, but Father Petar believed it all came down to using the time still being granted by God in a propitious way.

"We can't put it off!" Ljubicic emphasized to me.

"Now is the most important time and we must use it. That's the main point. We can't put it off…for it will be too late!"[39]

CHAPTER EIGHTEEN

A Conversation with Father Petar Ljubicic

"For there is nothing hidden that will not become visible, and nothingsecret that will not be known and come to light."
—Lk 8:17

Surprisingly tall, innately pleasant, and filled with zeal for the Lord and his mission; if the Ten Secrets of Medjugorje are said to have some harshness in them, their chosen presenter certainly doesn't have any in him.

Swinging through the northeastern United States in early February of 2000, Father Petar Ljubicic presented a talk on a cold winter afternoon at Franciscan University in Steubenville, Ohio, and spent a couple of days, along with his translator, defrosting at our home in the suburbs of nearby Pittsburgh.

Ljubicic was a delight to be around; one found his humility came as natural as his smile and unpretentious graciousness. His prominent glasses made up as much of his persona as his brown Franciscan robe, and one can't imagine what he would be like without them.

Our children were blessed to meet him, and my wife and I were left with no doubts that he was the perfect ambassador for the message of Medjugorje. Love, peace—and that Croatian warmth one finds when in Medjugorje—all radiated from him in his short stay with us.

At the time, I was thinking about writing a small book on Medjugorje and publishing another edition of our internationally distributed Marian newspaper—one featuring Medjugorje—that would be released the following year.

Of course, if one wanted to address the Ten Secrets in these endeavors, Father Ljubicic was as good a source as it gets, perhaps even better than the visionaries, since they were long known by then to be carefully policing their every word.

Ljubicic's openness and enthusiasm in discussing Medjugorje and the Secrets with me was a little surprising, for I thought by then that he would be fatigued by it all. But he wasn't. Moreover, his candor left me feeling that what he said would be edifying to the reader, for the interview did not come off as another repetitious dialogue on Medjugorje.

The following is the entire interview, published here for the first time.

Ljubicic's translator, in my opinion, was excellent; he was unhesitating and clear in presenting my questions to Father Petar and confident in the delivery of Father's exact answers in return to me.

The interview was tape recorded and took place on the campus of Franciscan University in Steubenville, Ohio. It was conducted after Father Ljubicic had given a talk to the students that morning, which was followed by a lively question and answer session with them.[1]

Question: *Father, I thought we would begin with a prayer.*
Ljubicic: Good! Lord, we believe you are present with us here. You are always with us, if we know that or not. You are our Creator. You lead this world. Give us that gift-that grace- that we recognize You. That we come to know You. That we open ourselves to your Spirit. And that everything we do, we do for

your greatness, and for our salvation. Bless all of our work in this time. Bless all of those we will be meeting tonight. Bless all of those who are opening themselves to you and want to come to know You. We pray too, Lord Jesus: save all people. You came to be our Saviour, to be the Saviour of everyone. Mary, Queen of Peace, pray for us. Pray for all those who look for your Son that they may find Him. Thank you for coming as our Mother and that you want to bring us Jesus, so that in Him we can have everything that we need. [Father Petar then led us in praying a Hail Mary and a Glory Be.]

Question: *Father, can you tell us a little bit about where you grew up in Croatia, you know, your early days, your childhood?*

Ljubicic: I was born in a little village about a hundred kilometers from Medjugorje.

Question: *What's the name of that village?*

Ljubicic: Prisoje. I am the first child of parents who waited a long time. My mother didn't have children for five years. She was in fear that she wouldn't have children at all. And she prayed to God and said to the Lord, "Lord, if you give me children, I'll consecrate all of them to you. And that's how I was born. The first child of ten.

Question: *In what year?*

Ljubicic: 1946. I finished grade school there (Prisoje) and then went to the minor seminary. Then to Split and onto Dubrovnik. Then I began studying theology in Sarajevo and went on to finish in Germany. I became a priest in 1972. I'm a Franciscan priest 28 years now. What I know of myself is that I knew I wanted to be a priest. I had a strong desire to preach the "Good News."

Question: *Good! Father, I have a lot of documentation on the early days of Medjugorje. So, I'm not going to really ask much. We'll talk a little bit about that, but I just kind of would like to know what your thinking is today, of the memories of those first days. Our Lady continues to speak to us at Medjugorje. She said this is "a time of grace." Father, what is your opinion of the apparitions today after almost twenty years? And why are they continuing? Why are they still continuing? Why do you think these apparitions are still going on?*

Ljubicic: The world—and we—are in great danger. There are horrible things around us. There is poverty and sickness. There's a great crisis in the world. And it's right for help to come from Heaven- to help get us out of this crisis. God wants all people to be saved. That is why I think these apparitions are a great help, for God to show us how much He loves us. That's why I see, that's the reason, that the apparitions have been lasting so long. Our Lady wants all people to realize they are God's children, that God loves them, and that He waits to see all of them in Heaven.

Question: *When did you first hear about the apparitions? They began on June 24,1981. How much longer after that did you first hear of these apparitions?*

Ljubicic: The first couple of days I heard of it. But I wasn't able to go right away.

Question: *When did you go?*

Ljubicic: I was helping the people for their Confirmation at my location. I went on the 27th of June. From the beginning. I believed that God is at work there, especially when she (Mary) spoke to Vicka and Ivanka. My feeling was these children can't be lying. I went with a priest then. And then, in the first months, we heard confessions in the Church. Through these confessions, I truly came to see how open people were and how much confession meant to them.

Question: *When did you first meet Mirjana?*

Ljubicic: I saw her just like the other visionaries. I didn't know any of them before the apparitions started. I saw her after a couple of times there and had a couple of words with her. But I wasn't especially tied to her. But she saw something in me, and I don't know what it was, but others told me she saw something in me, and she wanted…she was going to pick me as the one to give the Secrets to. I thought that those people were joking with me. But then she came to me and told me to get ready because I'll be the one to tell the world the Secrets when it comes to that time. The Secrets are about certain happenings that will happen, certain things that will happen at a certain time and certain places. She received something from Our Lady like a "sheet"—kind of like paper or cloth—but it's not something that looks…it looks sort of like…

Question: *Have you seen this?*

Ljubicic: No. I haven't. A few people have seen it. All of the Secrets are written on that sheet. Everything is written on it- what will happen and when. Ten days before the first Secret happens, the Secret will be able to be read. It will appear on that sheet. Now it's invisible. And then the Secrets…Every time another Secret comes-ten days before-it will show up on that sheet. The first two Secrets are warnings. The third Secret is of a Sign that will appear on Apparition Hill.

Question: *How did you feel when you first heard the news for sure that Mirjana said, "Yes—it's you." How did you feel personally inside? Did you feel worthy? Did you go into prayer?*

Ljubicic: On one hand, I felt joy. On the other hand, I felt a great responsibility. Why was it me? By what reason did she have? What does this mean?

Question: *Did you have any fear?*

Ljubicic: Maybe I'm not even conscious of the responsibility that is upon me. No. I don't fear it. It's something on the outside. It's almost like it doesn't really concern me. I won't let it affect me.

Question: *Now, to announce these Secrets—because you are the one that Mirjana chose—did you need to have your*

"Superior"—and this is just an example, because this would affect all the Franciscans throughout the world, since this a Franciscan parish—did you need to tell the Bishop or your superior about this, so that they weren't afraid of any embarrassment?

Ljubicic: This is a private thing. I don't have to clear it with anyone.

Question: *Why must you fast to announce these Secrets?*

Ljubicic: That's what Our Lady asks for Mirjana. Seven days of prayer and fasting.

Question: *So how will you fast? Just on bread and water those seven days?*

Ljubicic: Yes. Bread and water and then the three days before making public the Secrets, also.

Question: *So, there will be ten days that you'll fast?*

Ljubicic; The three days before the Secrets, I don't have to fast. It's just the seven days before revealing.[2]

Question: *Ok.*

Ljubicic: Three days before the Secret, I tell the world.

Question: *Where will you reveal it at? In Medjugorje?*

Ljubicic: Yes, I'll tell it in Medjugorje.

Question: *And then, will you be available to answer questions when people ask? You know, there's going to be worldwide media there. Are you prepared? Do you understand the media is going to be coming?*

Ljubicic: I'll give Croatian television the monopoly of my interviews if the Communists aren't back in power at that time.[3]

Question: *I figure the media in the United States, the Western media, is going to converge on this.*

Ljubicic: I don't have to [do interviews].

Question: *Has Mirjana talked to you about what you are to do as far as announcing it?*

Ljubicic: Nothing special when it comes to this. Then, she'll tell me what I have to do.

Question: *Have you been closer to Mirjana since you began your involvement with the apparitions?*

Ljubicic: I was in Medjugorje for ten years. So, I saw her very often and often talked to her. What we are waiting for now is the time for the Secrets to be revealed, to come.

Question: *Father, do you remember the time that they saw the fire on the hill, not where the cross is on Mt. Krizevac, and when they went up there the fire was gone. Reportedly, Our Lady said that's a sign of the Great Sign. Do you remember anything about that? What can you tell me about that?*

Ljubicic: There was a great fire on "Apparition Hill", and at the time that the fire appeared on Apparition Hill, the Communists wouldn't allow people to go up there. But the fire appeared. This was at the beginning of the apparitions. There was also a sign in the sky written—"MIR", which means "peace"—between Apparition Hill and Mt. Krizevac. About five hundred people saw that.

Question: *Did you see that also?*

Ljubicic: I didn't see that.

Question: *There was reportedly another sign, or fire, on the hill where the Cross is too. Do you know about this?*

Ljubicic: I don't know of a fire but oftentimes the cross on Mt. Krizevac used to disappear and there was a silhouette that appeared of the Blessed Mother, in place of the cross. Many people saw the silhouette of Our Lady.

Question: *The priest who sent the letter to the Pope, Father Tomislav Vlašić, do you know if he had ever gotten a response from the Pope, because that letter dealt with Mirjana and the Secrets?*[4]

Ljubicic: I don't know.

Question: *You don't know?*

Ljubicic: No.

Question: *Has Mirjana shared anything about these Secrets with you at all, other than what she has shared publicly?*

Ljubicic: [**Author's Note:** I have at this time decided to not publish Fr. Petar Ljubicic's response to this question and to two follow-up questions related to his reply. My decision was based on the fact that his answers were both surprising and remarkable, and on the fact that I have been—and remain—unable to find anywhere else what he revealed to me. Consequently, I did not want this singular issue to distract and possibly overwhelm the paramount essence and greater purpose of this book.]

Question: *Fr. Rene Laurentin, Fr. Michael O'Carroll, Fr. Ljudevit Rupčić. They have all talked about some of the Secrets possibly containing a nuclear element. Do you think that's possible? Have you heard anything like that?*

Ljubicic: No. I don't know of anything about that.

Question: *Our Lady said that when she came to Medjugorje, that she came—and she said this on August 25, 1991—"I have come to fulfill the Secrets I began at Fátima." What is your feeling on what this means?*

Ljubicic: They say that Medjugorje is the fulfillment or a continuation of Fátima. Maybe this means the finishing off of what has started at Fátima. The realization of everything that Out Lady started there.

Question: *Well, she (Mary) promised an "Era of Peace" there. So, do you think that she's come to Medjugorje to bring people to the level of prayer that will finally cause this to happen?*

Ljubicic: What was the end of the question?

Question: *I think Our Lady at Fátima gave a plan of peace which was really a plan of prayer. In Medjugorje, is she trying to get more prayer to finally bring the "Era of Peace?"*

Ljubicic: It's conversion. The call to prayer and the Rosary. A call to a strong faith and for penance. Because in Fátima, she said, "Penance, penance, penance!"

Question: *Mirjana has said that the 9th and 10th Secrets are very serious. You talked today about the first three Secrets. What can you tell us about the remaining Secrets?*

Ljubicic: I have asked [Mirjana] about the first three, and the others I have not been too concerned with. When the time comes, I'll get more information about them.

Question: *Our Lady spoke about "a century of peace" in her message of December 25,1999. What do you think she means by "a century of peace"? That was the last message of the last year of the millennium.*

Ljubicic: In the future… this next century… a century of peace. I don't know how to explain it, except that all of us are hoping and want that peace to come.

Question: *Our Lady said, "The world must convert while there is still time." What do you think she means by that? Is it the time before the Secrets? The time before the end of the "period of grace"?*

Ljubicic: What that means is this. What man puts off for more and more-he then has less time to convert. Because we must always think about that. That if I don't use the graces that our Lord gives me now, then I am even less ready to accept the grace that God gives me tomorrow. Because I'm just putting it off more and more. That's what we see when they asked Jesus for a sign for the Jews to convert. Jesus told them that another sign won't be given to them. The prophet Jonah, he was in the stomach of a fish for three days and the Son of Man will be in a tomb for three days. This means he will die and rise again. And when Jesus rose, those who wanted to convert, converted. And those who didn't want to believe, paid the guards to say that the Apostles stole him while they were sleeping. They don't want to convert. Who doesn't convert now, there's little hope they will convert tomorrow. Now is the most important time and we must use it. That's the main point. We can't put it off…for it will be too late.

Question: *One last question. Mirjana's has ten Secrets. The other five visionaries have nine or ten Secrets. Are they all the same Secrets? Or, are the other visionaries going to announce their own Secrets too?*

Ljubicic: None of the others have said anything. None of them have said anything but it has come to the conclusion that everyone has the Secret of the Sign that will appear on Apparition Hill. They don't talk about the Secrets amongst themselves, so they don't know whether they are the same ones or not.

Question: *Ok. So, Mirjana is the only one who's going to announce her Secrets?*

Ljubicic: I don't know anything, except for Mirjana.

Question: *Thank you Father.*

Jacov Colo

"Many wonder what Our Lady is saying in these Secrets. What will happen? I think the most important thing is that we accept her messages. If we have accepted them and have God in our hearts and in our lives, we need worry about nothing."

Photo Credit: Pittsburgh Center for Peace

CHAPTER NINETEEN

The Conversion of the World?

*"Repent, therefore, and be converted, that your sins may
be wiped away, and that the Lord may grant you times of
refreshment and send you the Messiah already appointed for
you, Jesus, whom heaven must receive until the times of
restoration of which God spoke through the mouth of
his holy prophets of old."*

—Acts 3:19-21

Jacov Colo is extremely reserved about the Secrets.

When asked if the world should convert now, however, he doesn't hesitate.

"That is why Mary is here."[1]

She has come, he then offers without prompting, to convert and reconcile the *whole* world.

Will such an unfathomable transformation of humanity happen?

"Yes," he calmly answers.[2]

Since June 25, 1981, Jacov Čolo—who turned ten years old just three weeks before—has been receiving apparitions of the Virgin Mary.

Being the youngest of the six visionaries, the early photographs of him in ecstasy were fascinating. The sight of a child, totally consumed in mystical wonder, was not something one sees every day.

But in contrast to such a blessing at that young age, comes the fact his mother died just two years later, and his father was nowhere to be found to raise him.

From the beginning, Jacov has gone out of his way to avoid publicity.

He does not desire attention and never will. To his credit, he shunned the role of the quasi-celebrity that the visions tried to cast upon him in the early years. And he didn't relish speaking much back then. Although he was the youngest of the six by far, he clearly identified his calling:

"My role is not as a prophet. I am a witness to the messages the Blessed Mother is bringing to the whole world here at Medjugorje."[3]

Consequently, there is little of substance on record from him during the early years of the apparitions, especially with regards to the Secrets, which he almost totally refused to speak about.

Father Milan Mikulich of Portland, Oregon—born just 25 miles from Medjugorje—was one of the first priests from America to visit Medjugorje. He headed there in November 1981, just five months after the apparitions began.

By 1983, Mikulich had published articles on the visions in the journal, *Orthodoxy of the Catholic Doctrine*. On February 6, 1984, the Franciscan interviewed little Jacov and asked him a couple of questions about the Secrets—which proved an exercise in futility.

Mikulich: *Are the nature of these Secrets more positive or negative for us?*
Jacov: There are some that are good, and some are not so good, but there are more that are good.
Mikulich: *What number are good and bad?*
Jacov: That I may not say.[4]

Almost ten years later, Jacov remained silent as ever concerning the Ten Secrets.

In the early 90s—around the time of the start of the war in the former Yugoslavia—I presented Jacov with a list of questions in an interview that took place in Medjugorje.

The following is an excerpt of that dialogue. It has not been published before:

Question: *Our Lady said this is the last time she will ever appear. What does this mean?*

Jacov: Our Lady didn't say this to me.

Question: *What does Mary ask of the world today that is different from the beginning of the apparitions?*

Jacov: During these twelve years, she is always calling us to pray. But she especially calls us to pray for peace.

Question: *It has been written that when the first Secret of Medjugorje is revealed, Satan's powers will be broken. Is this true? What is going to happen?*

Jacov: I don't want to talk about the Secrets.

Question: *Will all the Secrets take place before the end of this decade?*

Jacov: I don't want to talk about that.

Question: *Has Our Lady spoken to you about the Pope lately?*

Jacov: Not to me personally.

Question: *Is the world making progress in its conversion?*

Jacov: Our Lady never said anything about that. But she is very happy if people come here to pray.

Question: *Has Our Lady ever wept tears? Has she ever wept tears of blood?"*

Jacov: I have seen Our Lady weeping. But never tears of blood.

Question: *Is the Second Coming of Jesus part of the Secrets?*

Jacov: I don't know that.

Question: *Tell us about the Great Sign?*

Jacov: Our Lady promised us that she will leave a Great Sign on the Hill of Apparitions and we know when it will be.

Question: *It has been twelve years since the apparitions began. Has the Gospa indicated the apparitions may end soon?*

Jacov: I don't know anything about that.

Question: *Tell us about God's peace?*

Jacov: Our Lady invites us all the time to peace. This is the reason for her coming here. That is why she came here—for peace. First, she calls us to peace in our hearts. And, if we have peace in our hearts, we can start to pray and to love everybody. We can do anything!

Question: *Has Mary spoken to you of the Fátima message, the consecration of Russia and the era of peace that is promised the world?*

Jacov: Never.

Question: *Many say the Church and the Pope must suffer much. Has Mary spoken of this to you?*

Jacov: There is no message to me especially for this. One time, she gave a message for priests.

Question: *Has Mary spoken about abortion to you?*

Jacov: Not to me personally.

Question: *Did Our Lady and the prayers of her children bring about the fall of Communism?*

Jacov: She hasn't said anything special about this.

Question: *Jacov, the whole world has sunken into a deep darkness, and Mary is said to be concerned about the whole world as much as much as the war that is taking place here. What does all this mean to us? What should we do?*

Jacov: When Our Lady came twelve years ago, right at the beginning of the apparitions, she said we should pray for peace, and that her messages are not only messages for Medjugorje, they are messages for the whole world.

Question: *Is there anything special you would like to tell Americans?*

Jacov: I would just like to call all people to pray. Our Lady calls us for these twelve years to pray, especially now, for peace in our country. And, of course, for all the world.[5]

⤛⤜

In reading between the lines, one begins to notice how the visionaries at Medjugorje often speak of the Ten Secrets as much as from what they do not know, as they know.

They understand what the Secrets contain.

But they don't know the total breadth or outcome of the events. They don't know because it is unlikely it has been revealed to them.

At Fátima, the Virgin Mary did not tell the three shepherds all the details of the nightmare that World War II and Communism would launch upon the world. Mary did not tell them seventy million would die from the war. She did not explain how Communism would come to cover a third of the planet. She refrained from explaining the errors of Marxism, how nuclear weapons would come to haunt life on earth.

Similarly, the visionaries at Medjugorje are given only so much.

As a result, it appears they have adopted a careful, resigned approach. This helps them maintain a positive outlook and the optimism needed to speak about the Secrets.

Most of all, they understand it is senseless to worry.

At a Marian conference in the United States in November of 1997, Jacov revealed his steady approach with regards to the contents of the Secrets.

I know many of you are wondering, "What are the Secrets?" I can't tell you what they are. Many wonder what Our Lady is saying in these Secrets. What will happen? I think the most important thing is that we accept her messages. If we have accepted them and have God in our hearts and in our lives, we need worry about nothing. We should not think or worry about the Secrets.[6]

~∞~

Less than a year later, while visiting a friend, Marija Paulic, in Sunrise, Florida, Jacov Čolo received the surprise of his life.[7]

As he waited in prayer for his daily apparition that afternoon in Marija's home, the Virgin suddenly appeared. She carried with her a major announcement for him.

Author and filmmaker Sean Bloomfield wrote about this significant day:

> The Virgin finally appeared—a blissful moment which, according to the six seers, is impossible to describe in earthly terms no matter how many times it happens. To Jacov's shock, however, the Blessed Mother announced that this would be her last regular apparition to him. No reason was given. She concluded their meeting by requesting that Jacov prepare to receive the Tenth and final Secret during a special apparition the following morning.[8]

The startling apparition that day proved pivotal in Jacov's life. As was the date it took place—September 11, 1998—the same date the terrorist attack on the United States would come three years later.

The following morning at 11:15 a.m., the Virgin returned to Jacov:

> When she came, she greeted me as always with '*Praise be Jesus.*' While she was confiding the Tenth Secret to me, she was sad. Then with a gentle smile, she said to me:[9] "*...From today, I will not be appearing to you every day, but only on Christmas, the*

birthday of my Son. Do not be sad…Let people always see in you an example of how God acts on people and how God acts through them. I bless you with my motherly blessing and I thank you for having responded to my call."[10]

The apparition ended at 11:45 a.m. According to a witness, Jacov was overwhelmed with grief, not just because of the Tenth Secret,[11] but because it meant the end to his daily apparitions.[12]

A long and hard struggle for him would now begin. Not surprisingly, the news spread swiftly across the globe.

Bloomfield picks up the story:

The parishioners and priests of Medjugorje, including the late Fr. Slavko, were taken aback when they received word of Jacov's last daily apparition occurring in the USA. They had always thought it would take place in Medjugorje, where Mirjana and Ivanka had each received the Tenth Secret.

No one, however, was more affected than Jacov. He became depressed and withdrawn for many months, struggling with the absence of seeing Our Lady every day. Eventually, through ardent prayer, he came to understand that he had to be like everyone else who did not see the Virgin every day. Anyone, he allotted, could be close to her praying with their hearts.

Three years later, the symbolic reason for the date and location of Jacov's last daily apparition became apparent on September 11, 2001. Al Qaeda terrorists crashed hijacked planes into the World Trade Center buildings and the Pentagon. The attacks killed thousands and ushered in a new era of war, fear and uncertainty. It would later be revealed that many of the terrorists who piloted the planes had spent a substantial amount of time in Florida, preparing for the attacks and attending flight schools. Their plans, in fact, were being hatched at the same time that Jacov received the Tenth Secret.

A beautiful statue of Our Lady sits in Marija Paulic's living room where Jacov received his Tenth Secret. The statue often weeps inexplicably leaving the believer to decipher what it could mean.

When asked in 2003 if the Secrets he has received have anything to do with 9/11 attacks and the problem of Islamic terrorism, Jacov paused and then reluctantly said, "I should not answer that."[13]

~✕~

Jacov's last daily apparitions in the United States—and potential association with the coming 9/11 terrorist attacks in 2001—leaves much to ponder and more questions.

Are the Secrets associated with Islam?

Does the United States play a role in some way?

Is the weeping statue in Florida a sign of something to come?

Most of all, one can't help but read between the lines of Jacov's reply concerning the Secrets and terrorism: "I should not answer that."

From his response, it seems as if there was a desire in his heart to affirm that the question was perhaps on the right track.

Jacov last reported he and the Virgin talked about the Secrets in 2010.

After which, Mary said to him, "Pray, pray, pray."[14]

CHAPTER TWENTY

Time of Decision

*"Then the kingship and dominion and majesty of all the
kingdoms under the heavens shall be given to the holy people
of the Most High, whose kingdom shall be everlasting:
all dominions shall serve and obey him."*

—Dn 7:27

A group visiting Medjugorje one day was told the story of the Ten
Secrets by a tour guide while visiting Mt. Podbrdo, the hill of
the apparitions.

The man explained the role of the Secrets, the celestial parchment
with its cryptic writing, that the Secrets will be revealed three days in
advance, and how each one will be announced by a priest.[1]

One pilgrim inquired whether the Secrets held benign or dangerous events, and whether or not it would be a good idea to be in
Medjugorje at that time.

The guide just shrugged.

"Let's put it this way," he replied, "you'll get three days to get to
Medjugorje—or three days to get out!"[2]

"Totally bad."

In stark imagery, Mirjana's choice of words to describe the Tenth Secret is disconcerting.

But when the source of her words—the complete, original interview from 1983 is examined—another picture emerges. In fact, this document reveals a profoundly clearer understanding.

The Secrets of Medjugorje are not so much about physical chastisements—as at Fátima—as they are about God's intent to use the events in the Secrets to alter the direction of life on Earth.

The Secrets, it becomes clear, are going to move the world and the Church into a new time. It is to be an era, wrote Wayne Weible, that has been foretold by saints and mystics for centuries.

"The Blessed Mother," wrote Weible, "has said at various times in her messages that once all the Secrets occur, the Earth will be purified. The Tenth Secret will bring this purification. The Ten Secrets are in reality a great merciful grace. They are not about punishments, but about love—holy, divine love."[3]

Of course—when seen in this light—this then changes the Secrets from something "totally bad" to totally good.

~∞~

The Ten Secrets, the visionaries tell people, must be understood this way.

They are to transform the world for the better, while their harsher side can still be significantly lessened.[4]

They will bring—as not just Weible, but others point out—a climax to the Virgin's intervention on Earth.

And, say both Mirjana and Ivanka, every human being will play a part in the unfolding of the Secrets.[5] The assertion that every person on Earth will play a role is significant. This is because it shows the proper approach to the great mystery of the Secrets.

Viewed by many as a string of intense events that God will permit to purify the world, the Secrets, as the visionaries came to realize, are actually a gift to mankind through the mercy of God.

This is why every person will be involved.

In some manner, people will be confronted individually, as the Secrets come to pass, with a better understanding of the meaning of life on Earth, of the presence of sin and evil in the world, and of their own reality of God. They then will see the need to respond appropriately.

Mirjana, perhaps differently than the other visionaries, came to a deeper understanding of this truth about the Secrets in an ironic way—through her prayerful quest to have the Seventh Secret mitigated by God.

She received the Seventh Secret in her parent's apartment in Sarajevo and its contents troubled her greatly. So, she asked Mary if it was possible for the Secret to be lessened. After the Virgin replied "Pray," she rallied family and friends to pray with sincere conviction and intensity for this intention over a period of eight months.[6]

Told the Secret was softened, the Virgin Mary then said to her,

"But you must never ask such things again."[7]

Mirjana explained to the friars that the Virgin said this to her because "God has His plan" for the conversion of the world—a plan that strongly "necessitates the unfolding of the Secrets."[8]

In these words, we discover that only in the unfolding of the Secrets—God's plan—will there come peace, the *era of peace* prophesied at Fátima.

In essence, as Scripture holds, justice and peace will kiss.[9]

<hr/>

After this time comes to pass, will the Virgin Mary ever appear on Earth again?

This question stems from two of the messages Mary gave in the early days of the apparitions that stated these would be her "last apparitions."[10]

Over the years, five of the six visionaries are on record confirming that Mary did say this to them. As noted, some of them have emphasized that they are not certain what this means.

Perhaps Vicka helps put this curious issue in the proper perspective:

For me, the message that the Madonna has given is very clear: this is the last time that she will be present here on Earth *in the way* she has been present at Medjugorje for such a long period of time. I heard her speak those words, because I was the one who received them personally.[11]

But that does not mean we should be troubled or frightened. After all, God rules the world. He is present in this world, and we must always be ready for His will. If these then must be the last apparitions of Mary, it means that God wants it so…and we must recognize this will, this love of God, as always, with joy and serenity.[12]

Marija, in a revealing interview with *Caritas of Birmingham* on February 24, 2004, shed more light on this mystery:

Question: *Marija, several of the visionaries on various occasions said that these are the last apparitions on Earth. What did Our Lady say to you about this?*

Marija: Our Lady said from the beginning that these are the last apparitions on Earth in which we can hear Our Lady, touch Our Lady, speak with Our Lady; where we can pray with Our Lady; apparitions where it is possible that we 'have' Our Lady. In other apparitions—people have spiritual experiences—but not like us, the six visionaries in Medjugorje, where Our Lady speaks to us. This is really the last and special grace. Normally, one person may see Our Lady [like Bernadette or St. Catherine of the Miraculous Medal, who also touched Our Lady.] But here, six visionaries are a number which is very credible. But this is the last where we can touch Our Lady, speak to her, etc., in this way.13

Question: *Also, is it after the Secrets are revealed, will there not be any need for the apparitions?*

Marija: Our Lady is with us so she can give us knowledge of the Secrets and to help us through the Secrets. After the Secrets are realized, Our Lady will not need to come anymore.[14]

Mirjana is found to be in agreement with this assertion. She told author Jan Connell that she received the same understanding, "She (Mary) said after the Secrets are realized she won't need to come again."[15]

On January 2, 2008, Father Livio Fanzaga interviewed Vicka on *Radio Maria Italia*. The two talked about the Ten Secrets, the end of the Virgin Mary's apparitions, and how people need to use the remaining time of grace for conversion.

Fanzaga: *When the time of the Secrets comes, the Fourth through the Tenth Secrets—Secrets which are evidently very difficult, it means that in any event, in the time of the Secrets—we will always have the Sign of Our Lady which will comfort us. But you also said the last time, last year, that during the time of the Ten Secrets, one of the visionaries will still have the daily apparitions of the Madonna.*

Vicka: Yes, it is certain, it is something I repeat now. We will see who it is. There is still me, Marija, and Ivan. Afterwards, we will see who the Madonna has chosen, who of us three remains with the apparitions. Or, maybe it will be someone else that the Madonna has chosen.

Fanzaga: *So, you, Ivan, and Marija, one of you three. Someone said something to Mirjana like, "Vicka said that during the time of the Ten Secrets there will be one visionary who will continue to have the daily apparitions" but Mirjana said that she didn't know anything about this. What does that mean? That this was told personally to you by the Madonna?*

Vicka: Yes, the Madonna told me personally. Afterwards, we shall see. The Madonna didn't say, "Vicka, it will be you." Now, we just wait to see who it will be. She said that when the time comes, to the person who will continue to have the apparitions, she will explain every 'how and what' to that person.

Fanzaga: *The Madonna also spoke of false prophets, "Those who make catastrophic predictions are false prophets. They say: in that particular year, on that particular day, there will be a catastrophe. I have always said that the chastisements will come if the world does not convert. Therefore, I invite everyone to conversion. Everything depends on your conversion." So, now I ask you, if we convert, will there still be the Ten Secrets, or no?*

Vicka: No, no. The Ten Secrets will take place for sure. The Madonna has already given them. She has described nine of them to me and now I am waiting for the last one. I can only tell you about the Secret which is the Sign on the mountain which I already spoke about and now I only want to say this about the Seventh Secret: The Madonna said that half of the Seventh Secret has been canceled because of our prayers. She recommends that we continue praying because with our prayers we can lessen other Secrets.

Fanzaga: *So, in essence, the discourse is this: The Madonna urges us to convert, she tells us not to wait for the Sign on the mountain, and in any event, "All the Secrets I have confided will be realized and also the visible Sign will be made manifest. When the visible Sign comes, for many it will already be too late (December 23, 1982)." What does that mean?*

Vicka: The Madonna did not explain why it will be "too late" and I did not ask. She only said that we are now living "in a time of grace."

Fanzaga: *So, it is important to convert before the Sign is manifest?*

Vicka: Every day the Madonna calls us to conversion, to the conversion of hearts, you understand? And twenty-seven and a half years later the Madonna is still among us, and our hearts are still too closed, too distant. I don't know. I don't know what it could be, but "too late" could be right.

Fanzaga: *You have always said, and also the Madonna of Medjugorje, that when we talk about the Ten Secrets, we must do so always inviting everyone to hope. In fact, in one of the Madonna's messages, she said, "We must never take away hope." The Madonna didn't come to frighten us but to call us back to responsibility and to conversion in a context which always inspires hope. The Madonna even once said, in the first year of the apparitions: "For the Christian, there is only one attitude with regard to the future: hope of salvation." (June 10, 1982)*

Vicka: Well, you see, the Madonna is here among us to save our souls, truly; she did not come in order to boss us, 'do this, do that or else'—she is here to occupy herself with our souls, she says she is the Mother of everyone and loves everyone. "You do not know how much I love you; If you knew you would cry for joy." We are still a long way away from her joy—you understand? All those things, simple things—she always gives us hope. And then you read her face which she shows you—it is so sad! But she gives you so much joy! She lifts you up, she gives you strength! And this is so encouraging.

Fanzaga: *In all my radio broadcasts, I try to underline this fact too, that the Ten Secrets are a "time of grace" because it is at this time that the power of the Evil One will be conquered by the Madonna. The Madonna is here as "Queen."*

Vicka: The Madonna many times has told us that the Evil One knows where we are the weakest and he looks for empty places not dedicated to God that he can inhabit and he has found many places among the young and in families, breaking them up. The Evil One does a lot of things like this you know. But the Madonna has said that when we feel peace in our hearts and joy and tranquility, then you can see very clearly that this comes from God. If, instead, there is fear in our hearts and we feel disturbed, then we must be very careful, because this doesn't come from God. We must be able to distinguish immediately that which comes from God and that which does not. We need to keep awake and persevere with making the change in our lives so that we can keep the Evil One at bay.

Fanzaga: *This means that if we stay close to the Madonna, we will feel joy in our hearts and we will not feel anxious fear about our future. In fact, the Madonna once said that he who prays has no fear about the future.*

Vicka: Certainly, he who prays has no fear about the future and he who fasts has no fear of the Evil One. We have a great grace—we are living in "a time of grace." I have never heard a word come from the Madonna that created fear—she always gives you hope. She gives joy and tranquility. You can see that the Madonna and her Son defeat all that evil that exists. We shouldn't have any fear, but we must follow what They want. He who follows the Madonna and lives her messages has no motive for being afraid. He who has fear, is afraid even of himself—he must do something to start himself going in the right direction and then he can follow the messages of the Madonna.

Fanzaga: *Power is of God; evil is dangerous, and Satan is strong. Anxious fear for the future certainly is not befitting of believers, but today there exists a worrying concern which is not to be undervalued. On two occasions, John Paul II affirmed that the world was in danger of destroying itself. The seer Ivan declared in a video broadcast that the Madonna had said the very same thing to him, that is, that the world was at risk of destroying itself. So, it's not wise to be too superficial. In one message, the Madonna said, "I will pray to my Son to not punish the world, but I beg you: convert yourselves. You cannot imagine what will happen and neither that which God the Father will send upon the Earth. For this, I repeat, convert yourselves. Renounce everything. Do penance (April 25, 1983)." Here one sees how hope and concern can coexist.*

Vicka: The Madonna has been with us all these many years precisely so that we might come near to God and convert ourselves. As a mother, the Madonna does not want to lose even one of her children. She comes from Heaven to the Earth to save us, but we are still too far away from her. But she never forces anyone. She never says, "You must convert, you must do this and that." No, she doesn't force anyone. She says to each one of us, "*My son, do what your heart tells you to do.*" And she waits for us like a mother. She waits for everyone. She does all that she can do, but apparently our hearts are still very, very hard.[16]

⤖

The Secrets of Medjugorje are secret.

Needless to say, they will remain so until otherwise.

After more than forty years, expecting to learn something new at this time is folly. It is also unwise to place any trust in those who offer whimsical predictions as to when the Secrets will unfold. Theologians say that God is often found to move slow and with a divine precision that dictates the schedule of His plan.

The present age of the visionaries at Medjugorje, seen in this light, is not a determining factor with the coming of the Secrets, even though they have all indicated that the Secrets will unfold in their lifetimes.

Many key biblical characters were quite old when some important events found in Scripture took place in their lives.

It should also be pointed out that Sister Lúcia was seventy-seven years old when Pope John II performed the 1984 consecration; she was ninety-three years of age when the third part of the Secret of Fátima was at last revealed in 2000.

With this in mind, Father Slavko Barbarić says people should try to temper their curiosity about the arrival time of the Secrets:

> The language of Secrets is like a mother speaking to a child... the words refer to something other than what the words them- selves suggest...So don't be a "literalist" about the Secrets. The rule here is "the less you know, the better."

> I've had discussions with some people who've written books about Medjugorje...Some of these have spoken about the "de- lay of the Secrets." I've said to them, "Look, who's late, in your view? God? Well, surely, He knows His ways. And what pre- cisely do you think you know, in any case, about the Secrets, or about some sort of timetable? Hypothetically?"

> No, it's a great mistake to focus on these things. After all, the very reason they're called Secrets is to make it clear that no one except the visionaries knows anything about them at all.[17]

One point about the Secrets of Medjugorje may be surprising to some.

God has protected the visionaries from disclosing too much about them. In fact, asserts Mirjana, the visionaries are "incapable" of divulg- ing the Secrets.[18]

Furthermore, stresses Ivanka, although the Secrets hold some chal- lenging moments, they are not what the Virgin Mary wants anyone to be thinking about:

"The Blessed Mother told us never to focus on bad things. She told us to stay focused on God—on His love for us and on the future, He has planned for us."[19]

This proper focus, emphasizes Father Barbarić, is the *true* message of Medjugorje, the real purpose behind the Secrets.

"If you knew something about the Secrets," asks Barbarić hypothetically, "would it make it easier to say fifteen decades of the Rosary each day? I think not. Would it make it easier to fast two days a week? No. Well, these things—prayer, fasting, making peace, going to confession—this is the real message, the heart of the message of Medjugorje!"[20]

"The biggest secret has been revealed," adds Barbarić, "Peace is possible, it depends on you!"[21]

The visionaries agree.

If people are to focus on anything with regard to the future and the Secrets, it's the Virgin Mary's promise of a welcomed outcome in the end—that the world is going to change for the better, and peace is to come.

But people must begin to decide for God to bring that peace.

As Mirjana wrote in her book, "Now, is the time of decision."

Mary's many conversations with the visionaries about the future is the greatest testament to this truth.[22] Ivan, in a talk given in Australia in 2003, spoke passionately of the Virgin's great hope for the future:

> She wants to lift up this weary world, the weary families, the weary Church. She desires to lift us up and strengthen us. She says, "Dear children, if you are strong, the Church will be strong. If you are weak, the Church will be weak. You are the living Church. Dear children, this world, this mankind, has hope and has a future. But you have to begin to change. You have to come back to God."[23] *

"What the Madonna started in Fátima," Mirjana is often heard to say, "She will finish in Medjugorje."[24]

At the annual National Conference on Medjugorje at Notre Dame University on May 30, 2004, Mirjana participated in a question-and-answer forum that saw her give perhaps the best explanation of this prophetic promise.

"From what I know about Fátima," Mirjana told the large gathering there that day, "everything continues in Medjugorje. What she said in Fátima—what she started—I think through these Ten Secrets, it will be finished in Medjugorje. Her heart will win—she will win the part in this war. Everything will be finished in Medjugorje."[25] †

Mirjana's reasoning is thought provoking.

This is because she has connected—whether she meant to or not—the Secrets of Fátima with the Secrets of Medjugorje.

The Virgin Mary said at Medjugorje in 1991 that she has come to fulfill "the Secrets she began at Fátima," now we see from Mirjana's words that this will only be accomplished "through the Secrets" of Medjugorje.

---

* The future of the Church, according to Ivan, is part of the Ten Secrets. In his book, *Fear of Fire*, author Michael Brown writes: "At Medjugorje, one reputed seer, Ivan Dragićević, when asked if when the Blessed Mother's Secrets unfold there will be a great trial for the Church, said, "Yes, absolutely so." (*Fear of Fire*, p. 229)

† On January 25, 2023, the Virgin Mary, for only the second time in her public messages at Medjugorje, spoke of Fatima: "Dear children! Pray with me for peace, because Satan wants war and hatred in hearts and peoples. Therefore, pray and sacrifice your days by fasting and penance, that God may give you peace. The future is at a crossroads, because modern man does not want God. That is why mankind is heading to perdition. You, little children, are my hope. Pray with me, that what I began in Fátima and here may be realized. Be prayer and witness peace in your surroundings, and be people of peace. Thank you for having responded to my call."

"I cannot divulge much more about the contents of the Secrets," wrote Mirjana about the coming end of an age of evil in her book, *My Heart Will Triumph*, "but I can say this—Our Lady is planning to change the world. She did not come to announce our destruction; she came to save us, and with her Son, she will triumph over evil."[26]

"I'm not personally called to interpret the Secrets of Fátima, but Our Lady affirmed in Medjugorje that both apparitions are connected to the Triumph of her Heart.[27]

⋙⋘

Yes, Fátima and Medjugorje are "both" connected to the Triumph of Mary's Immaculate Heart. And this truth is becoming a more visible reality.

As with so many historical events related to Fátima that mysteriously fall on the anniversary date—May 13—of the Virgin's first apparition there, the proof that Mary's Triumph is unfolding in the world through Medjugorje is often identifiable in the same manner.

This happened again in 2022.

On June 24, 2022—the anniversary date of Mary's first apparition at Medjugorje in 1981—the United States Supreme Court overturned *Roe Vs Wade*, the 1973 case which legalized abortion in the United States. *

For decades, the faithful had beseeched the intercession of the Virgin to help end this holocaust, and now it could be said that she had heard their anguished cry.

---

* In another curious sidebar, the Supreme Court case that overthrew Roe V Wade (Dobbs versus Jackson Women's Health Organization) is known simply as the Dobb's decision, which can easily be viewed as an acronym standing for "Date of Birth," which 65 million Americans never experienced due in great part to Roe V Wade.

But what made the announcement of this court decision even more attributable to Mary was the fact that June 24th is not just the anniversary date of Medjugorje. It holds another intimate connection to the issue at hand—one even more target specific.

June 24th is the date of the annual feast in the Catholic Church of the birth of John the Baptist, who as an "unborn" baby "leapt in the womb" (Lk 1:41) upon hearing the Virgin Mary greet his mother, Elizabeth.[28] †

---

† The June 24 date of the Supreme Court ruling in the overturning of *Roe Vs Wade* holds further significance in the spiritual war at hand. It is the same date as the official founding of Freemasonry. On June 24, 1717, four lodges came together in London to form the Premier Grand Lodge of England, which became the Grand Lodge of England, the first Masonic Grand Lodge in history. Freemasonry—whose principles are still considered irreconcilable with the teachings of the Catholic Church (See *Quaesitum est*, November 26, 1983, by Joseph Cardinal Ratzinger)—is understood to have exercised considerable influence on the U.S. Supreme Court over the years. (See *Behind the Lodge Door* by Paul Fisher and *Hope of the Wicked* by Ted Flynn.)

CHAPTER TWENTY-ONE

————————

"The Victory of the Blessed Mother"

"Fear not, for I have redeemed you; I have called you by name: you are mine."

—Is 43:1

The Ten Secrets of Medjugorje are a plea for action.

Needless to say, the entire world needs to know not just about the Secrets, but about Medjugorje's urgent call to peace, prayer, fasting, and especially, conversion.

The visionaries consistently stress this point.[1]

But there is an important consideration that must be remembered.

One that can't be ignored.

No matter how miraculous an apparition, visionary or mystic is found to be, even Catholics are not required by the Church to entertain, yet alone follow, any messages such as those emanating from Medjugorje—or even the approved revelations of Fátima—regardless of their reported urgency.

Such heavenly pronouncements are not considered official Church teachings, and no matter how serious they sound—no matter if they are sanctioned by the Church—*no one* is warranted to put their faith in them.

Here in lies, some Church officials claim, a difficult situation.

It is a perplexity that especially surrounds the Marian apparitions of the past century and their prophecies, which often strike a dire tone.

⸺⟁⸺

The Catholic Church teaches that public revelation concluded with the death of the last Apostle, St. John.

Known as Divine Revelation, the Church teaches that these revelations are given to people for all ages, and they are preserved in Sacred Scripture and Sacred Tradition. They make up the foundation of the Church, its doctrines and dogmas.[2]

However, there are also what are known as private revelations.

These are messages from God that are given to individuals to inspire them to live more faithfully, and ultimately to draw people closer to Him. But these revelations, even when sanctioned by the Church, have no binding resolution upon the faithful, as explained in the *Catechism of the Catholic Church* (N.67).

Fátima, however, brought into question the level of importance to be given private revelations. This is because the Secret of Fátima came to involve the decisions of a series of popes over time that had far-reaching effects on the Church, and in the eyes of many, the world.[3]

"It was the first time that the Church has officially recognized the historic incisiveness of a prophecy whose source was an apparition of the Virgin. A prophecy that Cardinal Sodano has defined as 'the greatest of modern times,'" writes Fátima author Renzo Allegri.[4]

Indeed, Pope John Paul II was adamant about the importance of Fátima.

He strongly held that Fátima "imposes an obligation on the Church" and is "not optional." It is one, asserted the Holy Father, that "commands the Church"; one that is "more current and even more urgent than before."[5]

Like Medjugorje, Fátima also came to be viewed by many as eschatological in make-up and, therefore, of great significance to the Church's mission. Pope Paul VI was the first to truly see this new reality emerging in regard to Fátima, the Church, and the times at hand.

Paul VI believed the falling sun at Fátima was *not only* a warning of a possible nuclear war if mankind refused to change, but more. The Miracle of the Sun, he thought, conjured up images of the end times as revealed in Scripture.[6]

"It was eschatological in the sense that it was like a repletion or an annunciation of a scene at the end of time for all humanity, assembled together," the Holy Father told the French philosopher, Jean Guitton, on May 28, 1967, which Guitton quoted in *Journal de ma Vie*, one of his fifty books.[7]

A number of Church hierarchy echoed the Pope's view in the 1970s.

Cardinal Ciappi, Papal Theologian, revealed that he shared Paul VI's conviction, and talked about it at the International Seminar at Fátima in 1971:

"The apocalyptic imagery of the woman glowing with the sun's light may well be applied to the person of the Mother of God, seen by the beloved Apostle as crowned with twelve stars and at the same time crying as she labored in birth."[8]

The Cardinal Patriarch of Lisbon, Antonio Ribeiro, said much the same at the 8th Fátima Congress at Kevelaer, Germany, on September 18, 1977:

"Fátima appears like a great supernatural light. It is God who reveals Himself with the impressive majesty of Sinai."[9]

Two years later, Abbé André Richard, the French philosopher, was even more expansive on the eschatological significance of Fátima:

Fátima is an intervention to change the march of the entire caravan of mankind...How can any of us fail to be conscious of

Our Lady appearing in the sky, reminding us of the Great Sign in Chapters 11 and 12 of the *Apocalypse*? How can any of us consider Fátima to be less than the presentation of that apocalyptic message of Our Lady, dressed with the sun and announcing her triumph over the dragon?[10]

⚬

The implications of such thinking are clear.

Fátima, and consequently its contemporary peer, Medjugorje, appear to be much too important, much too critical to our present times— an age when a potential nuclear holocaust hangs over the world—to be casually framed as *private revelation* and cast aside.

Father Louis Kondor, the noted theologian and former vice-postulator of the Causes of Francisco and Jacinta, expressed his conviction concerning this conundrum.

In the 1975 July-August edition of the Fátima newsletter, *Seers of Fátima*, Kondor wrote,

"In view of this similarity, which seems to be a telling fulfillment of Apocalypse 12, who would venture any longer to speak of a 'private revelation'? Fátima is an eschatological Sign that reveals the saving victory of the 12th chapter of the *Apocalypse*."[11]

Kondor argued that though not Divine Revelation, some private revelations hold great importance to the will of God for His people as He guides them through history. Fátima, he pointed out, is the model for this emerging truth:[12]

We can consider Fátima as the great eschatological Sign given by God in our times, so that we will not deserve the rebuke that Our Lord made to the Jews: "You know how to read the face of the sky, but you cannot read the sign of the times (Mt 16:4)." Fátima is the sign of the times.[13]

Father Paul Kramer, a Fátima historian and author, echoes Kondor's argument that some apparitions are not merely private revelation:

> The (Fátima) message was conveyed in a manner that is unique in Church history, and its form and content are also unique. This puts it in a class by itself; it can't be relegated to the broad category of "private revelations." Ignoring this particular message is impossible for Catholics and may also be unwise for everyone else on this troubled planet.[14]

$\approx$

"Do you believe in Fátima?" Pope Pius XII asked a group of American pilgrims in Rome led by Father Leo Goode in late August 1958, just months before he died.

When they answered in the affirmative, the Holy Father asked, "Will you do what Our Lady asked at Fátima?"

On hearing their assent, Pius stated, "If we are to have peace, we must obey the request made at Fátima. The time for doubting Fátima is long past. It is now time to take action."[15]

Not only was it time to take action, wrote acclaimed Fátima author Francis Johnston, but it was time for the Church to take action on a large, national scale.

Fátima needed, he believed, to be seen as a matter of "privileged priority" by the Church.[16]

"Why are we not hearing," Johnston bemoaned in his book, *Fatima, the Great Sign*, "the message of Fátima proclaimed loudly and clearly, as the world lurches deeper into the black mire of iniquity and the threat of a global holocaust?"[17]

$\approx$

To a great degree, this need *was* recognized and acted upon on a grand scale in Portugal in the late 1920s and early 1930s.[18]

On May 13, 1931, all of the country's bishops responded to the call of Fátima and, before 300,000 gathered at the Cova da Iria, consecrated the nation to the Immaculate Heart of Mary.[19] They would repeat the consecration in 1938 and 1940.

Their bold action, Sister Lúcia noted, kept Portugal out of World War II:

"In this horrible war, Portugal will be spared because of the national consecration to the Immaculate Heart of Mary made by the Bishops."[20]

But within Portugal, the consecrations did much more.

Over the next ten years, a Catholic renaissance unfolded in the country like never before seen. Seminaries throughout the nation were filled with hundreds of students, new schools opened, and religious communities abounded. By 1941, there were 3,815 professed nuns.

Moreover, a renewal of Christian life spread throughout the nation in every way. Spiritual retreats, pilgrimages, Catholic radio shows—along with a complete political and social transformation—swept through Portugal.[21]

Cardinal Manuel Gonçalves Cerejeira—who did not at first believe in Fátima and called it a "bad counterfeit of Lourdes"—told a French journalist in 1942:[22]

"In the whole country (Portugal), you can hardly manage to gather a handful of enemies of religion."[23]

In Poland, the Church also took action on a national level.

According to Grzegorz Gorny and Janusz Rosikon, in their book, *Fatima Mysteries*, it was no accident that the collapse of Communism began there.

The Catholic Church's position in Poland, they write, was better than in any other nation under Communist rule in Eastern Europe. Its Marian devotion was very strong.[24]

And, the authors' note, because of its former primate—Cardinal August Hlond—Poland had long before taken the urgency of Fátima to heart.[25]

While in exile during World War II, Hlond had witnessed Pope Pius XII consecrate the world in 1942 to the Immaculate Heart of Mary.[26] From this, he took very seriously Pius's call for other bishops to do the same in their countries. Consequently, he made up his mind to do just that when he returned to Poland.[27]

Poland, after Portugal, became the first country to practice the First Saturdays' devotion and to be consecrated to the Immaculate Heart of Mary, which was decided by the episcopate during Advent of 1946, and then performed in three stages.[28]

The first stage of the consecration was done in all the parishes together on July 7, 1946. All of the bishops then performed the consecration in their own diocese on August 15. Finally, on September 8, the Polish episcopate gathered together in Częstochowa and performed the consecration in the presence of pilgrims from all over Poland.[29] Over one million assembled in the town that day, delivering a great shock to the Communist authorities.[30]

Over the years, the Polish Church actively disseminated literature about Fátima throughout the country, to the point that the name Fátima became censored by the government.[31]

All of this can be seen to be the mystical seeds of what led to the fall of Communism in 1989, and subsequently throughout Eastern Europe and beyond.

Cardinal August Hlond—on his deathbed many years later—related to Cardinal Wyszyński a prophetic vision of the Virgin battling the fiery dragon of *The Book of the Revelation*.

"Pray!" Hlond told Wyszyński, "difficult times are coming, difficult times. Call out! Victory, when it comes, will be the victory of Our Blessed Mother!"[32]

Today, at Medjugorje, a similar reality surfaces.

Action needs to be taken before the Ten Secrets unfold, before it's—as Mary warns—"too late."

The times at hand, as the six visionaries constantly note, are urgent, serious and grave.

While the apparitions at Medjugorje remain to be sanctioned by the Church, Medjugorje's call to peace, prayer, penance, and conversion—as with the call at Fátima—is in desperate need to be proclaimed to a world submerged in atheism.

Moreover, an important question arises.

When the events contained in the First Secret of Medjugorje come to pass—after having been publicly announced just days before at Medjugorje—will the faithful be prepared to voice an urgent call to the nations? To all mankind?

Indeed, after the First Secret unfolds—before the Great Sign (The Third Secret) appears on Mt. Podbrdo—there will be a need to act swiftly and boldly to seize the moment at hand. Such a moment must become the great return to God of pilgrim humanity—the penultimate fulfillment of the parable of the Prodigal Son.

In essence, mankind will be at the Red Sea, and it will be time to leave the bondage of sin, to cross over into a new world, a new time, into the "Era of Peace" promised at Fátima.

In 1917, Fátima sounded this call of universal metanoia.

Now, the Madonna of Medjugorje—the Queen of Peace—hopes to see it brought to fruition with all the nations.[33]

⁓∞⁓

"One day a lady from Vietnam came up to me and told me how hard it was when she was forced to leave her home during the war," said Father Jozo Zovko in a homily he delivered at St. Elijah Church in Tihaljina, a village about twenty miles from Medjugorje.

"As she was leaving, she turned and gave one last look. In her yard, she saw the statue of Mary still sitting there. It seemed to say to her, 'Don't leave me behind.'

She went back for it.

CHAPTER TWENTY-ONE

"Don't leave Mary behind here in Medjugorje.

"Let her be the Mother of your family, your parish, your community, of your nation."[34]

Medjugorje and the Prophet Elijah

"Lo, I will send you Elijah, the prophet, before the day of the Lord comes, the great and terrible day, to turn the hearts of the fathers to their children, and hearts of the children to their fathers, lest I come and strike the land with doom."

—Mal 3:23-24

The mysterious fire that appeared on Mt. Podbrdo at Medjugorje on October 27, 1981, just months after the apparitions began there, was a singular event.

Witnesses say it burned brightly for fifteen minutes—was observable from a considerable distance—and looked as real as any fire. Over five hundred people, scattered about the five villages below, attested to seeing it.[1]

In a village that would become known over the years as a haven for the unexplainable, the massive blaze on the hilltop that suddenly vanished still sits close to the top of the list.

But while it was mysterious, its origin is no mystery.

"The fire seen by the faithful was of a supernatural character," the Virgin Mary revealed to the visionaries the following day. "It's one of the signs; a forerunner of the Great Sign."[2]

That the Virgin Mary revealed this fire was a forerunner of the Great Sign—the Third Secret of the Ten Secrets of Medjugorje—does not imply that the Great Sign at Medjugorje will necessarily consist of fire itself.

But it does have significant implications.

⌁

As in the Old Testament, the manifestation of this supernatural fire on a mountain, like the glowing Sinai, clearly appears to confirm the presence of God from whom the Great Sign will directly come.

And, as in the ancient days of old, one cannot help but wonder if the fire was intended to convey the certainty of God's approaching victory over His enemies.

Marian writers say the reality of this coming victory was already prophetically symbolized at Fátima during the Miracle of the Sun on October 13, 1917.

On that terrifying day—as the sun left its mooring in the sky and descended upon the thousands huddled in fear in the Cova da Iria—the children were shown three visions.

First, Saint Joseph with the Child Jesus appeared in the sky, blessing the world, as Mary stood beside them clothed in a white tunic and blue mantle.

Next, Christ appeared in His glorified manhood and again made the sign of the cross. This time, Mary stood beside Him as Our Lady of Sorrows.

Finally, in the third and last vision, the Virgin Mary appeared as Our Lady of Mt. Carmel.

This final vision is of prophetic significance.[3]

The vision of Our Lady of Mt. Carmel, Fátima historians write, was intended to symbolically reveal the presence of a twofold message in the Miracle of the Sun that was taking place at that moment.

Seen only by the three children, the vision of Our Lady of Mt. Carmel conveyed what Mary promised the future held—God's coming victory in the world over evil:

"In the end my Immaculate Heart will triumph."

Mt. Carmel—where the prophet Elijah called fire down from Heaven—was being recalled by the appearance of Mary as Our Lady of Mt. Carmel for a reason: to evoke the immortal moment recorded in *The First Book of Kings* when God intervened in the affairs of ancient Israel to bring victory over the false prophets of Baal.[4]

~∞~

At that time, Israel was on the verge of annihilation from a punishment sent by God for their idolatry.

Elijah the Tishbite—one of the most illustrious figures in the Old Testament, who, along with Moses, appeared at the Transfiguration of Jesus on Mt. Tabor—told the people that if they did not destroy their idols and return to God, they would experience a severe drought:

"As the Lord, the God of Israel lives, whom I serve, during these years there shall be no dew or rain except at my word."[5]

Facing the extinction of his nation after years of no rain, King Ahab met with Elijah, who asked for the meeting by request of the Lord. Confronting the prophet face-to-face, Ahab said,

"Is it you?—you disturber of Israel."

Elijah replied,

"It is not I who disturb Israel but you and your family, by forsaking the commands of the Lord and following the Baals. Now summon all Israel to me on Mt. Carmel, as well as the four hundred and fifty prophets of Baal and the four hundred prophets of Asherah who eat at Jezebel's table."[6]

⤜⤛

With all of Israel and the false prophets gathered on Mt. Carmel, Elijah presented them with a challenge.

The pagan priests would erect an altar, place a young bull upon it, and pray to Baal to send down fire to consume the sacrifice.[7]

At the same time, Elijah—the only surviving prophet of God left in Israel—would build another altar, dig a trench filled with water around it, and place a sacrifice upon it, too.[8] Then, like the prophets of Baal, he was to call upon the one true God of Israel:

"You shall call on your gods, and I will call on the Lord. The God who answers with fire is God," declared Elijah.

All the people answered, "Agreed!"[9]

As the day unfolded, the pagan priests hopped around their altar and pleaded with Baal from morning to noon to demonstrate his power. They even self-mutilated themselves with swords and spears until blood gushed over them, all in the hope of triggering a response.[10]

Elijah, all the while, taunted them on,

"Call louder, for he is a god…perhaps he is asleep and must be awakened."[11]

Finally, as it was evident that their petition was in vain, Elijah called upon Heaven in a singular prayer:

"Lord, God of Abraham, Isaac, and Israel, let it be known this day that you are God in Israel and that I am your servant and have done all these things by your command. Answer me, Lord! Answer me, that this people may know that you, Lord, are God and that you have brought them back to their senses."[12]

Immediately, fire fell from the sky and consumed not only Elijah's sacrifice but the wood and stony altar, as well as the water in the trench. With this, the people of Israel fell to their knees,

"The Lord is God! The Lord is God!" they cried out.[13]

Ordering the prophets of Baal to be seized, Elijah then had them all slain. God's victory over the false gods of the age was complete and the people returned to the Lord.[14]

〜✕〜

At Fátima, theologians say God was letting the world know that the fiery sun falling from the sky not only confirmed Mary's powerful presence, but also that His enemies of today—like the prophets of Baal—were destined to suffer the same humiliating defeat as His enemies of yesterday.

"Our Lady came under her ancient title of Mt. Carmel,"[15] explains Fátima author John Haffert of the symbolism behind the vision, "Elijah had performed a miracle to show God is God, and now Mary had just done the same on this mountain of Fátima."[16]

Now, at Medjugorje, the Virgin Mary will fulfill the Secrets she began at Fátima.

The appearance of the forerunning sign, the supernatural fire at Medjugorje—on a mountain top like at Carmel and Fátima—appears to confirm God's approaching victory, a victory to be forever immortalized by the manifestation of the Third Secret, the Great Sign there.

Indeed, with the Great Sign's appearance on Mt. Podbrdo, an unparalleled moment in the history of mankind will have arrived.

The era of universal atheism as never seen before; the era of massive death as never experienced before; the era of sin and Satan as never known before will be brought to its prophesied demise, defeated through the blood and tears of its tragic victims—and the faith and prayers of the Virgin Mary's children.

At last, the era of peace foretold at Fátima will begin to manifest, and the presence of the Great Sign at Medjugorje will prove to the world, as did Elijah on Mt. Carmel, that "the Lord is God."

It is to be an era presented to humanity as a gift from the hands of the Father through the Immaculate Heart of the Mother.

Indeed, Mary's Immaculate Heart, the ultimate symbol of the Triumph, will now secure its rightful place in the Church next to the Sacred Heart of her Son, as people throughout the world come to realize that she—*the Woman Clothed in the Sun*—secured the grace that delivered God's victory.[17]

This coming honor of the Queen of Heaven and Earth, Church tradition holds, was also previewed in Scripture that memorable day on Mt. Carmel by the prophet Elijah.

<hr />

"Go up, eat and drink," Elijah told King Ahab after the false prophets of Baal were slain, "for there is the sound of a heavy rain."[18]

With these words, the time of the three-year drought in Israel was now to be over, and as Elijah called down the fire, so now he announced to Ahab the coming of the rain, which the people of the nation so desperately longed to see.[19]

Perched on the highest point of Mt. Carmel, Elijah instructed his servant to look out over the waters of the Mediterranean Sea to see if the storm was nearby.

"There is nothing," the servant reported to the prophet after six attempts to spot the coming rain.

But on the seventh attempt, the youth told Elijah,

"There is a cloud as small as a man's hand arising from the sea."[20]

That cloud, tradition has long held, symbolized the coming of the Immaculate Conception—the coming of the Virgin Mary—who at a future time would shower God's healing graces from her Immaculate Heart upon a needy world, like the cloud that day showered rain upon Mt. Carmel and all of Israel.[21]

Tradition further holds that Elijah beheld a vision that day on Mt. Carmel of the coming of the Blessed Virgin Mary.[22]

<hr />

If such were the case, we know today why Mary and the presence of Elijah and Mt. Carmel has been linked together at many of her apparition sites over the centuries.

It is a mystery especially noted at Lourdes, where Mary's last apparition there was on July 16, 1858, the Feast of Our Lady of Mt. Carmel.[23]

It is seen again at Fátima, where Mary's final appearance to the three children on October 13,1917, was as Our Lady of Mt. Carmel.[24]

At Lourdes, Mary shocked the Church by declaring,

"I am the Immaculate Conception."

At Fátima, she stunned the world by performing the greatest foretold miracle in history, the "Miracle of the Sun."

Now, at Medjugorje, where another supernatural fire on a mountain top set the stage, the faithful are left to wait and wonder what is to come.

Are ancient biblical prophecies about to be fulfilled in the times that are near?

Is Elijah's shadowing, mystical presence being revealed once again in what may be the last apparitions of the Virgin Mary, who first appeared at Medjugorje on the feast day of John the Baptist, the prophet who the Gospels say came in "the spirit and power of Elijah?"

Is Medjugorje to take its place next to Lourdes and Fátima in a transcendent mystery involving this great prophet?

It is a mystery that deepens with the reality that the patron saint of Bosnia and Herzegovina is none other than Elijah, the only nation in the world to proclaim him as such.

And—to add to the intrigue—he was declared patron saint in 1752 by a Franciscan Bishop named Pavao "Dragićević."

Yes, the same name as the one who is to reveal the Ten Secrets of Medjugorje to the world—Mirjana Dragićević [Soldo]—the Secrets that will bring the crushing defeat of evil in these times, as Elijah brought defeat to the prophets of Baal.[25]

"Lo, I will send you Elijah," Scripture reads.

Many believe these words are being fulfilled at Medjugorje.

ACKNOWLEDGEMENTS

Since I began this book—as well as my previous one, *Twilight of Marxism*—some twenty years ago, there were those at the time who helped me that I wish to thank: Denis Nolan—whose letter encouraged me to write this book, Bishop Pavel Hnilica, and his two assistants, Fr. Paul Sigl and Fr. Lucia Maria Alimandi, Stan and Marge Karminski, Joan Smith, Jan and Ed Connell, Carole McElwain, Dr. Rosalie Turton of the 101 Foundation, Sister Agnes McCormick, Sister Emanuel Maillard, Michael Fontecchio, Fr. Rene Laurentin, June Klins, Fr. Richard Foley, Fr. Michael O'Carroll, Fr. Robert Herrmann, Fr. Kenny Keene, Fr. Ed O'Conner, Fr. John O' Shea, Fr. Richard Whetstone, Fr. Jozo Zovko, and Fr. Petar Ljubicic.

More recently, I want to thank John Davis and Don Kirkwood, who both did a masterful job editing the book. Likewise, Fr. David Tourville and Fr. Bill McCarthy were instrumental in their spiritual support and guidance. I am also indebted to Amanda DeFazio for her tireless assistance on every possible need that arose.

Dr. Frank Novasack Jr, Mary Lou Sokol, Brad Fassenbender, Noah Ostlund, Gerard Beer, Barbara and Richard Nozewski, my daughter Dominique and my son, Joshua, all agreed to read the manuscript and were very helpful with their insights, observations and corrections.

Finally, my wife, Emily, was once more at my side, covering for my failures in countless ways. A special thank you to my six children, who I can always count on for their encouragement, love and prayers: Maria Meyers and her husband, Adam, and our first grandson, Theo, Sarah, Joshua, Natasha, Dominique and Jesse.

Eternal appreciation to my parents, Andrew and Mary, along with my uncle Michael Petrisko, good old Sammy, who was like a brother.

NOTES

PROLOGUE: THE PATH TO PEACE

1   Fr. René Laurentin and Fr. René Lejeune, *Messages and Teachings of Mary at Medjugorje* (Milford, Ohio: Riehle Foundation, 1988) 55.
2   Chris Marshall, "Divine Justice as Restorative Justice," Center for Christian Ethics, 2012, pp 11-19, https://restorativejustice.org.
3   Ibid.
4   Ibid.
5   Ibid.
6   Ibid.
7   Ibid.
8   Ibid.
9   Antonio Socci, *The Fourth Secret of Fatima* (Fitzwilliam, NH: Loreto Publications, English language translation, 2009), 217.
10   Ibid.
11   Ibid.
12   Ted Flynn, "Medjugorje and the Great Spiritual Reset," *Signs and Wonders for Our Times*, Vol. 31, Spring/Summer, 2021, 46-54.
13   Joseph A. Pelletier, A.A., *The Queen of Peace Visits Medjugorje* (Worcester, MA: Assumption Publications, 1985), 145.
14   Thomas Petrisko, Twilight of Marxism (Pittsburgh, PA: St.Andrew's Productions,2022), 153.
15   Jan Connell, *Queen of the Cosmos*, Brewster, MA:Paraclete Press,1990, Revised Edition 2004), 144, 145.
16   Fulton J. Sheen, *Communism and the Conscience of the West* (New York: Garden City Books, 1948), 15.

CHAPTER 1: "THE SECRETS ARE THEIR DESTINY"

1   Ljudevit Rupčić, *Is the Virgin Mary Appearing in Medjugorje? An Urgent Message Given to the World in a Marxist Country* (Washington, D.C.: The Word Among Us Press, 1984), 73.
2   Ibid.
3   Ibid., 28.

4   Mirjana Soldo, *My Heart Will Triumph* (Cocoa, Fl: Catholic Shop Publishing, 2016), 136. Through Father Petar Ljubicic, Mirjana will reveal the Ten Secrets, one by one. The question arose many years ago as to whether the visionaries could reveal the Secrets to anyone beforehand, such as Church authorities, as occurred at La Salette and Fátima. Jacov Marin, a Croatian priest, in his 1989 book, *Queen of Peace Visits Medjugorje*, writes: "None of the Secrets can be revealed by the seers to anyone, not even to the Holy Father. At the suggestion of the local pastor, the visionaries asked Our Lady whether they could at least reveal the Secrets to the Church superiors. Our Lady answered that she herself will tell them when, to whom, and how they should reveal the Secrets." (p. 35). In her 2016 book (p. 187), Mirjana writes that if the Pope asked for the Secrets, she could not say "no."

5   Father Richard Foley SJ, *The Drama of Medjugorje* (Dublin: Veritas Publications, 1992), 16.

6   Lucy Rooney SND and Robert Faricy SJ, *Medjugorje Up Close: Mary Speaks to the World* (Chicago, IL: Franciscan Herald Books, 1985), 87.

7   Pelletier, *The Queen of Peace Visits Medjugorje*, 192.

8   Albert J. Hebert, *Medjugorje: An Affirmation and Defense* (Pauline, LA: Albert Hebert, S.M., 1990), 48,76.

9   René Laurentin, *The Latest News of Medjugorje* (Milford, OH: The Riehle Foundation,1987), 36-37. As Father Bianchi notes, Fátima and Medjugorje share much in common. The children were kidnapped by the authorities; persecuted by atheist governments; shown Hell; given Secrets; and told by the Virgin of her coming Triumph. Medjugorje is to bring to an end Fátima's Secret. But Medjugorje does not exactly share in that end. Its end involves a beginning; the beginning of the future of the world as revealed in parts to all the visionaries. As Father Bubalo notes in his book, "Vicka then told me that the Virgin said: 'So, today you are coming to the end of your first notebook wherein you are recording my narration of the future of the world.'"

10   Soldo, *My Heart Will Triumph*, 84.

11   Svetozar Kraljevic, O.F.M., *The Apparitions of Our Lady at Medjugorje, 1981-1983;* An Historical Account with Interviews (Chicago, IL: Franciscan Press, 1984), 128.

12   Transcript of interview with Ivan Dragićević by Fr. Zoran Ostojich in Chicago on November 19, 1989.

13   Medjugorje.Org., *The Medjugorje Messages: 1981-2013* (DeKalb, IL: The Medjugorje Web, 2013), 261.

14   Medjugorje.Org., *The Medjugorje Messages: 1981-2013*, 270.

15 Finbar O'Leary, *Vicka: Her Story* (Dublin, Ireland: The Columbia Press, 2015), 48.

16 Michael O'Carroll, CSSp, *Medjugorje: Facts, Documents and Theology* (Dublin, Ireland: Veritas, Publishers, 1991), 189.

17 Denis Nolan, *Medjugorje: A Time for Truth, A Time for Action* (Santa Barbara, CA: Queenship Publishing, 1993), 10.

18 Pelletier, *The Queen of Peace Visits Medjugorje*, 145.

19 Laurentin and Lejeune, *Messages and Teachings of Mary at Medjugorje*, 204.

CHAPTER 2: "NEVER TELL THE SECRETS TO ANYONE"

1 Lucy Rooney, S.N.D. and Robert Faricy SJ, *Mary Queen of Peace* (New York: Alba House, 1984), 42.

2 Ibid.

3 Peter Heintz, *A Guide to Apparitions* (Sacramento, CA: Gabriel Press, 1993), 59-67. Ivan spoke at Beauraing on August 24, 1994.

4 Thomas W. Petrisko, *The Fatima Prophecies, At the Doorstep of the World* (Pittsburgh, PA: St. Andrew's Productions, 1998), 249.

5 Lúcia dos Santos, *Fatima in Lucia's Own Words: Sister Lucia's Memoirs* [Edited by Fr. Louis Kondor, SVD]. Translated by Dominican Nuns of the Perpetual Rosary (Fátima, Portugal: Postulation Centre, 1976), 46. Lúcia was very protective of the Secret. This was due to an order from the Virgin herself not to not talk about the Secret given on July 13, 1917. It was a command that was of the greatest concern to her. Then, after Jacinta was exhumed on September 12, 1935, and a picture of her corpse was sent to her from the Bishop, the beginning of the revelation of the Secret begins to unfold. Lúcia responds with a letter to the Bishop, who is inspired to order Lúcia to write down her memories of Jacinta. This leads to Lúcia 's four memoirs. The first, on December 25, 1935, concerns Jacinta. The *Second Memoir* was written between November 7th and the 21st of 1937. The third was written on August 31, 1941, and the last on December 8th of the same year. [Several decades later, she would pen a 5th and a 6th memoir.] The revelation of the Secret begins now to see some light, but Lúcia is still reluctant to speak of it, claiming at different times that she was not asked by her superiors or did not have permission from Heaven. But beginning with the *First Memoir* and throughout the next three, the greatest mystery of the 20th century begins to have a public face. One Fátima author, Kevin Symonds, described the early glimpses of the Secret seen in the *First Memoir*, "In said Memoir, Lúcia halts her narrative on Jacinta at one point in order to tell the Bishop that some

details touch upon the Secret and she will proceed cautiously. After this note, the narrative on Jacinta largely concerns her processing the vision of Hell and her heroic sacrifices for sinners up to her death in 1920. Still, however, Lúcia provides scant information about the "Secret" of July,1917. In fact, very close to the end of the *First Memoir*, Lúcia relays one of the last words from Jacinta: never to reveal the Secret." Symonds writes that by the *Third Memoir* in 1941, Lúcia begins to tell more, but is still very guarded in exactly what she reveals. In this memoir, though, she states that she believes Heaven gave her permission to reveal the Secret, and so begins to explain there are three parts to it, of which she will reveal the first two. After the 4th memoir, the Bishop was well aware of Lúcia's wish to not disclose the third part of the Secret and he was inclined not to force her. But Lúcia became seriously ill in 1943, and out of concern she might die, he ordered her to write the third part of the Secret, which she did on January 3, 1944. It was then kept by the Bishop in the diocese until 1957, when it was transferred to Rome. For her part, Lúcia remained vigilant in her silence concerning this part of the Secret and its contents. (See Kevin Symonds's *On the Third Part of the Secret of Fatima*.)

6   Eph 3:1-6.

7   Joseph Dirvin I.C.M., *St. Catherine Laboure of the Miraculous Medal* (Rockford, IL: TAN Books & Publishers, 1987).

8   Sandra Zimdals-Swartz, *Encountering Mary: From LaSalette to Medjugorje* (Princeton, New Jersey: Princeton University Press, 1991), 165-189.

9   Ibid.

10   Ibid.

11   Ibid.

12   Ibid.

13   Ibid.

14   Ibid.

15   Ibid.

16   Ibid.

17   Ibid.

18   Ibid.

19   Ibid.

20   Ibid.

21   Ibid.

22   Ibid.

23   Ibid.

24 Ibid. While the apparitions of the Virgin Mary at La Salette received full approval of the Church, the Secret of La Salette did not. The contents of the Secret, however, continued to be circulated, with eventually Mélanie herself releasing a version. This version of Mélanie Calvat's secret message is actually what is known today as the "Secret of La Salette." This is because Mélanie's long secret message contained the apocalyptic language only, not Maxim's. As time went by, the Church moved to silence all versions of the Secret by issuing official Church decrees ordering the faithful to "refrain from treating and discussing the matter in any form." The last decree came in 1923, more than seventy-five years after the apparition at La Salette. To this day, however, the Secret of La Salette still circulates among the faithful and beyond.

25 Michael Brown, *The Day Will Come* (Ann Arbor, MI: Servant Publications, 1996), 49.

26 Abbe Francois Trochu, *Saint Bernadette Soubirous* 1844-1879 (Rockford, IL: TAN Books and Publishers, 1957), 89-100.

27 Grzegorz Gorny and Janusz Rosikon, *Fatima Mysteries* (San Francisco and Warsaw, Poland: Rosikon and Ignatius Press, 2017), back cover.

CHAPTER 3: THE WINTER OF TOMORROW

1 Laurentin and Lejeune, *Messages and Teachings of Mary at Medjugorje*, 55.

2 Pelletier, *The Queen of Peace Visits Medjugorje*, 143. The magical effects of Mary's secrets that Father Pelletier speaks of is undeniable. Investigative journalist Randall Sullivan, in questioning Mirjana about the Secrets, says she told him that what makes Secrets necessary is "part of the Secrets." The ultimate Catch 22, Sullivan says he thought to himself.

3 Ibid, 240. Laurentin writes that the messages of Medjugorje have an "apocalyptic propensity." (See Laurentin's, *The Apparitions of Medjugorje Prolonged*.)

4 Rooney and Faricy, *Medjugorje Up Close*, 87.

5 Ibid.

6 Ibid.

7 Ibid.

8 Ibid.

9 Ibid.

10 Ibid.

11 Ibid.

12 Ibid.

13 Ibid., 90-91.

14 Laurentin and Lejeune, *Messages and Teachings of Mary at Medjugorje*, 194.

15 Mary Craig, *Spark from Heaven: The Mystery of the Madonna of Medjugorje* (Notre Dame, IN: Ave Maria Press, 1988), 104.

16 *Queen of Peace Newsletter*, Vol. 1, No. 3 (Coraopolis, PA, Pittsburgh Center for Peace, 1988), p.5.

17 Medjugorje.Org, *The Medjugorje Messages: 1981-2013*, 88. In essence, at Medjugorje, the revelations reveal a countdown has begun to transition the world from one era to another—from an era of unprecedented evil to an era of relative harmony. The transitory stage is referred to as a "period of grace" in the revelations. The many special graces emanating from Medjugorje throughout the world are meant to illuminate God's call "to change willingly." This call, which comes from God's love, also harbors his approaching justice, the consequence of refusing "to change willingly."

18 Laurentin and Lejeune, *Messages and Teachings of Mary at Medjugorje*,269.

19 Medjugorje.Org, *The Medjugorje Messages:1981-2013*, 195.

20 John Paul II, Apostolic Letter, *Tertio Millennio Adveniente*, 1994.

21 Medjugorje.org., *The Medjugorje Messages: 1981-2013*, 82.

CHAPTER 4: A VOICE CRYING IN THE WILDERNESS

1 Lk 1:15.

2 Soldo, *My Heart Will Triumph*, 327.

3 Sabrina Smetko, "The Time in Which We Live is a Time of Decision," *Medjugorje Magazine*, Vol. 17, No.1, Spring, 2007, p. 26. Originally printed in *Glas Mira*. Translated by Marianne Sajn. Also see Mirjana's book, *My Heart Will Triumph*, p. 337.

4 Soldo, *My Heart Will Triumph*, 148. Many false visionaries, even religious and those who claim ties to Medjugorje, have called for physical places of refuge and to accumulate goods. Mary has made clear through her authentic voices that the safest refuge is her Immaculate Heart, nothing else.

5 1 Thes 5:2.

6 Soldo, *My Heart Will Triumph*, 191.

7 Lefevbre-Filleau, J.P., *L'Affaire Bernadette Soubirous*, Cerf, 1972, p.152; Ivonides, L., *Fatima, da ili ne?* (*Fatima, Yes or No*), Zagreb,1997, p.17. Both footnotes are cited according to D. Klanac, *Medjugorje: Responses aux Objections*, op.cit., p. 66., as documented in *Once Again the Truth About Medjugorje* by Dr. Ljudevit Rupčić and Dr. Viktor Nuić, p. 97.

8 John De Marchi, *Fatima: From the Beginning* (Torres Novas, Portugal: Missoes Consolata,1950), 169.

9 Ibid.

10 Transcript of interview with Father Svetozar Kraljevic at the Franciscan Monastery in Ljubuski, Yugoslavia, circa 1985, 1-2.

11 Soldo, *My Heart Will Triumph*, 101. Father Rupčić was imprisoned by the Communists in 1945, 1947, and again from 1952 through 1956.

12 Ibid.

13 *Center for Peace Newsletter*, Concord, MA: February 1986.

14 Laurentin and Rupčić, *Is the Virgin Mary Appearing at Medjugorje?* 17.

15 Fr. René Laurentin, *Ten Years of Apparitions: New Growth and Recognition of Pilgrimages* (Milford, OH: Faith Publishing Company, 1991), 124.

16 Laurentin and Rupčić, *Is the Virgin Mary Appearing at Medjugorje?* 20.

CHAPTER 5: THE LAST APPARITION?

1 Laurentin and Lejeune, *Messages and Teachings of Mary at Medjugorje*, 7.

2 Ibid., 146-147, 354-355; Dr. Ljudevit Rupčić and Dr. Viktor Nuić, *Once Again, The Truth About Medjugorje* (Zagreb, Croatia: K. Kresimir, 2002), 63.

3 Laurentin and Lejeune, *Messages and Teachings of Mary at Medjugorje*, 145.

4 Rupčić and Nuić, *Once Again, The Truth About Medjugorje*, 169.

5 Joaquin Maria Alonso, C.M.F., *The Secret of Fatima* (Cambridge: Ravengate Press, 1976), 108-110.

6 Heintz, *A Guide to Apparitions*, 61.

7 Tomislav Vlašić O.F.M., and Slavko Barbarić O.F.M., *Open Your Hearts to Mary Queen of Peace* (Milan, Italy: The Association of the Friends of Medjugorje, 1986), 12. Establishing an accurate timeline on the revelation of the Secrets is challenging. Jacov Marin in his *Queen of Peace Visits Medjugorje*, writes, "Our Lady promised the visionaries that she will reveal ten secrets to each of them. The first three Secrets she told them when they were *all* together. By the beginning of September 1982, Ivanka received eight Secrets all together, and of the remaining visionaries, some had received seven and some had received six Secrets. On the Feast of the Assumption, 1982, the other seers received the Secret which was the eighth one for Ivanka." If Jacov Marin's timeline is accurate, this would mean the Secrets were being revealed very early in the apparitions, before Mirjana returned to Sarajevo at the end of August. (Mirjana reports in her book [p. 98] that she was ordered to Čitluk, locked in a holding cell, and then driven three hours to her parents' home in Sarajevo by the authorities near the end of August 1981.)

8 Connell, *Queen of the Cosmos*, 15.

9 Laurentin and Lejeune, *Messages and Teachings of Mary at Medjugorje*, 216.

10 Ibid., 50.

11   Laurentin and Rupčić, *Is the Virgin Mary Appearing at Medjugorje?* 142-144. Rupčić and Nuić report there were other written letters to the Pope besides the December 2, 1983 letter. See *Once Again, The Truth About Medjugorje*, p. 46.

CHAPTER 6: A TIME OF GRACE

1   Alonso, *The Secret of Fatima*, 68-71. Lúcia wrote an initial draft of the first two parts of the Secret in 1927.

2   Frere de Marie des Agnes Francois, *Fatima: Tragedy and Triumph* (Buffalo, NY: Immaculate Heart Publications,1994), 24.

3   Unpublished original transcript of Fr. Rupčić's interview of the six visionaries in December 1982. It was titled: *"Questions Asked of the Six Visionaries in Medjugorje, Yugoslavia."* See Laurentin's, *Is the Virgin Mary Appearing at Medjugorje?* (pp.42-62), for the edited version of the same interview.

4   Kraljevic, *The Apparitions of Our Lady at Medjugorje*, 121-140. This interview with Mirjana was published in its entirety in the June, July, August, and September issues of the *Medjugorje Herald* in 1988. Father Vlašić found himself at the eye of the storm not long after his interview with Mirjana— not because of the interview, but due to everything that was going on in Medjugorje at that time. Criticized by the Bishop for what was unfolding in the village, he would be transferred out of Medjugorje to a parish in Vitina nine miles down the road in July of 1984. But the overwhelming mystery of the Secrets was upon Vlašić. He understood that the world and the Church were at a crossroad in history. Vlašić's ears were the first to pick up the apparent magnitude of the implications of Medjugorje and the Secrets, and it appears from everything that unfolded with him, the extremely amiable priest was never the same after his time there. Fr. Vlašić was laicized in 2009 and, primarily because he reportedly continued to carry out priestly activities, was excommunicated in 2020. The critics of Medjugorje in the media seized upon this news and immediately attempted to use it to discredit the apparitions even though Vlašić had only been in Medjugorje for a little more than 2 years and had not been involved there since 1984, some 36 years prior.

5   Sister Emmanuel, "Sister Emmanuel's Medjugorje Network," *Medjugorje Gebetsaktion*, No. 30, Vienna, Austria, October 1993, p. 31.

6   Kraljevic, *The Apparitions of Our Lady in Medjugorje*,141-150.

7   Jacov Marin, *Queen of Peace in Medjugorje* (Milford. OH: Riehle Foundation, 1989), 109.

CHAPTER:7 "THE FINAL BATTLE"

1   Unpublished interviews with the Franciscan priests at Medjugorje by a French journalist in 1984 who chose not to put his name on the interviews.

2   Gabriel Meyer, *A Portrait of Medjugorje* (Studio City, CA: Twin Circle Publishing Company, 1990), 63.

3   Fr. Janko Bubalo, O.F.M., *A Thousand Encounters with the Blessed Virgin Mary in Medjugorje* (Chicago, IL: Friends of Medjugorje, 1987), xiii. All of the visionaries, it was written early on, have been told by Mary of some of the events that occurred in her own earthly life. It is unclear at this point which of them, like Vicka, are going to release what they have learned in a book, or some other type of report. Vicka says she was given "something like a complete biography of Mary." Some of it was shown to her, as Mirjana often says, "like a movie, in pictures, as in a film."

4   Ibid, 152-155.

5   Fr. René Laurentin, *Medjugorje: 12 Years Later, Love Your Enemies* (Santa Barbara, CA: Queenship Publishing, 1993), 120-121.

6   Medjugorje. Org., *The Medjugorje Messages: 1981-2013*, 151. Message of June 25,1991. This message was given by Mary just two months before her singular message announcing that she would fulfill at Medjugorje "the secrets I began at Fátima." Perhaps, there is more than what meets the eye here. The Medjugorje messages from May through December of 1991 are of particular significance in understanding Medjugorje in terms of its mission to fulfill Fátima.

7   Brown, *The Final Hour* (Milford, OH: Faith Publishing Company, 1992), 251.

8   Janice T. Connell, *The Visions of the Children* (New York: St. Martin's Press, 1992, Revised Edition, 2007), xvii-xviii.

9   Ibid., 23.

10 Hebert, *Medjugorje: An Affirmation and a Defense*, 43.

11 Francis Johnston, *Fatima: The Great Sign* (Rockford: IL: TAN Books and Publishers, 1980), 8.

12 Ibid., 70.; Socci., *The Fourth Secret of Fatima*, 8. See also Chapter 55 of my book, *Call of the Ages*, for a more in-depth look at this question.

13 Alonso, *The Secret of Fatima*, 170.

14 "Fatima Visionary Predicted 'Final Battle' Would Be Over Marriage, Family," December 31, 2016, https://www.catholicnewsagency.com/news/fatima-visionary-predicted-final-battle-would-be-over-marriage-family-17760.

15 Diane Montagna, "(Exclusive) Cardinal Caffarra: 'What Sr. Lucia Wrote to Me Is Being Fulfilled Today," May 19,2017, https://aleteia.org/2017/05/19/

exclusive-cardinal-caffarra-what-sr-lucia-wrote-to-me-is-being-fulfilled-today/.

16 Ibid.

17 Jonathan Liedl, "Back to the Sixties? Pontifical Academy for Life Pushes for Departure from Doctrine on Contraceptive Sex," July 13, 2022, National Catholic Register, https://www.ncregister.com/news/analysis-pontifical-academy-for-life-pushes-to-change-churchs-opposition-to-contraception.

CHAPTER 8: THE FALL OF SATAN

1 Andrew Thull, ed., *What They Say About Medjugorje:1981-1991* (Cincinnati, OH: Precision Built Corporation, 1991), 121-122. Draga Ivanković is a cousin to three of the visionaries. She lived in Bijakovići at the time of the first apparition.

2 The visionaries speak often about the joys of the afterlife. They speak of the virtues of the next world over this one. Spoken by them in all sincerity, their remarks, however, inadvertently sometimes add to the apocalyptic suspicions of readers or listeners. Some have said they get the feeling that the visionaries know the harsh future, and so this is why they stress the positive view of the next life.

3 Connell, *Queen of the Cosmos*, 30.

4 Randall Sullivan, *The Miracle Detective* (New York: Grove Press, 2004), 189.

5 Kraljevic, *The Apparitions of Our Lady at Medjugorje*, 126. There is no specific message directly attributable to the Virgin Mary at Medjugorje concerning the "First Secret" breaking the power of Satan. In the December 16, 1983, letter to Pope John Paul II, the report states that Mirjana said that the Virgin Mary told her, "This century is under the power of the Devil, but when the Secrets confided to you come to pass, his power will be destroyed." The original source of the understanding that the "First Secret" will end Satan's power is from Mirjana's interview of January 10, 1983, that was initially published in Fr. Kraljević's book (p. 126). In this interview, Mirjana states that the Devil "will rule until the first Secret is unfolded." In an interview with Archbishop Frane Franic of Split in Medjugorje on January 24, 1985, it is again repeated that the Devil's power will end with the unfolding of the First Secret: "His power will end when the Secret comes true." Confirmation of this disclosure by Mirjana is found again eight years later in an interview that Janice T. Connell did with Mirjana for her book, *Queen of the Cosmos* (p. 23). Mirjana tells Connell that Satan will rule "until the First Secret is unfolded." Several

years after this, in another interview with Connell for her second book on Medjugorje, Visions *of the Children* (p. 67), Mirjana again tells Connell that "the First Secret will break the power of Satan." Connell is seen to be clear with this exact understanding, as she repeats it in a question to Marija in the same book (p. 145): "Marija, Mirjana told me that one of the reasons Satan is so aggressive right now is that he has little time left since his power will be broken when the "First Secret" happens. Will life be more pleasant after the "First Secret" occurs?" For the record, no one knows when the "century of Satan" began or when it will end. But it is, according to Mirjana's words, not an officially designated calendar century, such as the 20th century. This is found to be clearly understood by Mirjana's answer to a question posed during her January 20, 1983, interview. Question: "You mean the century until the year 2000, or generally speaking?" Mirjana: "Generally, *part* of which is in the twentieth century, until the First Secret is unfolded. The Devil will rule till then." With this answer—"part of which is in the twentieth century"—Mirjana was inadvertently revealing in1983, although not understood by anyone at the time, that the Ten Secrets would not begin to be revealed until at least after the year 2000. (See *The Apparitions of Our Lady at Medjugorje*, by Fr. Svetozar Kraljevic, p. 138.)

6   Ibid., 124.

7   Kevin Symonds, *Pope Leo XIII and the Prayer to St. Michael* (Boonville, NY: Preserving Christian Publications, 2018), 1-264. There is no known definitive Vatican documentation on Pope Leo XIII's reported vision involving the Devil. But it is often repeated in Catholic publications, especially Marian publications. (See *Soul Magazine*, May 1, 1984.) However, the *Prayer to St. Michael*, which is often said to have originated from Leo's vision, is directly attributable to him and was authorized to be said after every Mass. The *Prayer to St. Michael* continued to be recited after Mass through the remainder of the 19th century and into the 20th century until September 26, 1964, when the Congregation of the Sacred Liturgy decreed: "*The Last Gospel is omitted; the Leonine prayers after Mass are no longer to be said.*" (See Chapter Four, note N. 27, in Kevin Symonds's book, *Pope Leo XIII and the Prayer to St. Michael*, for a summary on the question of Pope Leo's vision. This book is the only known work on the subject. It is well researched, and highly recommended.)

8   Laurentin and Rupčić, *Is the Virgin Mary Appearing in Medjugorje?* 142-144.

9   Kraljevic, *The Apparitions of Our Lady at Medjugorje*, 126.

10 Laurentin and Lejeune, *Messages and Teachings of Mary at Medjugorje*,194; Soldo, *My Heart Will Triumph*, 136.

11 Soldo, *My Heart Will Triumph*, 137. As noted, Mirjana has stated that her annual apparition on her birthday, March 18th, has nothing to do with her birthday. The real reason for that date, she says, will eventually become known with unfolding of the Secrets. (See Chapter 16 of this book, "The Mystery of the Number "18," for a more in-depth look at this whole issue.)

12 Laurentin, *The Apparitions at Medjugorje Prolonged*, 25.

13 Soldo, *My Heart Will Triumph*, 191. With the addition of the 2nd of the month apparitions in 1987, Mirjana would now be receiving a total of 13 apparitions a year (12 monthly apparitions on the 2nd of the month and her annual apparition on the 18th of the month.) Perhaps, some would say, a fitting number in lieu of the Medjugorje connection to Fátima.

14 Rooney and Faricy, *Mary Queen of Peace*, 93.

15 Ibid.

16 Laurentin, *The Apparition at Medjugorje Prolonged*, 25.

17 Ibid.

18 Craig, *Spark from Heaven*,165.

19 Laurentin, *The Apparitions at Medjugorje Prolonged*, 25.

20 Ibid., 26-27. The twelve dates Mirjana experienced locutions or apparitions in 1985 were: end of February; March 18; March 19; June 1; June 15; July 19; July 27; August 11; August 17; September 13; October 25; and December 25. In her book (p.191), Mirjana states that her locutions continued throughout 1985. This could mean there were perhaps more than what was documented by the Franciscans.

21 Thull, ed., *What They Say About Medjugorje*, 34.

22 Laurentin and Lejeune, *Messages and Teachings of Mary at Medjugorje*,271-272.

23 Fr. René Laurentin, *The Apparitions at Medjugorje Prolonged* (Milford, OH: Riehle Foundation, 1987), 29-30; "Maria Konigin des Friedens," *Medjugorje Gebetsaktion*, 1986, No.2, 25.

24 Lucy Rooney S.N.D. and Robert Faricy SJ, Medjugorje Journal (Essex, England: McCremmon Publishing Co., Ltd., 1987), 9.

25 Ibid., 34.

26 Laurentin, *The Apparitions at Medjugorje Prolonged*, 30.

27 Rooney and Faricy, *Medjugorje Journal*, 39.

28 Vlašić and Barbarić, *I Beseech You, Listen to My Messages and Live Them* (Milan, Italy: The Association of the Friends of Medjugorje, 1987), 23.

29 Rooney and Faricy, *Medjugorje Journal*, 136.

30 Thull, ed., *What They Say About Medjugorje*, 841.

31 Soldo, *My Heart Will Triumph*, 121.

CHAPTER 9: "IT WILL BE TOO LATE"

1 Sullivan, *The Miracle Detective*, 189.

2 Michael Brown, *The Tower of Light* (Palm Coast, FL: Spirit Daily Publishing, 2013), 208- 303; Brown, *The Final Hour*, 246; "Seer at Famous Apparition Gave Enthralling Hints of What May Be Her First 'Secrets,'" *Spirit Daily*, June 24, 2011, www.spiritdaily.org/mirjanainterview.htm.

3 Brown, *The Day Will Come*, 223; Brown, *The Tower of Light*, 303-305; "Seer at Famous Apparition Gave Enthralling Hints of What May Be Her First Secrets,"; *Spirit Daily*, June 24, 2011, www.spiritdaily.org/mirjanainterview. htm. The Virgin Mary gave Mirjana the last indications of the realization of the First Secret on June 4, 1986, according to the June 1986, *Queen of Peace Newsletter* of St. Laurent, Quebec, Canada.

4 Fr. Petar Ljubicic, "The Secrets," *Medjugorje Herald*, Volume 3, N.2, February 1989, p.16.

5 Connell, *The Visions of the Children*, 145.

CHAPTER 10: AN APOCALYPTIC MOOD

1 Ivan Kordic, *The Apparitions of Medjugorje* (Zagreb, Croatia: K. Kresimir, 1994), 56. Kordic's quote of Pervan is out of K. Knotzinger's, *Antwort auf Medjugorje*, p. 191.

2 Wintz, "The Secret of Medjugorje," *St. Anthony's Messenger*, August, 1988, 33.

3 Sullivan, *The Miracle Detective 191*; *Queen of Peace Newsletter*, Vol. 1, No 3, p 5. Over the centuries, many visionaries have received startling revelations and have been asked to convey them to the world. Each does so in their own way, according to how they interpret what they have received. Though it is important to take seriously what true visionaries reveal, it must be remembered that their personal subjectivity is always involved, as every visionary sees, comprehends, and communicates their visions and revelations differently. "Whatever is received," wrote the Dominican friar St. Thomas Aquinas in the thirteenth century, "is received according to the measure of the receiver." (Cf. *Summa Theologiae*, la, q.75, a.5; 3a, q.5). This understanding is especially significant when dealing with prophecy, because prophecy is not etched in stone. Father René Laurentin explains, "Predictions, even those inspired by God, are not infallible because they are subjected to human

confusion on the part of the seers. The first Christians waited for the return of Christ in their lifetime, and He has not yet returned." Medjugorje, adds Laurentin, is especially challenging because of the Ten Secrets, a fact that he believes must be kept in perspective. "The Secrets are not the essence of the message." writes Laurentin. "They are prophecies, words given in the name of God for the reality of the world and its future. Prophecies and forecasts have always played an important role, in order to guide the lives of the people of God—in the Bible and in our days—with discontinuance. But one needs to be careful. Predictions are not made in order to satisfy one's curiosity. They are always given in clear obscurity, or light and shade, that has the function of forecasting, a guide to the future. In itself, it is of the future, but a provision which cannot be history before history exists. Further, it is incomprehensible before existing, according to its cultural context."

4   Vlašić and Barbarić, *Pray with Your Heart* (Milan, Italy: The Association of the Friends of Medjugorje, 1986), 185-186.

5   Ibid., 212.

6   Connell, *Queen of the Cosmos*, 144.

7   Wintz, "The Secret of Medjugorje," *St. Anthony's Messenger*, p.36.

8   Vlašić and Barbarić, *Pray with Your Heart*, 162-163.

9   Ibid., 168-169.

10 Ibid., 173-175.

11 I have seen at least four versions of the account of the October 25, 1985, apparition/vision. Fr. Laurentin's account, which I used, was obtained from the official parish logue kept by the Franciscans.

12 Connell, *The Visions of the Children*, 67-68.

13 Ibid. A man named Brother David Lopez from Texas visited Medjugorje in August of 1987 and reported that while there on August 15th, he received a locution from the Virgin Mary that spoke of the "Three Days of Darkness." At the time, and for years after, this purported revelation continued to experience widespread circulation. Brother David died in February 1988. (For more information see *The Michael Journal, Rougemon*t, Canada, January-February 1990.)

14 Michael H. Brown, *Fear of Fire* (Palm Coast, FL: *Spirit Daily Publishing*, 2013), 103.

15 Connell, *Visions of the Children*, 143.

16 June Klins, "Ivan's Talk," *Spirit of Medjugorje*, Vol. 17, No. 9, September 2004, p.3. From Ivan's talk given in Mentor, Ohio, April 20, 2004.

17 June Klins, "Ivan Speaks of Family Prayer", *Spirit of Medjugorje*, May 2009, p. 3. Klins article is from a talk given by Ivan in Chagrin Falls, Ohio, on April 26, 2008.

18 June Klins, *The Best of the Spirit of Medjugorje, Vol. I, 1988-1997* (Bloomington, IN: Authorhouse, 2005), 28. This quote is from a talk given by Ivan in Windsor, Ohio, on September 8, 1996.

19 Linda Rogers recorded and transcribed this talk given by Ivan in Seattle, Washington, on October 29, 1997. It was published in the *Children of Mary Center for Peace* newsletter in November 1997, and reprinted in the *Spirit of Medjugorje* newsletter of February 2006.

20 The first stage of the Russian Revolution took place from February 24 to 28, 1917. At this time, the Romanov monarchy of Czar Nicholas II was over-thrown and replaced by a provisional government formed by the Duma, an elected semi-representative body in Russia. The October Revolution, the second stage of the Russian Revolution, is officially known in Soviet his-tory as the Great October Socialist Revolution. It is also called the October Uprising, the October Coup, the Bolshevik Revolution, the Bolshevik Coup, and Red October. It successfully overthrew the provisional government of the Duma. The October 25th date of the Bolshevik Revolution in Russia is according to the Julian calendar which was still in effect in the country at the time. According to the Gregorian calendar used in the West, the date of the revolution was November 7, 1917. Curiously, 'thirteen days' separate the dates of the different calendars, which again reminds of Fátima. On February 14, 1918, the Communists converted Russia from the Julian calendar to the Gregorian calendar pursuant to a decree signed by Lenin on January 24, 1918. The Orthodox Church, however, stubbornly retained the Julian cal-endar. In 1923, the government dropped both calendars and a new calen-dar was introduced in which the weeks were changed, and religious feasts and holy days were replaced by five national public holidays associated with the October Revolution. The October 25th date appears at other memorable times in Catholic Church history. One of the most significant is that it is the date that St. Bernadette Soubirous made her religious vows, October 25, 1866. (October 25th is also the date of my own birthday, which may attribute to my fascination with the date and this matter in general.)

21 Sullivan, *The Miracle Detective*, 189.

22 Wayne Weible, *The Last Apparition: How it Will Change the World* (Hiawassee, GA: New Hope Press, 2013), 208-212.

23 Thomas W. Petrisko, *The Miracle of the Illumination of All Consciences* (Pittsburgh, PA: St. Andrews Productions, 2000).

24 June Klins, ed., "Fr. Petar Speaks About the Secrets," *Spirit of Medjugorje*, Vol. 20, No.7, July 2007. Transcript of a panel discussion at the Notre Dame Conference on Medjugorje held on May 27, 2007.

CHAPTER 11: THE GREAT SIGN

1 Laurentin and Lejeune, *Messages and Teachings of Mary at Medjugorje*, 53. At Fátima, the third part of the Secret was mostly hidden, and the rest of the Secret revealed. At Medjugorje, the Third Secret (The Great Sign) is relatively revealed, and the rest of the Secrets hidden.

2 Ibid., 169.

3 Ibid., 54.

4 Rooney and Faricy, *Mary Queen of Peace*, 97.

5 The prediction concerning the Adriatic Sea circulated far and wide during the 1990s. Some even claimed one of the visionaries said it. There is no evidence of such a statement on record. A man named Mate Sago who lived in Bijakovići and died in 1979, two years before the apparitions, predicted that the Gospa was coming and someday the town would be a holy place where hotels would be constructed for the many visitors. He foretold there would be a large lake in Medjugorje, so big it would have boats moored in it. Mate also envisioned that hundreds of steps would run up Podbrdo, like a staircase in the hillside, which has virtually taken shape today from all the pilgrim traffic up the hill over the years. While it did not directly concern the Great Sign, Mary Craig, in her book, *Spark from Heaven*, writes that Padre Pio reportedly told a group of pilgrims from Mostar that the Blessed Mother will "soon be visiting your land." Craig conjectures that possibly this prophecy inspired the painting that hung above the main door in St James at the time of the commencing of the apparitions. Painted in1974 by a parishioner, seven years before the apparitions, it depicts the Blessed Virgin Mary in a white robe, blue girdle, white veil, and blue cloak floating in the sky above the church and the village of Medjugorje. In the background, on the Madonna's left side, can be seen Mt. Krizevac with the massive cross at its peak.

6 Bruce Cyr, *After the Warning* (Alberta, Canada: Bruce A. Cyr, 2013), 142.

7 Rooney and Faricy, *Mary Queen of Peace*, 97.

8 James Mulligan, *Medjugorje: What's Happening?* (Brewster, MA: Paraclete Press, 2008), 212.

9   Ibid.

10 Connell, The Visions of the Children, 146.

11 Bubalo, A Thousand Encounters with the Blessed Virgin Mary in Medjugorje, 158.

12 Ibid.

13 Laurentin and Rupčić, Is the Virgin Mary Appearing at Medjugorje? 142-143.

14 Bubalo, A Thousand Encounters with the Blessed Virgin Mary in Medjugorje, 158.

15 Ibid., 158-159.

16 Connell, Queen of the Cosmos, 30.

17 Bubalo, A Thousand Encounters with the Blessed Virgin Mary in Medjugorje, 158.

18 Ibid.

19 Connell, Queen of the Cosmos, 30.

20 Brown, The Day Will Come, 229.

21 Connell, Queen of the Cosmos, 78; Kraljevic, The Apparitions of Our Lady at Medjugorje, 59. There is reportedly a promise from Mary to the visionaries that when the Great Sign appears a man from the parish will have his leg miraculously healed. He had it severely injured in a farm accident.

22 Bubalo, A Thousand Encounters with the Blessed Virgin Mary in Medjugorje? 158.

23 Ibid., 159. In Vlašić's and Barbarić's book, Open Your Hearts to Mary Queen of Peace, it is reported on April 22, 1984, that five of the six children know the date on which the Sign will occur. By this time, all six were certainly aware of the coming of the Great Sign on Podbrdo. It is not known which of the visionaries reported to not know the date, or if known, perhaps simply chose not to disclose such an awareness at the time.

24 Ibid.

25 Laurentin and Rupčić, Is the Virgin Mary Appearing at Medjugorje? 143.

26 Ibid.

27 Connell, The Visions of the Children, 108.

28 Ibid.

29 Ibid., 146.

30 Ibid., 145.

31 Ibid., 146; Connell, Queen of the Cosmos, 21.

32 Connell., The Visions of the Children, 108.

33 Soldo, My Heart Will Triumph, 120.

34 Ibid.

35 Ibid.

36 Ibid.

37 Ibid.

38 Michael Brown, *The Tower of Light: The 1990 Prophecy* (Palm Coast, FL: Spirit Daily Publishing, 2007), 298-305.

39 June Klins, ed., "The Period of Conversion and the Ten Secrets," *The Spirit of Medjugorje*, Vol. 22, No. 8, August 2009, p. 6-7. (Transcript of radio broadcast by *Radio Maria Italia* from Medjugorje, January 2, 2008.)

40 Bubalo, *A Thousand Encounters with the Blessed Virgin Mary in Medjugorje*, 156-159.

41 Brown, *The Day Will Come*, 225. Brown writes: "She (Vicka) believes she'll see the Virgin less than an hour before the Sign appears…"

42 June Klins, ed., "The Period of Conversion and the Ten Secrets," *Spirit of Medjugorje*, Vol. 22, No. 8, August 2009, p. 6-7. (Transcript of radio broadcast by *Radio Maria Italia* from Medjugorje, January 2, 2008.)

43 Fr. René Laurentin, *Medjugorje-Thirteen Years Later* (Milford, OH: The Riehle Foundation, 1994), 27, 117.

44 *Medjugorje* Network, August 1, 1995.

45 Sister Emmanuel Maillard, *Medjugorje, The 1990s* (Pittsburgh, PA: St. Andrew's Productions, 1997), 93.

46 Ibid.

CHAPTER 12: A CALL TO ATHEISTS

1 Michael Brown, *The Tower of Light: The 1990 Prophecy*, 298-305. According to two of the visionaries, Vicka and Maria, the Great Sign will occur at a time when belief and interest in Medjugorje will have extremely waned. Marija reportedly told Father Lube Kurtosis, O.F.M., an assistant pastor at Medjugorje who arrived after Father Slavko died, that even the most loyal will become skeptical: "The Sign on Apparition Hill will appear when even the most convinced believers doubt in the authenticity of the messages." (See Father James Mulligan's Medjugorje: What's Happening?)

2 Helen Sarcevic, (translator), "A Talk by Petar Ljubicic: April 22, 1989", *Queen of Peace Journal: Medjugorje Center of Poughkeepsie*, New York, No. XI, December 1989, 8-9.

3 Laurentin, *The Apparitions at Medjugorje Prolonged*, 32.

4 Unpublished parts of the original transcript of the interview of Mirjana on January 10, 1983, which was originally published in books by Father Kraljevic and Father Laurentin, contained footnotes of observations concerning

Mirjana's testimony that day. The final, published form of the interview in the two books is an edited version that can be seen to be missing these notes, some of which are insightful and valuable in better understanding Mirjana's words and experiences. A second interview, dated June 16, 1984, is also part of this original transcript. It is titled: "How Mirjana Prays Now that Our Lady Has Stopped Appearing to Her." It discusses her daily prayer life and her advice to people who write to her, such as a man from Sarajevo who could not walk and was partially healed through "Mirjana's prayers to Our Lady for help."

5   Fr. Tomislav Vlašić, *Our Lady Queen of Peace, Queen of Apostles is Teaching us the Way to the Truth and Life at Medjugorje, Yugoslavia* (East Sussex, England: Peter Batty / Pika Print Limited, 1984), 10.

6   Fr. René Laurentin, *Eight Years: Reconciliation, Analysis, the Future* (Milford, OH: Riehle Foundation, 1989), 102.

7   Ibid. Father Rupčić's second interview with the visionaries—a repetition of the same 60 questions as previous—conducted in 1987, was published in its entirety in Father René Laurentin's 1989 book, *Eight Years: Reconciliation, Analysis, the Future* (pp. 102-130). Rupčić was indeed one of Medjugorje's greatest advocates and defenders. Father Ljudevit Rupčić died on June 25, 2003, the 22nd anniversary of the Medjugorje apparitions.

8   Ibid., 118.

9   Ibid.

10 John Thavis, *The Vatican Prophecies: Investigating Supernatural Signs, Apparitions, and Miracles in the Modern Age* (New York, NY: Viking Press, 2015), 57.

11 Kraljevic, *The Apparitions of Our Lady at Medjugorje*, 148; Medjugorje Torino, July,1995.

12 Ibid. Laurentin says Mirjana once told him, "After the Sign will be shown, one will be obliged to believe." It was an indication to Laurentin of the confidence the visionaries have in the overwhelming impact the Sign will have on those with faith. (See Laurentin, *The Apparitions at Medjugorje Prolonged*.)

13 Connell, *The Visions of the Children*, 107.

14 Rupčić, "The Silenced Situation of the Catholic Church in Bosnia and Herzegovina," 22.

15 Thull, ed., *What They Say About Medjugorje*, 171-172.

16 Ibid.

17 Ibid. The December 16-17, 1984, interview with Archbishop Frane Franic was also published and distributed by the Center for Peace in Boston as a special 13-page report in 1985.

18 Connell, *Queen of the Cosmos*, 20-21.

CHAPTER 13: "I KNOW THE FUTURE OF THE WORLD"

1 Laurentin and Lejeune, *Messages and Teachings of Mary at Medjugorje*, 291.

2 Thull, ed., *What They Say About Medjugorje*, 277. Thull quotes British Theologian Fr. Richard Foley, "The ten secrets being confided to the visionaries out-number anything given in other apparitions." There is a possible exception, although somewhat circumspect. In Gala, Croatia, apparitions were reported beginning on August 27, 1983. One visionary reported receiving 12 secrets, others 10. (See Brown, *The Day Will Come*, 267.)

3 Sullivan, *The Miracle Detective*, 189. The Virgin, as noted, has continued over the years to speak with Mirjana about the Secrets and to give her public messages. However, on the 2nd of the month in June 2006, Mirjana stated, "Our Lady did not give a message." Mirjana said Mary explained some things that are supposed to happen and that her face reflected concern.

4 Connell, *Queen of the Cosmos*, 53.

5 Connell, *Queen of the Cosmos*, 44.

6 Tomislav Vlašić, O.F.M. and Slavko Barbarić O.F.M., *Open Your Hearts to Mary Queen of Peace*, (Milan, Italy: The Association of the Friends of Medjugorje, 1986), 12.

7 Laurentin, *Eight Years*, 95.

8 Ibid., 93.

9 Ibid., 94.

10 Connell, *Queen of the Cosmos*, 45.

11 Ibid.

12 Ibid., 46. Ivanka's statement, "I know the future of the world—not just my own history—but the future of the world," is revealing. Janice Connell has written that Ivanka is God's choice for a "great project" involving the future. Likewise, many of Ivanka's comments also appear to hint of something ahead for her that is of significance with regards to the future and the Secrets. Ivanka was the first to see Mary on day one, and on day two. She was also the first to speak to her. This was of significance. It must be remembered that although Mirjana is the visionary who will announce the Ten Secrets, all six are receiving them. This is for a reason. It is not far-fetched to believe that each of them has some role to play in the unfolding of the Secrets that has not yet been revealed. Some of Vicka's later interviews appear to allude to this possibility. Perhaps Mirjana, due to unforeseen circumstances, may not be the one who reveals the Secrets. In her book, she speculates on different

scenarios arising that can change our present expectations and assumptions. Mirjana went so far as to write, "Of course, there is no guarantee I will be alive when the Secrets are revealed." (See *My Heart Will Triumph*, p. 327)

13   Ibid., 48.

14   Ibid.

CHAPTER 14: THE SECRETS AND THE CHURCH

1   Laurentin and Rupčić, *Is the Virgin Mary Appearing at Medjugorje?* 54.

2   Ibid.

3   Ibid.

4   Ibid.

5   Bubalo, *A Thousand Encounters with the Blessed Virgin Mary in Medjugorje*, xiii.

6   Laurentin and Rupčić, *Is the Virgin Mary Appearing in Medjugorje*, 54.

7   Brown, *The Final Hour*, 249. Author Michael Brown quotes Ivan, from an August 14, 2012, *Radio Maria* interview with Father Livio Fanzaga, as saying, "When the prophetic Secrets of the Blessed Mother are revealed in Medjugorje, the Catholic Church will find itself in a great ordeal, as much for the world as the faithful, and a little of this suffering has already started." (See Brown's *Fear of Fire*, p. 93).

8   Weible, *Medjugorje: The Last Apparition*, 213.

9   Laurentin, *The Apparitions at Medjugorje Prolonged*, 97. Maria Pavlović told Father Rupčić that "all her Secrets concern the world." This is the same as what Mirjana has stated about her Secrets. However, some early statements by the visionaries, particularly Vicka, are on record as saying that they have received secrets that are personal, or not just for themselves, but for the Franciscans and others.

10   Laurentin and Rupčić, *Is the Virgin Mary Appearing at Medjugorje?* 55.

11   Transcript of interview with Archbishop Frane Franic on January 24, 1985. This document was released by Father Serra to the Center for Peace in Concord, Massachusetts.

12   Soldo, *My Heart Will Triumph*, 325.

13   Linda Rogers, "Question and Answer Session with Ivan," *Children of Mary Center for Peace Newsletter*," November 1997. (Ivan's talk and Q & A session was on October 29, 1997, in Seattle, Washington.) Reprinted in *Spirit of Medjugorje* newsletter, February 2006, p.7.

14   Connell, *Queen of the Cosmos*, 19.

15   Ibid., 21.

16 Ibid., 30.

17 René Laurentin and Henri Joyeux, *Scientific & Medical Studies on the Apparitions at Medjugorje* (Dublin, Ireland: Veritas Publications, 1987), 112.

18 Ibid., 114.

19 Ibid.

20 Soldo, *My Heart Will Triumph*, 120.

21 Kraljevic, *The Apparitions of Our Lady at Medjugorje*, 148.

CHAPTER 15: THE "SERIOUS" SECRETS

1 Connell, *The Visions of the Children*, 91.

2 Ibid., 108.

3 June Klins, ed., *Spirit of Medjugorje*, Vol. 24, No. 9., Erie, PA, September 5, 2011, 6-7. Concerning the Seventh Secret, Sister Emmanuel Maillard writes, "This reminds me of something Marthe Robin [a French mystic/stigmatist from Chateauneuf-de-Galaure,1902-1981] said to a priest of my community: 'The prophecy in the *Apocalypse*, concerning the death of two-thirds of the human race, does not refer to an atomic war or any other catastrophe, but to a spiritual death.' Prayer and fasting can alleviate and even prevent chastisements. This is the case for the Seventh Secret in Medjugorje." (See Sister Emmanuel's *Medjugorje the 90s*, p. 92-93.)

4 Marin, *Queen of Peace in Medjugorje*, 77.

5 Ibid.

6 Marin, *Queen of Peace in Medjugorje*, 121; Sullivan, *Miracle Detective*, 191. Marin has this event occurring on August 22, 1986, while Sullivan has it on April 22. Marin relied on Bubalo's first book, *Testimonies: Medjugorje Blessed Land*, and is more likely to be accurate.

7 Bubalo, *A Thousand Encounters with the Virgin Mary in Medjugorje*, 153.

8 All of the annual apparitions in which the Virgin Mary and Ivanka reviewed the Secrets can be found in Medjugorje.Org., *The Medjugorje Messages :1981-2013*, 253-271.

9 Connell, *The Visions of the Children*, 47.

10 Soldo, *My Heart Will Triumph*, 192.

11 Ibid., 209, 336.

12 Kraljevic, *The Apparitions of Our Lady at Medjugorje*, 128,129.

13 Laurentin and Lejeune, *Messages and Teachings of Mary at Medjugorje*, 51.

14 O'Carroll, *Medjugorje: Facts, Documents and Theology*, 189.

15 Laurentin and Lejeune, *Messages and Teachings of Mary at Medjugorje*, 269. Mirjana received this message by interior locution as reported in the *MIR Recorder*, January 5, 1986, p.3.

16 Connell, *Queen of the Cosmos*, 53.

17 Ibid., 75.

18 Connell, *The Visions of the Children*, 129.

19 Klins, ed., *The Best of the Spirit of Medjugorje*, Vol. I, 75. Ivanka's statement is from an interview on June 6, 1996, at St. George's Church in Erie, Pa. Writes Laurentin, "On the evening of May 6, 1985, Ivanka was in the rectory with Marija, Ivan and Jacov, for the apparition. At the end of two minutes, the apparition terminated for the three others. They got back up. Ivanka still sees the apparition. The others were stupefied, for they had never seen another of their group in this kind of ecstasy. For Ivanka, the apparition lasted for six minutes after which she explained: 'The Virgin has ended her messages to me on the coming chastisement of the world. She confided to me the Tenth Secret. Our Lady said to me, 'The apparitions are finished for you, but I will see you again every year on the anniversary of the first apparition (June 25th) starting the next year (1986).' She will come to say her good-byes tomorrow at my house at the same time.' 'Can we come?' asks Fr. Slavko. 'The Gospa asked to see me alone,' she answered." Ivanka's use of the word chastisement here should not be viewed as contradicting her statement that Mary had never said anything about chastisements. But it does reveal perhaps a level of innocence and naivety for her age at the time about the meaning of the word in the first place. (See Laurentin's, *The Apparitions at Medjugorje Prolonged*.)

20 Bubalo, *A Thousand Encounters with the Blessed Virgin Mary in Medjugorje*, 194.

21 John Haffert, *To Prevent This* (Asbury, NJ: The 101 Foundation Inc., 1993), 11,12.

22 Sister Lucia of Jesus and of the Immaculate Heart, *'Calls' from the Message of Fatima* (Still River, MA: The Ravengate Press, 2001), 53.

23 Vlašić and Barbarić, *Pray with Your Heart*, 185

24 Gal 4: 4-7.

25 Nolan, *Medjugorje: A Time for Truth, A Time for Action*, xxx.

26 Laurentin, *Latest News of Medjugorje*, 37.

27 Laurentin and Lejeune, Messages and *Teachings of Mary at Medjugorje*, 130.

28 Bubalo, *A Thousand Encounters with the Blessed Virgin Mary in Medjugorje*, 270.

29 *Catechism of the Catholic Church* (New Hope, Kentucky: Et Orbi Communications,1994), N. 1040.

30 Laurentin, *Medjugorje*: 12 Years Later, 121.

31 Laurentin, *Ten Years of Apparitions*, 121. Ivan was interviewed by *The National Catholic Register* (published in the newspaper's *Mary's People* supplement of January 27, 1991) at a gathering in Herndon, Virginia, in November 1990.

32 Connell, *Queen of the Cosmos*, 19.

33 Ibid., 163.

34 Vlašić and Barbarić, *Pray with Your Heart*,185-186.

35 Ibid., 204-205.

CHAPTER 16: THE MYSTERY OF THE NUMBER '18'

1 Soldo, *My Heart Will Triumph*,137.

2 Ibid.,157.

3 Ibid.,136.

4 Ibid.,137.

5 CLR James, "Karl Marx and the Paris Commune," January 3, 2006, https://libcom.orglarticle//karl-marx-and-paris-commune-clr-james.

6 Katherine Connolly, "Karl Marx and the Paris Commune," March 17, 2021, https://www.counterfire.org/articles/history/22167-karl-marx-and -the-paris-commune.

7 Ibid.

8 Ibid.

9 Vladimir Lenin, "The Experience of the Paris Commune of 1871: Marx's Analysis" (Chapter 3, *The State and Revolution* by Vladimir Lenin), Summer,1917, https://www.wsws.org/en/special/library/lenin-state-and-revolution/experience-paris-commune-html.

10 John Westmoreland, "The Paris Commune: When Workers Ran a City," March 10, 2021, https://www.counterfire.org//articles/history/21095-the-paris-commune-150-when-workers-ran-a-city; Marx, Karl. *The Civil War in France: The Paris Commune.* (New York, NY: International Publishers Co.,1968).

CHAPTER 17: TIME IS SHORT

1 Craig, *Spark from Heaven*, 152-153. The controversy surrounding Ivan while in the seminary was in regard to his response to the Bishop's request for the visionaries to write down on a piece of paper everything they knew about the Great Sign. Separated from the other visionaries, who all refused to answer

the question, Ivan said at first that he wrote nothing on the paper. He later admitted to writing something. What he did write did not reveal the Great Sign or anything about it, but still led to a lot of trouble for him, and indirectly, the apparition itself. (For a full account of this matter, see Nolan's *Medjugorje: A Time for Truth, A Time for Action*.)

2   Ivan's remarks were made on March 25,1988, and are quoted in *St. Anthony Messenger*, Cincinnati, OH, August 1988, p. 32.

3   "Excerpts from an Interview with Ivan Dragićević", Pittsburgh Center for Peace, *Queen of Peace* newsletter, Vol. I, N. 4., 1990. (Interview of Ivan Dragićević conducted by Jan Connell on August 5, 1989, in Medjugorje.); Connell, *Queen of the Cosmos*, 90.

4   "I Am Striving to Be Better: Conversation with Ivan at the Franciscan Monastery of Vienna," *Medjugorje Gebetsaktion*, No. 28, January 1993, 12-16.

5   Klins, ed., *Spirit of Medjugorje*, Vol. 24, No. 9., 6-7. Ivan's remark about "physical changes in the world," followed almost immediately by his mentioning of the Secrets, is a perfect example of how the visionaries often subtly allude to the contents of the Secrets. This remark is especially revealing, as it seems to clearly indicate that something in the Secrets is going to contain an event that will result in a physical alteration of the planet as we presently know it. It hints of a sizable occurrence that will have universal recognition.

6   Carolanne Kilichowski, "Message to Ivan's Prayer Group: September 10, 2004," *Spirit of Medjugorje*, Vol. 17, No. 10, October 2004, p. 3.

7   June Klins, "Ivan Speaks About Family Prayer," *Spirit of Medjugorje*, Vol. 22, No. 5., May ,2009, p.3. Talk given by Ivan on April 26, 2008, in Chagrin Falls, Ohio. Because of Ivan marrying an American and thereby living in the United States half of every year, he has perhaps given the most talks outside of Medjugorje. There are a good number of recordings and transcripts of his talks throughout the United States over the last 25 years. In many ways, he has become somewhat of an American, even in support of some of the sports teams such as the Chicago Bulls and the Pittsburgh Steelers, whose t-shirt he has been photographed wearing. When in St. Mary's, Pa. (of all places), he was taken to meet the Steeler players and received a jacket and a miniature replica of Heinz Field, the stadium the team plays in at Pittsburgh. (Source: *Spirit of Medjugorje*, February 2010.)

8   Connell, *Queen of the Cosmos*, 49.

9   Medjugorje.Org, *The Medjugorje Messages: 1981-2013*, 263.

10 Ibid., 264.

11 Ibid.

12 Ibid., 262.

13 June Klins, ed., "Question and Answer Session with Ivanka," *Spirit of Medjugorje*, Vol. 19, No. 7., p. 3, July 2006. Interview with Ivanka conducted in Medjugorje on August 6, 2001. Videotaped by Mark Dicarlo of Michigan.

14 Laurentin, *Medjugorje-13 Years Later*, 13-14.

15 Ibid., 14.

16 Ibid.

17 Ibid.

18 Fr. Edward O'Conner, C.S.C., "The Lady Behind the Iron Curtain," *Queen*, Nov-Dec 1986, 23.

19 Connell, *The Visions of the Children*, 143.

20 Ibid., 145.

21 Ibid., 146.

22 "We Should Grow from Day to Day: Interview with Marija Pavlović on January 2, 1994, in Medjugorje," *Medjugorje Gebetsaktion*, No.33, October,1994, 10-13.

23 "Interview of Marija Pavlović," Pittsburgh Center for Peace, *Queen of Peace Newsletter*, Vol.1, N.2., p .9, July 1988. (Interview conducted by Janice Connell on January 25, 1988, in Medjugorje.)

24 "Special Message," *Medjugorje Herald*, October 1987, 4.

25 Renzo Allegri, "Marija Tells Her Story," *Medjugorje Torino* (English Edition), Vol. 10, No.35, July 2001, 8-12.

26 Connell, *Queen of the Cosmos*, 53,54.

27 Laurentin, *Medjugorje: 12 Years Later*, 16.

28 Connell, *Queen of the Cosmos*,75

29 Ibid.,120-121.

30 Ratzinger, "*The Message of Fatima*," published in *The Fatima Prophecies*, 271-298.

31 Laurentin, *Medjugorje: Twelve Years Later*, 120.

32 Socci, *The Secret of Benedict XVI*, 155.

33 Tomislav Vlašić O.F.M., and Slavko Barbarić O.F.M., *I Beseech You, Listen to My Messages and Live Them* (Milan, Italy: The Association of the Friends of Medjugorje, 1987), 69.

34 Medjugorje.Org, *The Medjugorje Messages 1981-2013*, 169. Message of January 25, 1997.

35 Ibid., 201, Message of October 25, 2008.

36 Ibid., 211. Message of July 25, 2012.

37 Medjugorje message of January 25, 2023. [Available through various Medjugorje web sources.]
38 Connell, *The Visions of the Children*, 66.
39 Author's interview of Father Petar Ljubicic, February 2, 2000.

CHAPTER 18: A CONVERSATION WITH FATHER PETAR LJUBICIC

1 The interview with Father Petar Ljubicic was conducted by the author on February 2, 2000, at Franciscan University in Steubenville, Ohio. It has not been previously published. Father Petar's talk that day at the college was recorded and is available through St. Andrew's Productions.
2 Father Petar Ljubicic and Mirjana, according to Mirjana, will fast for seven days. It seems Father Petar was perhaps indicating that he might fast the additional three days before a Secret comes to realization.
3 Father Petar's comment about the Communists being "back in power" was understood to be mostly in jest at the time.
4 Three visionaries are directly tied to the letter sent to the Pope. After the apparition of November 30, Marija Pavlović revealed that the Virgin wanted a letter sent to the Pope. According to Laurentin, much of the information in the letter was incorporated from a November 5,1983, meeting with Mirjana Dragićević. Vlašić writes in the letter that Ivan Dragićević reported to him that the visionaries had approved its contents. No response from the Pope has ever been publicly cited. At the time of my interview with Father Ljubicic, I was curious if he was aware if there ever was such a response from the Holy Father that had not been disclosed.

CHAPTER 19: THE CONVERSION OF THE WORLD?

1 Connell, *Queen of the Cosmos*, 104. The Virgin Mary's assertion at Medjugorje to the visionaries that she has "come for everybody" is in keeping with Christ's words in Scripture that not one of the Father's children be lost: "Now the will of him who sent me is that I should lose nothing of all that he has given to me, but I should raise it up on the last day. It is my Father's will that whoever sees the Son and believes in him should have eternal life, and that I should raise that person up on the last day" (Jn 6: 39-40).
2 Connell, *The Visions of the Children*, 108. Jacov's certainty here carries implications that are important to consider. It has been pointed out that the fulfillment of all of Mary's Secrets at Fátima were visible happenings in time—i.e., the end of World War I, World War II, Communism, religious persecutions, the attempted assassination of Pope John Paul II, etc. They were, as

author Antonio Socci writes, historical/political prophecies directly linked to Fátima that unfolded through undeniable realities, not hidden/rumored events. Consequently, it is expected with Medjugorje that this will continue, that the events that are to fulfill the Secrets will be visibly connectible to what was foretold. Jacov's words reflect a confidence that appears to imply that all will be able to see that what he is saying will come true. This means they will again be historical related prophecies in time, and that their fulfillment will be undeniable and directly related to the words of the Madonna of Medjugorje. The Triumph, in essence—through the fulfilled prophecies of Fátima and Medjugorje—is to be visible. Mirjana and Ivan, like Jacov, have also implied as much in their public comments.

3   Connell, *Queen of the Cosmos*, 101.

4   Father Milan Mikulich, "The Apparitions of Our Lady in Medjugorje, Croatia, Yugoslavia." From a talk given by Mikulich at St. Patrick's Church, Portland, Oregon, on April 4, 1984.

5   Unpublished interview with Jacov Čolo conducted by Robert Petrisko in Medjugorje for the Pittsburgh Center for Peace, April ,1992. The questions were written by the author.

6   Larry and Mary Sue Eck, "Jacov Čolo, the Youngest Visionary," *Medjugorje Magazine*, Winter 2001-2002, 10.

7   Sean Bloomfield, "Jacov's Last Daily Apparition and the Tenth Secret," *Spirit of Medjugorje*, Vol. 23, No.1, January 2010, p .3.

8   Ibid.

9   Ibid.

10   Medjugorje.Org., *The Medjugorje Messages: 1981-2013*, 206.

11   Connell, *The Visions of the Children*, xviii. Janice Connell was present that day in Florida and witnessed all that took place during and after Jacov's final daily apparition. In a June 21, 2006, interview, Jacov recalled that day: "You have to remember, I was having apparitions on a daily basis for seventeen years and I grew up with Our Lady. As you see, I knew only about this life. And, of course, it is normal when I was given the Tenth Secret and when Our Lady told me that she would not appear to me on a daily basis anymore, I cannot describe the pain I felt in my heart. And I tell you that was the most difficult moment in my life." (*Spirit of Medjugorje*, May 2007, p. 7.)

12   Fr. René Laurentin, *Medjugorje Testament: Hostility Abounds, Grace Superabounds* (Toronto, Ontario: Ave Maria Press, 1998), 216. Laurentin, at the time, was pondering the longevity of the apparitions and the fact that each of the visionaries was often experiencing the visions privately. This to

him posed a concern for different reasons, mostly being the lack of objective witnesses at the apparitions. Critics, at the time, were also casting doubts. The announcement of Jacov's final apparition served, he would write, as a conviction to him that the apparitions were truly still occurring. "The end of the apparitions for him (Jacov) not only destroys this hypothesis but also tends to confirm that Our Lady's apparitions were authentic." (See Laurentin's *Medjugorje Testament*, pp. 215-218).

13 Bloomfield, "Jacov's Last Daily Apparition and the Tenth Secret," *Spirit of Medjugorje*, Vol. 23, No. 1, January 2010, p .3.

14 Medjugorje.org, *The Medjugorje Messages:1981-2013*, 270.

CHAPTER 20: TIME OF DECISION

1   Thavis, *The Vatican Prophecies*, 65.

2   Ibid.

3   Wayne Weible, *Medjugorje, The Last Apparition: How It Will Change the World* (Hiawassee, GA: New Hope Press, 2013), 214-217.

4   Connell, *The Visions of the Children*, 129.

5   Connell, *Queen of the Cosmos*, 48. Mirjana is quoted by Connell as stating the exact same thing as Ivanka. See *The Visions of the Children* (2007, revised edition), p.81. In explaining to Connell how each person on Earth will have a role to play, Mirjana also revealed that those who follow the Virgin Mary's messages are going to be persecuted at some point. Question (Connell): Is this apparition just for the faithful ones? Answer (Mirjana): No. This apparition is for all people on Earth. Each person on Earth will have a role to play as the Secrets unfold. Many already know their role in this apparition, as I do. There will be suffering. Those who follow the Blessed Mother's messages will know persecution, but in the end all will be well. The rewards are great. They are worth every bit of persecution and suffering." See *The Visions of the Children* (2007, revised edition), p. 81.

6   Soldo, *My Heart Will Triumph*, 121.

7   Ibid.

8   Vlašić and Barbarić, *Open Your Hearts to Mary Queen of Peace*, 116. Mary's exact words were: "Do not ask for all the Secrets to be removed because God has His plan. You must be converted and live your faith."

9   Ps(s) 85, 11.

10 Laurentin and Lejeune, *Messages and Teachings of Mary at Medjugorje*, 186,188. Mary said this twice in early 1982, first on May 2nd and then on June 23rd.

11   June Klins, ed., "The Period of Conversion and the Ten Secrets," *Spirit of Medjugorje*, Vol. 22, No. 8, August 2009, p.6.

12   Laurentin, *Eight Years*, 135.

13   "Interview with Marija Lunetti," *Words of the Harvesters: Caritas of Birmingham*, Vol. 103, March 2004, p. 4.

14   Ibid.

15   Connell, *The Visions of the Children*, 56.

16   June Klins, ed., "An Interview with Vicka," *Spirit of Medjugorje*, Vol. 22, No. 2., Erie, PA, February 2009, 6-7. Father Albert Hebert reports that Vicka has said the apparitions will not only continue after the Secrets *begin* but will be still taking place after the Great Sign (the Third Secret) appears on Mt. Podbrdo. (See Hebert's *Medjugorje: An Affirmation and Defense*, p. 22.) One must suspect the crowds that will come for the apparitions at this time, especially after the Third Secret is fulfilled and the Great Sign manifests, will be tens, if not hundreds of thousands of people.

17   "An Interview with Father Slavko Barbarić," *Mary's People* (*The National Catholic Register*), October 25, 1992, p.16.

18   Brown, *The Day Will Come*, 233.

19   Ibid., 235.

20   Nolan, M*edjugorje: A Time for Truth, A Time for Action*, 10. (Nolan quoted Mary's People, October 25,1992.)

21   Thull, ed., *What They Say About Medjugorje*, 805. Father Slavko Barbarić's mark on the events at Medjugorje is immeasurable. Slavko died on Friday, November 24, 2000, immediately after completing the Way of the Cross near the top of Mt. Krizevac. In the monthly message of Mary at Medjugorje given the following day to Marija, Mary revealed that Slavko was "born into Heaven."

22   Throughout the many accounts of the visionaries reporting their conversations with Mary concerning the Secrets, talk of the future of the Church is found, especially with those visionaries that have received all ten Secrets and only experience annual apparitions. For example, there is the report of Ivanka Ivankovic Elez's annual apparition that took place on June 25, 2001: "The visionary Ivanka Elez had her annual apparition on June 25, 2001, in presence of her family. The Gospa was joyful and spoke to Ivanka about the future of the Church. Our Lady gave the following message: Dear angels, thank you for your prayers, because through them my plan is being realized. This is why, angels, pray, pray, pray, so that my plan may be realized. Receive my motherly blessing." Interviews with the visionaries reveal other

conversations with Mary that appear to concern the Church *after* the Ten Secrets are underway or have been fully realized.

23 June Klins, ed., "Interview with Ivan," Spirit of Medjugorje, Vol.16, No. 9, September 2003, p. 4. Interview with Ivan by Damir Govorcin of the *Catholic Weekly* in Australia, February 2003.

24 Mary Kemper, "Mirjana's Talk at the Medjugorje Conference in Irvine, California," *Spirit of Medjugorje*, Vol. 22, No. 3, March 2009, p.3. Mirjana has often repeated this statement about what Mary said to her concerning Fátima. On October 24, 2008, at the Medjugorje Conference in Irvine, California, Mirjana said, "The true faith is the faith that comes out of love. Our Lady said, 'What I started at Fátima, I will finish, accomplish, in Medjugorje; My heart will triumph.'"

25 June Klins, ed., "Mirjana's Question and Answer Session," *Spirit of Medjugorje*, Vol. 18, No. 4, April 2005, p.7. The question-and-answer forum took place on May 30 ,2004.

26 Soldo, *My Heart Will Triumph*, 142.

27 Ibid., 155.

28 June 24, 2022 was also the feast of the Sacred Heart of Jesus in 2022.The following day, June 25, 2022, was the feast of the Immaculate Heart of Mary and the annual feast of Our Lady of Medjugorje. All of these feasts together on June 24/25 send one message to the world: God's hand was on the overturning of Roe V Wade. Thus, any attempt to circumvent this court decision will not only fail, but be, as Gamaliel observed (Acts 5:33-41), a fight with God Himself.

CHAPTER 21: "THE VICTORY OF THE BLESSED MOTHER"

1 Connell, *Queen of the Cosmos*, 61-62.

2 *The New American Bible*, (Wichita, KS: Catholic Bible Publishers, 1994-95 Edition), xiii. See Dogmatic Constitution of Divine Revelation.

3 Siguenza, *John Paul II: The Pope Who Understood Fatima*, 51. Fr. Paul Kramer, who was critical of the Church's response to the importance of the message of Fátima to the world, writes, "To both insiders and outsiders, the Vatican's treatment of this matter seems strangely inconsistent with its own standards and traditions. It also seems to show a reckless disregard for the safety not only of the Catholic Church, but the rest of humanity as well. If the Fátima threat is genuine, the price of the Vatican's reluctance could be very high indeed—and it would be paid by all mankind." (See *The Devil's Final Battle*, p.ix).

4   Renzo Allegri, *The Pope of Fatima* (Milan, Italy: Mondadori, 2006), 21.

5   Socci, *The Fourth Secret of Fatima*, 8.

6   Johnston, *Fatima: The Great Sign*, 69.

7   Ibid., Socci. *The Fourth Secret of Fátima*, 8. Jean Guitton was very sensitive to the historical uniqueness of the times in relation to the theological implications of nuclear weapons. As he put it, "At the hinge of history, before and after Hiroshima, dividing history forever." (See *Portrait de Marthe Robin*, 1986, p. 248.) Guitton also told Paul VI, "Holy Father, Fátima is more interesting than Lourdes. It is both cosmic and historical…thus it is linked to the history of salvation, to universal history."

8   Johnson, *Fatima: The Great Sign*, 70.

9   Ibid.

10 Ibid., 70-71. Fátima became so significant that some Muslim factions claim it was not a Christian miracle but a Muslim miracle. *Inside the Vatican*, quoting the Lefebvrist bulletin *Si Si No No* (July, 1996), stated, "The news was first reported on October 25,1995, by the Italian newspaper *Il Giornale* (p.15), which wrote, "According to a documentary aired on Iranian television, what occurred in Fátima, Portugal, was not a Christian miracle but a Muslim miracle. In fact, Iranian TV affirms, it was not the Virgin Mary who appeared to three shepherd children, but Fatima herself, daughter of the prophet of Islam, Mohammed." (*Inside the Vatican*, November 1996, reports the full story.)

11 Ibid., 71.

12 Ibid.

13 Ibid.

14 Father Paul Kramer, *The Devil's Final Battle*, (Buffalo, NY: Good Counsel Publications,2002), vii. Fátima lay advocate John Vennari wrote that Fátima should not be considered just a private revelation, that it was in a different category. Wrote Vennari: "It is the notion that Fátima is supposedly only a private revelation. And because it is a private revelation, then it is not part of the Deposit of Faith, so you may take it or leave it. But Fátima is actually in a different category from that of a mere private revelation. It is in the category of a Public Prophetic Revelation that imposes an obligation upon the Church. I will quote what theologian Joseph de Sainte-Marie and Bishop Rudolph Graber had to say about it." (For Vennari's complete article see, "Prophecy and Miracle", The Fatima Crusader, Autumn, 2004, pp. 24-28.)

15 Johnson, *Fatima: The Great Sign*, 73.

16 Ibid.

17 Ibid.

18 Michel de la Saint Trinité, *The Whole Truth About Fatima*, 380-388.

19 Ibid., 390. In a letter to Pope Pius XII from Sister Lúcia, dated December 2, 1940, Lúcia notes that the action of Portugal's bishops has kept Portugal out of World War II, and "that this grace was available to other nations" if they would follow the bishops of Portugal's lead. She writes: "Most Holy Father, If I am not mistaken, it is in the union of my soul with God that Our Lord promised to be attentive to the consecration made by the bishops of our nation to the Immaculate Heart of Mary, that a special protection would be granted to our country in this war and this protection will be proof of graces that would be granted to other nations if they are consecrated to her."

20 Ibid., 429-434; Kramer, *The Devil's Final Battle*, 25. There is no greater lesson to be learned from the history surrounding the consecration to the Immaculate Heart than the fact that the grace attached to the act is available on a nation-to-nation basis. Moreover, it is granted on a diocese-to-diocese basis. The reason why Mary asked for all the Bishops to join in unison with the Pope was so that each nation, each diocese could be individually protected from the "errors of Russia." Like Portugal, each country, every diocese in each country, was being invited to experience what Portugal experienced in the 1930-40's.

21 Ibid., 405-410.

22 Ibid., 405-406.

23 Ibid., 410. Lucia 's revelation of how the consecration by the Bishops of Portugal helped to keep the country out of World War II and aided the nation as a whole in many positive ways, is thought provoking. When this truth is applied to the world as a whole in reverse, one must wonder if individual bishops, who refused to participate in the 1984 consecration of the world, have left their dioceses and nations in some degree of peril because of their decision.

24 Gorny and Rosikon, *Fatima Mysteries*, 233. In 1960, the Bishop of Leiria (Fátima), Joao Venancio, sent two small statues of Our Lady of Fátima to Cardinal Stefan Wyszynski in Poland. In order to prevent them from being seized by the Communist authorities, the little statues (designated as dolls on the shipping papers) were initially sent to Holland and then transferred by ship to Gdynia, a port city on the Baltic coast of Poland. Wyszynski gave one of the Fátima statues to the Warsaw Theological Seminary. He sent the other one to the Pallottine Order in Zakopane, where it was received by the young Bishop of Krakow in 1961- Karol Wojtyła. The Pallottines made their

chapel, where they kept the statue, the first Polish center of devotion to Our Lady of Fátima. They spread devotion to Our Lady of Fátima by secretly moving the statue from parish to parish in a suitcase. They called their effort the *Family Rosary Retreat*, carefully avoiding the use of the name of "Fátima."

25 Ibid., 233.

26 Ibid., 234.

27 Ibid.

28 Ibid.

29 Ibid.

30 Ibid.

31 Ibid., 237.

32 Ibid., 235.

33 Based on Mary's own words at Medjugorje, Fátima cannot be fulfilled without Medjugorje. The Virgin Mary said at Medjugorje on August 25, 1991, that she had "come to fulfill" the "Secrets I began at Fátima." She would not have said this if it were not true. She, therefore, needs Medjugorje to fulfill Fátima. At the time when Fátima could have been fulfilled, her wishes were opposed or not followed to the letter, as Saul failed to fully listen to Samuel. With Fátima, the consecration was unfortunately not done in a timely manner. The faithful also did not learn about the Five First Saturdays from the Church as requested, and then failed to respond in the numbers needed that the lay organizations tried to make up for after the fact. Although great good was done, it was not enough. Consequently, Mary has come to Medjugorje to finish the Triumph begun at Fátima. At Medjugorje, she can be seen going straight to the people. In essence, the focus shifts from the dangers of the "errors of Russia" to all nations, to the dangers of the "errors of Russia" to all people.

34 Thull, ed., *What They Say About Medjugorje*, 113.

EPILOGUE: MEDJUGORJE AND THE PROPHET ELIJAH

1 Craig, *Spark from Heaven*, 87; Laurentin and Lejeune, *Is the Virgin Mary Appearing at Medjugorje?* 34; Thul, ed., *What They Say About Medjugorje*, 499.

2 Laurentin and Lejeune, *Is the Virgin Mary Appearing at Medjugorje?* 169.

3 Haffert, *Her Own Words to the Nuclear Age*, 265. The final three visions at Fátima to the three children on October 13, 1917, are also seen as a warning of the coming spiritual attack on the family, the so-called "final battle" according to the words of Lúcia. She spoke of this on occasion. It is noted especially in her letter to Cardinal Carlo Caffarra, the founding President of the John

Paul II Institute for Studies on Marriage and the Family: "The final battle between the Lord and Satan will be about marriage and the family…because this is the decisive issue." The John Paul II Institute for Studies on Marriage and the Family was founded on December 13, 1981, at the Pontifical Lateran University in Rome, seven months after the attempted assassination of Pope John Paul II. Our Lady of Fátima is its patroness. It had been scheduled to be formally announced by Pope John Paul II on May 13, 1981, the day of his shooting in Vatican Square. The appearance of the Holy Family at Fátima in October of 1917 had been foretold at the September apparition. Today, the attack on the family is recognized as seen in many forms: divorce, infidelity, cohabitation, birth control, abortion, homosexual acts, same sex marriage, gender reassignment and more. The key to defeating this attack also lies in the model of the Holy Family.

4   1 Kgs 18: 20-40.
5   Ibid.
6   Ibid.
7   Ibid.
8   Ibid.
9   Ibid.
10   Ibid.
11   Ibid.
12   Ibid.
13   Ibid.
14   Ibid.
15   Haffert, *Her Own Words to the Nuclear Age*, 265.
16   John M. Haffert, *Her Glorious Title: Our Lady of Mount Carmel, Star of the Sea* (Washington, New Jersey: 101 Foundation, 1993), 6.
17   Apostoli, *Fatima for Today*, 170.
18   1 Kgs 18: 20-40.
19   Ibid.
20   Ibid. Haffert, in his book *Her Glorious Title*, writes that the cloud was "foot shaped" not "hand shaped." Haffert then further connects this to Genesis 3:15, where the woman is to crush the head of the serpent. The woman is Mary, traditionally seen as Our Lady of All Grace, which corresponds with the account on Mt Carmel. All contemporary Catholic bibles that I reviewed described the cloud as a hand, not a foot.
21   Ibid.

22 Haffert, *Sign of Her Heart* (Washington, New Jersey: 101 Foundation, 1998),136. Haffert's two books, *Sign of Her Heart and Her Glorious Title*, are both exceptional sources for the mystery of the prophet Elijah and his role in the coming of the Virgin Mary, and his role in the coming Triumph of the Immaculate Heart.

23 Haffert, *Her Glorious Title*, 12, 17. This understanding of Mt. Carmel and the Immaculate Conception was seen to be confirmed with the apparitions at Lourdes. In 1883, at the Silver Jubilee celebration at Lourdes, the Bishop of Nines(France), Francois-Nicolas Bessson, said in his address, "Lourdes is the new Carmel where Mary has deigned to appear. Mary Immaculate appeared to the prophet (Elijah) upon the height of Carmel, raising herself from the midst of the waves under the image of a light cloud. But at Lourdes the cloud assumes color, it is transfigured. Mary is arranged in light and splendor. She speaks and reveals her name. She designates herself, she declares, 'I am the Immaculate Conception.' O! Sacred Mountain of the Orient! Great though thy glory, thou hast beheld but the shadow of what here today we possess in reality!" At Lourdes, it has been noted that Bernadette wore the brown scapular of Our Lady of Mt. Carmel before the apparitions, as was common amongst the youth in France during the time.

24 Ibid., 60, 62. At Fátima, there were other signs that connected the Miracle of the Sun with the Miracle of Fire on Mt. Carmel. During both events, after the miracles occurred, all of the water on the ground was found to have been consumed by the force of the miracle—the water filled trench around the altar on Mt. Carmel, and the water from the days of rainfall that left the Cova da Iria at Fátima a virtual swamp on October 13, 1917. Likewise, at both Mt. Carmel and Fátima, the people immediately voiced aloud that what they experienced was truly of God. Finally, it is seven times that Elijah's young servant on Mt. Carmel went to look out over the Mediterranean to see if the clouds had appeared yet, and it was seven times that the Virgin Mary appeared at Fátima. At the first apparition on May 13th, Mary told the children she would appear "seven" times. The seventh apparition occurred on June 16, 1921, at the Cova da Iria to Lúcia only. It is also noted that Mary told the children on September 13th that she *would* appear in October as Our Lady of All Sorrows and as Our Lady of Mt. Carmel.

25 Elijah has been venerated as the patron saint of Bosnia and Herzegovina since August 26, 1752. He replaced Saint George of Lydia at the request of Bishop Pavao Dragićević. Pope Benedict XIV approved the request. It has been speculated in documents that Elijah was chosen because of his importance and

significance to all three main religious groups in Bosnia and Herzegovina—Muslims, Orthodox Christians and Catholics. Pope Benedict XIV is said to have granted Bishop Dragićević's request with the remark that "a wild nation deserved a wild patron." (For more information see: https://www.deviantart.com/stanoklee/art/Elijah-the-Prophet-830112981and https://en.wikipedia.org/wiki/Pavao_Dragi%C4%8Devi%C4%87.)

SCRIPTURAL QUOTATIONS

All Scriptural quotations, unless otherwise indicated, are from *The New American Bible*, (revised New Testament), Catholic Book Publishers, Wichita, Kansas,1994-1995 EDITION.

SELECTED BIBLIOGRAPHY

There is an extensive amount of literature on Medjugorje. The following are some of the primary sources drawn upon in researching this book.

ARTICLES AND DOCUMENTS
(CHRONOLOGICAL ORDER)

Christopher Civic, "A Fatima in a Communist Land," *Religion in Communist Lands*, Vol.10, No.1, Spring, 1982.

Fr. Ljudevit Rupčić, "Transcript of the 64 questions (with replies) asked of the six visionaries in Medjugorje, Yugoslavia," (unpublished), December 1982.

John Christopher Mathews, "Report [to the United Nations] on Gross Violations of Fundamental Human Rights in the Village of Medjugorje, Croatia, Yugoslavia since June 24, 1981," (unpublished), International Helsinki Federation for Human Rights, January 27, 1983.

Fr. Milan Mikulich, O.F.M., S.T.D., "Apparitions of Our Lady in Medjugorje, Croatia, Yugoslavia; Still are on Full Course," *Orthodoxy of the Catholic Doctrine*, June 1983.

Fr. Tomislav Vlašić, "The Message of Medjugorje," (unpublished draft), August 15, 1983.

Theresa Karminski, "Apparition Report: Both Plausible and Convincing," *The Catholic Standard and Times: The Official Newspaper of the Archdiocese of Philadelphia*, August 25, 1983.

Tomislav Vlašić, "Are the Apparitions in Yugoslavia for Real?", (unpublished), August 25, 1983.

"The Messages for the Parish of Medjugorje, 1984," (unpublished), circa 1984.

Unnamed French Journalist, "Interviews with the Franciscans: Frs. Bubalo, Vlasic, Pervan, Barbaric and Kraljevic." (unpublished), circa 1984.

Ann Hermans (translator), "At Medjugorje, the Inhabitants Believe, Pray and Fast," *Le Libre Belgique*, January 9, 1984.

Theresa M. Karminski, "Reported Apparitions of Mary to Six Young Yugoslavians Being Scrutinized," *Lake Shore Visitor-Catholic Diocese of Erie*, February 17, 1984.

Bonny Rodden, "Priest a Believer After Pilgrimage to Madonna Site," *Philadelphia Daily News*, March 13, 1984.

Robert and Annabelle Baldwin, "A Miracle in Medjugorje," *Our Sunday Visitor*, March 1984.

Dudley Plunkett, "Visions that can Contribute to the Peace of the World," *The Guardian*, July 9, 1984.

Peter Batty, "The Vision of Pope Leo XIII," *Peter Batty Newsletter*, July 26, 1984.

Fred Lilly, "What "Mr. Pentecost" Thinks About Medjugorje," *New Covenant*, October 1984.

Rev. Michael C. Crowdy (translator), "The Present (Unofficial) Position of the Episcopal Curia of Mostar Regarding the Events at Medjugorje," *Approaches*, No. 88, Mostar, 30 October 1984.

Jim Tibbets, "Interview of the Bishop of Mostar", (unpublished), November 8, 1984.

Fr. Milan Mikulich, O.F.M., S.T.D., "The Statement of the Commission on the Medjugorje Apparitions-March 23-24,1984," *Orthodoxy of the Catholic Doctrine*, October -December 1984.

V. Mess, "Have You Seen the Miracles in Medjugorje?" *Danitza* (Croatian publication), December 14, 1984. (This article was published in the review Jesus and was written by an Italian journalist after visiting Medjugorje in June 1984. The author's name is believed to be a pseudonym he used for the article.)

James Tibbets, "An Interview with Father Svetozar Kraljevic OFM at the Franciscan Monastery in Ljubuski, Yugoslavia," (unpublished), 1984.

Hans Urs von Balthasar (Translated by Fr. Milan Mikulich O.F.M., S.T.D.), "The Letter of Hans Urs von Balthasar, A Prominent Theologian from Switzerland, Sent to Pavao Zanic, Bishop of Mostar," *Orthodoxy of the Catholic Doctrine*, January-June 1985.

Fr. Milan Mikulich, O.F.M., S.T.D., "Chronological Analysis of the Case of the Medjugorje Apparitions," *Orthodoxy of the Catholic Doctrine*, January-June 1985.

Michael O'Carroll, CSSp. "Our Lady of Medjugorje–Hallucination or Apparition?", *The Sunday Press* (Dublin), January 20, 1985.

Fr. Serra, "Highlights of an Interview with One of the Visionaries by Archbishop Franic of Split and a Group of Italians," (unpublished interview conducted on January 24, 1985), Boston: MA: Center for Peace, February 1985.

Fred Lilly, "David Du Plessis: "This is a Working of the Holy Spirit," *The Catholic Digest*, February 1985.

Fr. Kvirin Vasily, O.F.M., "The Bishop of Mostar and the Facts," (unpublished), Beaver Falls, PA, Franciscan Fathers, March 1985.

Rev.Milan Mikulich, O.F.M., S.T.D., "Commentary: What Happened at Medjugorje?", *Fidelity*, March 1985.

Giorgio Sanguineti, "Critical Testimony About the Visionaries from Medjugorje", (unpublished), May 4, 1985.

Theresa Marie Karminski, "Scientists Investigate Medjugorje Apparitions," *National Catholic News Service*, May 10, 1985.

Giles Dimock, O.P., "Medjugorje: Fruits of the Spirit," *National Catholic Register*, June 16, 1985.

Mary Kenny, "Whatever is Here it Works," *The Sunday Press* (Ireland), July 28, 1985.

John Dart, "Explaining Visions of Mary: Professor Points to Psychological Origins," *The Philadelphia Inquirer*, August 4, 1985.

Orazio Petrosillo, "The Results of Scientific Tests of Two Medical Teams Agree that the Seers of Medjugorje are Neither Sick nor Deceivers," *Il Tempo* (p.21), October 9, 1985.

Fr. Slavko Barbarić, PhD, "Phenomenological Comparative Account of the 'Inner Locutions' of Jelena Vasilj and Marijana Vasilj," ['not for publication study'], October 1985.

Henry Kamm, "Yugoslavs are Abashed: Money from a 'Miracle," *The New York Times*, November 18, 1985.

John Primeau, "Medjugorje; Peace or Judgement?", *The Spirit and the Word*, November 1985.

Paul A. Fisher, "Our Lady's Secrets at Medjugorje," *The Wanderer*, December 26, 1985.

Gitta Sereny, "A Village Sees the Light," *Reader's Digest*, February 1986.

J. Rand McNally, "The Nuclear Tornado Effect." Unpublished research paper presented at *The American Physical Society*, Washington D.C., Spring Meeting: April 28-May 1, 1986.

Agostino Bono, "Vatican Will Pursue Apparition Claims," *The Catholic Standard and Times*, June 26, 1986.

Edward O'Connor, C.S.C., "The Lady Behind the Iron Curtain," *Queen*, Sept-Oct (Part I), Nov-Dec (Part II), 1986.

Bishop Paulo Hnilica, "By Their Fruits, You Will Know Them (Mt 7:16)," *Medjugorje Gebetsaktion*, No. 4, December 1986.

Richard Szczepanowski, "Medjugorje: Despite No Official Church Statement, Reported Marian Apparitions Draw Many," *Catholic Standard: Weekly Newspaper of the Archdiocese of Washington*, March 26, 1987.

Mark Miravalle, "Medjugorje and the Media," *National Catholic Register*, June 14, 1987.

Jackson Diehl, "Crowds Visit Vision Site: Rite Occurs Daily in Rural Yugoslavia," *Washington Post Foreign Service*, July 17, 1987.

Bishop Pavao Zanic, "Homily of Bishop of Mostar for Confirmation Day," (unpublished transcript), St. James Church, Medjugorje, July 25, 1987.

Julie Asher, "Medjugorje Fever: Alleged Apparitions have Supporters and Detractors," *The Catholic Standard and Times*, July 30, 1987.

Jeanine Jacob, "Medjugorje Experiences," *The Florida Catholic* (Diocese of St. Petersburg), July 31, 1987.

Sura Rubenstein, "Is it Really a Miracle at Medjugorje? Believers Say Virgin Mary Appears Daily in Yugoslavian Village," *The Sunday Oregonian*, December 6, 1987.

Deborah Daisy, "Medical Mystery: Teacher's Recovery is Investigated as Miracle," *The Pittsburgh Press*, January 24, 1988.

Dorothy Glojek (translator), "The President of America was Inspired with the Message of Medjugorje," *Sveta Bastina* (*Holy Inheritance* newspaper, Duvno, Hercegovina), February ,1988.

John Thavis, "Alleged Apparitions Can Be Headache for Vatican Office," *Catholic Standard*, March 10, 1988.

Fr. Tomislav Vlašić, "A Calling in the Marian Year," *Mariji K Isusu Association*, March 25, 1988.

John Thavis, "Medjugorje: Pilgrims Become 'Missionaries'," *Catholic Herald*, April 7, 1988.

Vittorio Messori, "A Modern Apologist for Mary: An Interview with Father René Laurentin," *Homiletic and Pastoral Review*, May 1988.

Richard McSorley, S.J., "Medjugorje Journal I, II, III," *Georgetown University Center for Peace* Studies, September 1986-May 1988.

Henry Rene Ayoub, "Medical and Scientific Studies of the Apparition at Medjugorje," *Editions of O.E.L.L.*, Paris, May 1988.

Peter Toscani, "Medjugorje Overview," *Homiletic & Pastoral Review*, May 1988.

Tomislav Vlašić O.F.M., "Documents: Interview with Mirjana Dragicevic," *Medjugorje Herald*, June, July, August, September 1988.

Rev. Louis Garbacik, "Medjugorje; Is It Another Fatima?", *Hazelton Standard-Speaker*, June 23, 1988.

Alberic Stacpoole O.S.B., "My Medjugorje Experience," *Priests and People*, July-August 1988.

Bishop Michael D. Pfeifer, O.M.I., "The Gospel, Mary and Medjugorje," *Catholic Diocese of San Angelo, Press Release*, Texas, August 5, 1988.

Jack Wintz, "The Secret of Medjugorje," *St. Anthony Messenger*, August 1988.

Ann Marie Hancock, "Medjugorje: Signs and Wonders of Her Love," *Venture Inward-The Magazine for the Association for Research and Enlightenment*, September-October 1988.

Rev. John Szantyr, "Medjugorje and the Miracle of the Sun," (unpublished), November 1988.

Jack Wintz, O.F.M., "What I Saw at Medjugorje," *Catholic Digest*, November 1988.

Fr. Tony Petrusic. "Interview with Visionary Vicka Ivankovic," (unpublished), December 12, 1988.

Fr. Slavko Barbarić, "The Immaculate Heart of Mary Will Triumph: An Interview with Cardinal Frantisek Tomasek," *Medjugorje Gebetsaktion*, No.1, 1988.

Zoran Krzelj, "Miracle of the Red Madonna," *Yugoslav Airlines Magazine*, 1988.

Fr. Tomislav Vlašić, "A Calling in the Marian Year," *Po Mariji K Isusu Association*, 1988.

Fr. Ljudevit Rupčić, "The Great Falsification: The Hidden Face of Medjugorje," (unpublished), circa 1989.

Father Robert F. Griffin, C.S.C., "Medjugorje, Miracles and a Bit of Smugness," *Our Sunday Visitor*, January 29, 1989.

Fr. Petar Ljubicic, "The Secrets", *Medjugorje Herald*, February 1989.

NC, "Bishop Quinn Sees 'Indisputable' Spiritual Energy in Medjugorje," *The Catholic Standard and Times*, February 16, 1989.

Loretta Seyer, "Catholic Controversy: Is Mary Appearing at Medjugorje?" *The Catholic Twin Circle National Weekly Magazine*, March 19, 1989.

Thomas C. Fox, "Medjugorje: Miracle or Hoax?", *National Catholic Reporter* (Forum), Vol 25, No.22., March 24, 1989.

Michael Davies, "Letter from London: More on Medjugorje," *The Remnant*, March 31, 1989.

Helen Sarcevic, "Apparitions in Split," *Mir Peace Group*, April 23, 1989.

Helen Sarcevic, "Interviews with Vicka, Mirjana, Ivan, Jelena, and Bishop Hnilica," (unpublished), April 18-25, 1989.

Zrinko Cuvalo, O.F.M., "The Spirit of Medjugorje…The Early Dawn Days," *Medjugorje Herald*, May 1989.

Richard Foley, "Mother Angelica Talks About Medjugorje-An Interview by Father Richard Foley, S.J.", *The Medjugorje Messenger –Canadian Edition*, May 1989.

Greg Burke, "Medjugorje: The View from Rome," *National Catholic Register*, December 10, 1989.

Peter Hyun and Barbara J. Tyner, "The Miracle of Medjugorje," *Morning Calm-Korean* Air, December 1989.

Rev. Leonard Orec O.F.M., "A Sanctuary in the Making," *Medjugorje Gebetsaktion*, No. 16, December,1989.

Gianni Cardinale, "Medjugorje Decision by Spring," *30 Days*, February 1990.

CNS, "Bishop Zanic Rejects Medjugorje Claims," *The Remnant*, April 30, 1990.

Riehle Foundation, ed., "The National Conference on Medjugorje: Report by R. Laurentin," *Riehle Foundation-Press Release*, May 12-13, 1990.

Lou Baldwin, "Medjugorje Defended: Yugoslavian Archbishop Confident Apparitions Are Genuine," *The Catholic Standard and Times of the Archdiocese of Philadelphia*, May 17, 1990.

René Laurentin, "Response by Fr. René Laurentin to the Most Recent Objections of His Excellency Bishop Zanic against Medjugorje," *The Riehle Foundation: Press Release*, May 1990.

Msgr. Pavao Zanic, "The Truth About Medjugorje," *Fidelity Magazine*, May 1990.

Steven Crabill, "A Little Piece of Heaven on Earth: Seeking a Miracle in Yugoslavia," *Passaic Record*, July 22, 1990.

Tihomir Karacic, "The Public Confession of a Perjured Witness" (Witness in the trial of Fr. Jozo Zovko), *Nasa Ognijista* (English translation: Fr. Chris Coric and Marie Leman), March 1991.

Inga Saffron, "Madonna in the Balkans," *The Philadelphia Inquirer Daily Magazine*, June 21, 1991.

Anne McGlone, "The Third Secret of Fatima," *Mary's People* (*The National Catholic Register*), October 25, 1992.

M.D., "I am Striving to be Better- A Conversation with Ivan," Medjugorje Gebetsaktion, No. 28, January 18, 1993.

Father Ljudevit Rupčić, "The Silenced Situation of the Catholic Church in Bosnia and Herzegovina," *Medjugorje Gebetsaktion*, No. 30, August 1993.

Uta Herrmann, "David Parkes Tells How He Was Healed on Yugoslav Trip," *Naples Daily News*, January 16, 1994.

I.D., "My Task is to be at the Disposal of the Pilgrims: Interview with Fr. Petar Ljubicic," *Medjugorje Gebetsaktion*, No. 33, January 19, 1994.

J. Rand McNally, "This Would Be the Ultimate Catastrophe," *Voice of the Sacred Hearts*, January-February 1994.

N.M., "Prayer is the Spiritual Nourishment for Every Person: Interview with Marija Pavlovic-Lunetti," *Medjugorje Gebetsaktion*, No. 37, September 9, 1994.

Robert Moynihan, "Why is Mary Weeping," *Inside the Vatican*, Year 3, No.5, March 1995.

VIS., "Vatican Issues Declaration on Pilgrimages to Medjugorje," The Wanderer, July 11, 1996.

Daniele Palmieri, "Our Lady of Akita," Inside the Vatican, Year 4, No.8, October 1996.

Antonio Gaspari," Medjugorje: Deception or Miracle?", Inside the Vatican, Year, 4, No.9, November 1996.

Inside the Vatican Staff, "The Third Secret: Is the End Near?", Inside the Vatican, Year 4, No. 9, November 1996.

Renzo Allegri, "An Interview with René Laurentin," Medjugorje -Torino, December 1996.

Antonio Gaspari, "Fatima: Faith, Marvels and Messages," Inside the Vatican, August-September 1997.

Antonio Gaspari, "Did the Statue Really Weep," Inside the Vatican, Year 6, No. 5, May 1998.

Robert Moynihan, "Editorial: The Fatima Prophecy", Inside the Vatican, Year 8, No.1, January 2000.

Christa Kramer von Reisswitz, "Will John Paul II Reveal the Third Fatima Secret," Inside the Vatican, Year 8, No. 3, March 2000.

Wlodziermierz Redzioch, "Seen from Fatima," Inside the Vatican, Year 8, No. 3, March 2000.

Raymond De Souza, "The Third Secret is Out," The National Catholic Register, May 21-27, 2000.

"Pope Reveals Third Secret", www.cwnews.com., May 23, 2000.

Brian McGuire, "The Third Secret: Doom or Triumph?", National Catholic Register, June 3, 2000.

Lucio Brunelli, "The Third Secret Involves Apostasy in the Church," www.fatima. org., June 5, 2000.

Michael Brown, "Fatima Mystery: How did a German Publication Guess at the Third Secret?" Spirit Daily, March 20, 2001.

Wlodzimierz Redzioch, "Assassination Attempt: 'I Reminded Him of Fatima," Inside the Vatican, Year 9, No.8, October 2001.

Joseph Pronechen, "Marian Apparitions, Why Fatima is the Key to Understand Them: She Still Warns Us,", Marian Helper, Winter, 2001-2002.

Rudy J. Rummel, "Mass Murder Under Communism: A Few Statistics," Inside the Vatican, Year 10, No.1, January 2002.

Wlodzimierz Redzioch, "Sister Lúcia Speaks," Inside the Vatican, Year 10, No.1, January 2002.

Father Gerard Mura, "The Third Secret of Fatima: Has it Been Completely Revealed?", *Transalpine Redemptorists* [Orkney Isles, Scotland (Great Britain)], March 2002.

Larry and Mary Sue Eck, "The Medjugorje 'First Family' in the United States," *Medjugorje Magazine*, Summer, 2006.

"Last Surviving Witness Says Third Fatima Secret is Fully Revealed," *CNA* (*Catholic News Agency*), September 12, 2007.

Inside the Vatican Staff, "Mary's Role in the Last Battle," *Inside the Vatican*, Year 16, No. 1, January 2008.

Andrea Torniella, "Medjugorje: Communists Against Apparitions," www.lastampa.com., July 9, 2011.

Daniel Klimek, "Fatima Visionary Saw and Confirmed the Apparitions of Our Lady of Medjugorje," www.medjugorjemiracles.com., July 21, 2011.

Joe Tremblay, "The 100 Year Test," *CNA* (*Catholic News Agency*), February 1, 2013.

Orth, Maureen, "Mary: The World's Most Powerful Woman," *National Geographic*, 30-59, December 2015.

"Alice Von Hildebrand Sheds New Light on Fatima," www.onepeterfive.com., May 12, 2016.

Dr. Maike Hickson, "Cardinal Ratzinger: We Have Not Published the Whole Secret of Fatima," www.onepeterfive.com., May 15, 2016.

Simcha Fisher, "The Lady of Medjugorje Is Not Your Mother," www.catholic weekly.com.,March 17, 2017.

Kevin Symonds, "Fatima and Fr. Dollinger: A Response," www.kevin symonds. com., May 17,2016.

Steve Skojec, "On Fatima Story: Pope Emeritus Benedict XVI Breaks Silence," www.onepeterfive.com., May 21, 2016.

George Weigel, "The Ostpolitik Failed. Get Over It," *First Things*, July 20, 2016.

Maike Hickson, "A Further Confirmation of Father Dollinger's Claim About Cardinal Ratzinger and Fatima, www.onepeterfive.com., March 10, 2017.

Jonathon Luxmoore, "Polish Archbishop thinks Vatican Will Recognize Medjugorje Apparitions," www.americamagazine.org.,August 22, 2017.

Jonathan and Clara Fleischmann, "Lúcia of Fatima, Part I: Marian Genius," www. onepeterfive.com., October 11, 2017.

Jonathan and Clara Fleischmann, "Lúcia of Fatima, Part II: The Vow of Perfection," www.onepeterfive.com.,October 12, 2017.

Jonathon and Clara Fleischmann, "Lúcia of Fatima, Part III: The Infamous Third Secret," www.onepeterfive.com.,October 13, 2017.

Jonathan and Clara Fleischmann, "Lúcia of Fatima, Part IV: Calls from Our Lady," www.onepeterfive.com., October 14, 2017.

Steve Skojec, "As 2017 Comes to a Close, Fatima Warnings Still Resonate," www.onepeterfive.com., November 21, 2017.

Michael K. Jones, "Is Medjugorje the Sequel to Fatima and the Woman Clothed with the Sun," http://www.medjugorjefatimasequel.htm., November 25, 2017.

Matthew Culligan Hoffman, "The Third Secret of Fatima and the "Hermeneutic of Conspiracy," www.catholic world report.com., November 27, 2017.

Antonio Socci, "Do the Hierarchies in the Church Still Have the Faith," www.rorate caeli.com., March 10, 2018.

Maike Hickson, "The Church and the World in Vertigo-We Are Still in Need of the Full Fatima Message," www.onepeterfive.com., April 3, 2018.

Fr. Richard Heilman, "Father Joseph Ratzinger's 1969 Prediction: What the Church Will Look Like in 2000," www.romanatholicman.com., April 10, 2018.

Jonathan Luxmoore, "Pope's Delegate Outlines Plans for Expansion at Medjugorje Shrine," Crux, September 20, 2018.

Fr. Richard Hellman, "Things Accelerate Toward the End: Prophecy of Archbishop Fulton Sheen," www.romancatholicman.com.,October 27, 2018.

Andrea Tornielli, "Fatima: The Prophecy, the Envelope, the Missing Words, and the Denial of Ratzinger," www.lastampa.com., October 27, 2018.

Sarah MacDonald, "Vatican Official: Church Must Be Prudent Judging Medjugorje Apparitions", www.Americamagazine.org., August 16,2019.

Richard Chonak, "A Leak from the Medjugorje Study Commission," *Catholic Light*, www.catholiclight.stblogs.org/Inc., February 12, 2020.

Pope Francis Tells Youth at Medjugorje: Be inspired by the Virgin Mary," *CNA* (*Catholic News Agency*), www.catholicnewsagency.com., August 2, 2020.

BOOKS

Allegri, Renzo. *The Pope of Fatima*. Milan, Italy: Arnoldo Mondadori Editore, 2006.

Alonso, Joaquin Maria, C.M.F. *The Secret of Fatima*. Cambridge: The Ravengate Press, 1976.

Alonso, Joaquin Maria and Ribeiro, Abilio Pina. F*atima: Message and Consecration*. Fatima, Portugal: Consolata Missions' Publications, 1984

Apostoli, Fr. Andrew, C.F.R. *Fatima for Today: The Urgent Marian Message of Hope*. San Francisco: Ignatius Press, 2010.

Ashton, Joan. *Mother of All Nations*. New York: Harper and Row, 1989.

——. *The People's Madonna: An Account of the Visions of Mary at Medjugorje*. London, UK: HarperCollins Publishers, 1991.

Baker, Peter and Glasser, Susan. *Kremlin Rising: Vladimir Putin's Russia and the End of Revolution*. Washington D.C.: Potomac Books, Inc., 2005, revised edition, 2007.

Barbarić, Fr. Slavko. *In the School of Love*. Milford, OH: Faith Publishing Company, 1993.

——. *Pearls of the Wounded Heart*. Medjugorje: Mir Information Center, 1998.

——. *Pray with the Heart*. Steubenville, OH: Franciscan University Press, 1988.

Bartholomew, Professor Courtney, M.D. *The Last Help Before the End of Time: The Ultimate message of Fatima*. Goleta, CA: Queenship Publishing Company, 2005.

Bartulica, Nicholas, M.D. *Are the Seers Telling the Truth?* Chicago, IL: Croatian Franciscan Press, 1991.

Bedard, Fr. Bob. *Medjugorje Reflections*. Toronto, Ontario: Koinonia Enterprises, 1989.

——. *Medjugorje: Prophecy for Our Time*. Ottawa, Canada: Catholic Renewal Centre, 1982.

——. *Medjugorje: A Second Look*. Ottawa, Canada: Catholic Renewal Centre, 1984.

Bertone, Cardinal Tarcisio. T*he Last Secret of Fatima*. New York: Image, Doubleday, 2008.

Beyer, Rev. Richard. *Medjugorje: Day by Day*. Notre Dame, IN: Ave Maria Press, 1993.

Bianchi, Fr. Luigi. *Fatima and Medjugorje* (4th Edition). Gera Lario, Italy: Bianchi, 1985.

Blackbourn, David. *Marpingen: Apparitions of the Virgin Mary in a Nineteenth Century German Village*. New York: Vintage Books, 1993.

Blue Army. *There is Nothing More*. Washington, NJ: AMI Press, circa 1975.

Borelli, Anthony A. and Spann, John R. *Our Lady at Fatima: Prophecies of Tragedy or Hope?* York, PA: The American Society for the Defense of Tradition, Family and Property, 1975.

Brochado, Costa, Boehrer, George C.A., ed. and trans. *Fatima in the Light of History*. Milwaukee, WI: Bruce Publishing Company, 1955.

Brockman, John, ed. *This Will Change Everything: Ideas That Will Shape the Future*. New York: Harper Perennial, 2009.

Brown, Hilary. *The Great War: History's Most Tragic Conflict,1914-1918*. London, UK: Go Entertainment Group, 2014.

Brown, Michael. *The Final Hour*. Milford, OH: Faith Publishing Company, 1992.

——. *Fear of Fire*. Palm Coast, FL: Spirit Daily Publishing, 2013.

——. *Sent to Earth*. Goleta, CA: Queenship Publishing, 2000.

——. *The Day Will Come*. Ann Arbor, MI: Servant Publications, 1996.

——. *The Last Secret*. Ann Arbor, MI: Servant Publications, 1998.

——. *Tower of Light*. Palm Coast, FL: Spirit Daily Publishing, 2007.

Brown, Wilmott G. *The Significance of Lourdes, Fatima, and Medjugorje as Explained in Scripture*. Winter Park, FL: Wilmot G. Brown, 1995.

Bubalo, Fr. Janko, O.F.M. *A Thousand Encounters with the Blessed Virgin Mary in Medjugorje*. Chicago, IL: Friends of Medjugorje, 1987.

——. *Testimonies: Medjugorje, Blessed Land*. Croatia: Jesla, 1986.

Cacella, Rev. Joseph. *Fatima and the Rosary: A Brief History of the Wonders of Fatima, Portugal*. New York: St. Anthony's Welfare Center, circa 1948.

Cappa, Alphonse M. S.S.P. *Fatima: Cove of Wonders*. Boston, MA: St. Paul Editions, circa 1980.

Carberry, Thomas F. *Medjugorje and Guadalupe: Parallels and Speculation. Will Medjugorje Lead to the Conversion of Russia?* Burlington, MA: T.F. Carberry, 1988.

Carmel of Coimbra. *A Pathway Under the Gaze of Mary: Biography of Sister Maria Lucia of Jesus and the Immaculate Heart*. Coimbra, Portugal: World Apostolate of Fatima, 2015.

Carroll, Rev. Msgr. Richard L. *Oasis of Peace: Our Refuge in the Tribulations*. Diamondhead, MI: Signs and Wonders, 2002.

Carroll, Warren H. *1917: Red Banners, White Mantle*. Front Royal, VA: Christendom Publications, 1981.

Carter, Rev. S.J. *The Spirituality of Fatima and Medjugorje.* Milford, OH: Faith Publishing Company, 1994.

Casaletto, Thomas. *A State of Emergency.* New York: Richardson & Steinman, 1987.

Catechism of the Catholic Church-Liberia Editrice Vaticana. New Hope, KY: Urbi et Orbi Communications, 1994.

Cheston, Sharon E. *Mary the Mother of All: Protestant Perspectives and Experiences of Medjugorje.* Chicago, IL: Loyola University Press, 1992.

Christian, William A. Jr. *Visionaries.* Berkeley, CA: University of California Press, 1996.

Cirrincione, Msgr. Joseph A. with Nelson, Thomas A. St. Joseph, *Fatima and Fatherhood: Reflections on the Miracle of the Sun.* Rockford, IL: TAN Books and Publishers, 1989.

——. *The Forgotten Secret of Fatima and the Silent Apostolate.* Rockford, IL: TAN Books and Publishers, 1988.

——. *The Rosary and the Crisis of Faith: Fatima and World Peace.* Rockford, IL: TAN Books and Publishers, 1986.

Cirrincione, Msgr. Joseph A. *Venerable Jacinta Marto of Fatima.* Rockford, IL: TAN Books and Publishers, 1992.

——. *Fatima's Message for Our Times.* Rockford, IL: TAN Books and Publishers, 1990.

Citrano, Louis J. *Jesus, Mary, Medjugorje, and Me.* Metairie, LA: New Writers' Inc., 2005.

Clissold, Stephen, ed. *A Short History of Yugoslavia.* Cambridge: Cambridge University Press, 1966.

Connell, Jan. *Queen of the Cosmos.* Orleans, MA: Paraclete Press, 1990.

Connell, Janice T. *The Secrets of Mary: Gifts from the Blessed Mother.* New York: St. Martin's Press, 2009.

——. *The Triumph of the Immaculate Heart.* Santa Barbara, CA: Queenship Publishing Company, 1993.

——. *The Visions of the Children.* New York: St. Martin's Griffin, 1992, Revised Edition, 2007.

Covic-Radojicic, Sabrina. *Mirjana Dragićević Soldo: Visionary of Our Lady in Medjugorje: Guardian of the Secrets.* Paris, France: Les Editions Sakramento, 2018.

Covic, Sabrina. *Encounters with Father Jozo.* Paris, France: Les Editions Sakramento, 2003.

Craig, Mary. *Spark from Heaven: The Mystery of the Madonna of Medjugorje.* Notre Dame, IN: Ave Maria Press, 1988.

Cyr, Bruce. *After the Warning 2016*. Alberta, Canada: Bruce A. Cyr, 2013.

Danish, Peter. *Medjugorje-The Final Prophecy*. Bulverde, TX: True North Publishing, 2015.

Davies, Michael. *Medjugorje, A Warning*. St. Paul, MN: The Remnant Press, 1988.

——. *Medjugorje: After Fifteen Years* (2nd Edition). St. Paul, MN: The Remnant Press, 1998.

——. *Medjugorje: After Twenty Twenty-One Years* (1981-2002). [Full text], Archive. Org. 2005.

Delaney, John J., ed. *A Woman Clothed with the Sun*. New York: Doubleday, 1961.

De Marchi, John. F*atima: From the Beginning*. Torres Novas, Portugal: Missoes Consolata, 1950.

De Marchi, John I.M.C. *Mother of Christ Crusade*. Billings, MT: Mother of Christ Crusade, Inc., 1947.

DeMers, John. *Invited to Light: A Search for the Good News in Medjugorje*. Chicago, IL: Trinakria Press, 1990.

De Oca, Rev. V. Montes CSSp. *More About Fatima*. USA: L. Owen Traynor, K.M., 1945.

Dinolfo, John. *A Place of Healing: The Virgin Mary in Medjugorje*. Toronto, Canada: Ave Maria Centre of Peace, 2001.

Dirvin, Joseph I.C.M. *St. Catherine Laboure of the Miraculous Medal*. Rockford, IL: TAN Books and Publishers, 1987.

Donia & Fine, Jr. *Bosnia &Hercegovina*. New York: Columbia University Press, 1994.

Dziwisz, Cardinal Stanislaw. *A Life with Karol: My Forty Year Friendship with the Man Who Became Pope*. New York: Image, Doubleday, 2008.

Eck, Larry & Mary Sue. *The Embrace of the Gospa: Miraculous Stories from Medjugorje Magazine*. Westmont, IL: Epiphany Formations, Inc., 1995.

——. *Will You Be My Priest? Stories of Men Who Said "Yes" to God's Call through Medjugorje*. Westmont, IL: Medjugorje Magazine, 2009.

Ellis, Sue. *Dear Children: Words from the Mother of God at Medjugorje*. Surrey, UK: Marian Spring Centre, 1993.

Emanuele; Lane, Edmund C., S.S.P., translator. *Medjugorje: A Portfolio of Images*. New York: Alba House, 1987.

Evaristo, Carlos. *Saint Michael and the Fatima Connection*. Fatima, Portugal: Evaristo, 1992.

——. *"Two Hours with Sister Lucia."* Fatima, Portugal: Evaristo, 1996.

Fellows, Mark. *Fatima in Twilight*. Niagara Falls, Canada-USA: Marmion Publications, 2003.

Ferrara, Christopher A. *The Secret Still Hidden*. Pound Ridge, New York: Good Counsel Publications, 2008.

Ficocelli, Elizabeth. *Bleeding Hands, Weeping Stone*. Charlotte, NC: Saint Benedict Press, 2009.

——. *The Fruits of Medjugorje: Stories of True and Lasting Conversion*. New York/Mahwah, N.J: Paulist Press, 2006.

Flynn, Ted and Maureen. *The Thunder of Justice*. Herndon, Virginia: MaxKol Communications, 1993, revised edition, 2010.

Flynn, Ted. *The Great Transformation*. Herndon, Virginia: MaxKol Communications, Inc., 2015.

Foley, Donel Anthony. *Medjugorje Revisited: 30 Years of Visions or Religious Fraud?* Nottingham, England: Theotokas Books, 2011.

Foley, Fr. Richard, SJ. T*he Drama of Medjugorje*. Dublin: Veritas Publications, 1992.

Fonseca, Luigi Gonzaga. *The Marvels of Fatima*. San Paulo, Italy: Cinisello Balsamo, 1997.

Fox, Rev.Robert J. *Rediscovering Fatima*. Huntington, IN: Our Sunday Visitor, Inc., 1982.

Fox, Father Robert J. *The Intimate Life of Sister Lucia*, Hanceville, AL: Fatima Family Apostolate, 2001.

Fox, Fr. Robert J. and Martins, Fr. Antonio Maria, S.J. *Documents on Fatima & the Memoirs of Sister Lucia: Pictorial Documentary & Historical Update* (English Edition). Waite Park, MN: Family Fatima Apostolate, Park Press, Inc., 1992.

Francois, Frere de Marie des Agnes. *Fatima: The Only Way to World Peace*. Buffalo, NY: Immaculate Heart Publications, 1993.

——. *Fatima: Tragedy and Triumph*. Buffalo, NY: Immaculate Heart Publications, 1994.

Galot, Jean, S.J. *ABBA, Father, We Long to See Your Face: Theological Insights into the First Person of the Trinity*. New York: Alba House, 1992.

Girard, Fr. Guy, S.SS.A.; Girard, Fr. Armand., S.SS.A. and Bubalo, Fr. Janko., O.F.M. *Mary Queen of Peace Stay with Us*. Montreal, Canada: Editions-Paulines, 1988.

Golob, D.R. *"Live the Messages": The Messages of Mary, Mother of Jesus Christ Lord God, Mary, Queen of Peace Medjugorje*. Harahan, LA: D.R. Golob, 1987.

Gorny, Grzegorz, and Rosikon, Janusz. *Fatima Mysteries*. San Francisco and Warsaw, Poland: Rosikon Press and Ignatius Press, 2017.

Gress, Carrie, Ph. D. *The Marian Option: God's Solution to a Civilization in Crisis*. Charlotte, NC: TAN Books, 2017.

Grillo, Bishop Girolamo. *Our Lady Weeps: Report on Civitavecchia.* Toronto, Ontario: Ave Maria Press, 1997.

Gruner, Father Nicholas, and other Fatima Experts. *World Enslavement or Peace...It's Up to the Pope.* Ontario, Canada: The Fatima Crusader, circa 1988.

Guerrera, Fr. Vittorio. *Medjugorje: A Closer Look.* Meriden, CT: Maryheart Crusaders, 1995.

Haffert, John M. *Deadline: The Third Secret of Fatima.* Asbury, NJ: The 101 Foundation, Inc., 2001.

——. *Dear Bishop: The History of the Blue Army.* Washington, NJ: AMI International Press, 1982.

——. *Explosion of the Supernatural.* Washington, NJ: Pillar, AMI Press, 1975.

——. *Finally, Russia!* Asbury, NJ: The 101 Foundation, Inc., 1993.

——. *From a Morning Prayer: Autobiography.* Washington, NJ: Ave Maria Institute, Inc., 1947.

——. *God's Final Effort.* Asbury NJ: The 101 Foundation, Inc., 1999.

——. *Her Own Words to the Nuclear Age.* Asbury, NJ: The 101 Foundation, Inc., 1993.

——. *Meet the Witnesses.* Washington, NJ: AMI Press, 1961.

——. *Night of Love.* Asbury, NJ: The 101 Foundation, Inc., 1996, revised edition, 1997.

——. *Now, The Woman Shall Conquer.* Asbury, NJ: The 101 Foundation, Inc., 1997.

——. *Sign of Her Heart.* Washington, NJ: Ave Maria Institute, 1971.

——. *The Brother and I.* Washington, NJ: Ave Maria Institute, 1971.

——. *The Day I Didn't Die.* Asbury NJ: Lay Apostolate Foundation, 1998.

——. *The Great Event.* Asbury, NJ: The 101 Foundation, Inc., 2000.

——. *The Hand of Fatima.* Washington, NJ: AMI Press, 1984.

——. *The World's Greatest Secret.* Washington, NJ: AMI Press, 1967.

——. *Too Late?* Asbury, NJ: Queen of the World Center, 1999.

——. *To Prevent This.* Asbury, NJ: The 101 Foundation, Inc., 1993.

——. *To Shake the World: Life of John Haffert.* Asbury, NJ: The 101 Foundation, Inc., 2001.

——. *You, Too, Go into the Vineyard.* Asbury, NJ: The 101 Foundation, Inc., 1989.

Hardiman, James. *The Incredible Story of the Song of Three Shepherds: A Non-Catholic Meets the Miracles of Fatima.* New Hope, KY: Family Fatima Apostolate, 1993.

Herbert, S.M., Albert J. *Medjugorje: An Affirmation and Defense.* Paulina, LA: Albert J. Herbert, S.M., 1990.

Heintz, Peter. *A Guide to Apparitions.* Sacramento, CA: Gabriel Press, 1993.

Howe, Cathy. *A Heavenly Promise: In Search of My Mother's Garden, I Found My Own.* Tarentum, PA: World Association Publishers, 2018.

Hummer, Franz. *Medjugorje.* West Concord, MA: Center for Peace, 1987.

Hummer, Franz, and Jungwirth, Christian. *Medjugorje, Reports, Pictures, Documents.* Duvno, Bosnia-Hercegovina: Sveta Rastina, 1986.

John Paul II, His Holiness. *Crossing the Threshold of Hope.* New York: Alfred A. Knopf, 1994.

John Paul, II. *Centesimus Annus.* London, UK: Catholic Truth Society, 1991.

——. *Memory and Identity: Conversations at the Dawn of the Millennium.* New York: Rizzoli, 2005.

Johnston, Francis. *Fatima: The Great Sign.* Rockford, IL: TAN Books and Publishers, 1980.

Jones, E. Michael, Ph.D. *Medjugorje: The Untold Story.* South Bend, IN: Fidelity Press, 1988.

Jones, E. Michael. *The Medjugorje Deception.* South Bend, IN: Fidelity Press, 2010.

Jones, Michael Kenneth. *Medjugorje Investigated.* Medjugorje, Bosnia & Hercegovina: Devotions, Catholic Books, Music, and Souvenir Shops, 2006.

Kaczmarek, Louis. *The Wonders She Performs.* Manassas, VA: Trinity Communications, 1986.

Kelly, Cynthia J., ed. *The Manhattan Project.* New York: Black Dog and Leventhal Publishers, 2007.

Kengor, Paul. A *Pope and a President.* Wilmington, DE: ISI Books, 2017.

——. T*he Devil and Karl Marx: Communism's Long March of Death, Deception, and Infiltration.* Gastonia, NC: TAN Books, 2020.

Klanac, D. *Medjugorje, Réponses aux Objections.* Canada: Le Serment, 2001.

Klaus, Rita. *Rita's Story.* Orleans, MA: Paraclete Press, 1993.

Klimek, Daniel Maria. *Medjugorje and the Supernatural: Science, Mysticism, and the Extraordinary Religious Experience.* Oxford, United Kingdom: Oxford University Press, 2018.

Klins, June. *The Best of "The Spirit of Medjugorje: Volume I, 1988-1997."* Bloomington, IN: Authorhouse, 2005.

Knotzinger, Kurt. *Antwort Auf Medjugorje* (*Answer to Medjugorje*). Germany: Styria Graf, 1985.

Kordic, Ivan, Ph.D. *The Apparitions of Medjugorje: A Critical Conclusion.* Zagreb, Croatia: K. Kresimir, 1994.

Kotkin, Stephen. *Armageddon Averted: The Soviet Collapse 1970-2000.* New York: Oxford University Press, 2001.

Kowalska, M. Faustina. *Diary of Sister Maria Faustina Kowalska: Divine Mercy in My Soul.* Stockbridge, MA: Marian Press, 1987.

Kraljevic, Svetozar, O.F.M. *In the Company of Mary.* Nashville, TN: St. Francis Press, 1988.

———. *Pilgrimage: Reflections of a Medjugorje Priest.* Orleans, MA: Paraclete Press, 1991.

———. *The Apparitions of Mary at Medjugorje.* Chicago, IL: Franciscan Herald Press, 1984.

Kramer, Father Paul. *The Devil's Final Battle.* Terryville, CT: Good Counsel Publications, 2002.

Krepinevich, Andrew F. *7 Deadly Scenarios: A Military Futurist Explores War in the Twenty-First Century.* New York: Bantam Books, 2010.

Kselman, Thomas A. *Miracles and Prophecies in Nineteenth Century France.* New Brunswick, NJ: Rutgers University Press, 1983.

Laurentin, Fr. René, and Joyeux, Henri. *Scientific and Medical Studies on the Apparitions at Medjugorje.* Dublin, Ireland: Veritas Publishers, 1987.

Laurentin, Fr. René, and Lejeune, Fr. René. *Messages and Teachings of Mary at Medjugorje.* Milford, OH: Riehle Foundation, 1988.

Laurentin, Fr. René. *Eight Years: Reconciliation, Analysis, the Future.* Milford, OH: Riehle Foundation, 1989.

———. *Is the Virgin Mary Appearing in Medjugorje?* Washington, D.C.: The Word Among Us Press, 1984.

———. *Latest News of Medjugorje: June 1987.* Milford, OH: Riehle Foundation, 1987.

———. *Learning from Medjugorje.* Gaithersburg, MD: The Word Among Us Press, 1988.

———. *Medjugorje Testament: Hostility Abounds, Grace Superabounds.* Toronto, Ontario: Ave Maria Press, 1998.

———. *Medjugorje -13 Years Later.* Milford, OH: The Riehle Foundation, 1994.

———. *Medjugorje: 12 Years Later, War, Love Your Enemies.* Santa Barbara: CA: Queenship Publishing, 1993.

———. *Nine Years of Apparitions.* Milford, OH: Riehle Foundation, 1991.

———. *Report on Apparitions.* Milford, OH, Riehle Foundation, 1989.

———. *Seven Years of Apparitions: Time for the Harvest?* Milford, OH: Riehle Foundation, 1988.

———. *Sixteen Years of Apparitions: Peace and Deepening in the Expectation of the Ten Secrets.* Paris, France: F.X. de Guibert, 1997.

———. *Ten Years of Apparitions: New Growth and Recognition of Pilgrimages.* Milford, OH: Faith Publishing Company, 1991.

——. *The Apparitions of Medjugorje Prolonged.* Milford, OH: Riehle Foundation, 1987.

——. *The Apparitions of the Blessed Virgin Mary Today.* Dublin, Ireland: Veritas Publishers, 1990.

——. *The Cause of Liberation in the USSR.* Santa Barbara, CA: Queenship Publishing Company, 1993.

——. *The Church and Apparitions - Their Status and Function: Criteria and Reception.* Milford, OH: Riehle Foundation, 1989.

Lindsey, David Michael. *The Woman and the Dragon.* Gretna, LA: Pelican Publishing Company, 2000.

Ljubicic, Petar. *The Call of the Queen of Peace.* Zagreb, Croatia: Glas Mira Medjugorje, 1996.

Lord, Bob and Penny. *The Many Faces of Mary: A Love Story.* Slidell, LA: Journeys of Faith, 1987.

Lynch, Dan. *The Ten Secrets of the Blessed Virgin Mary: How to Prepare for their Warnings.* St. Albans, VT: John Paul Press, 2011.

Maillard, Sister Emanuel. *Medjugorje: The 1990's.* Pittsburgh, PA: St. Andrew's Productions, 1997.

——. *Medjugorje: The War Day by Day.* Miami, FL: Florida Center for Peace, 1993.

Maillard, Sister Emanuel and Nolan, Denis. *Medjugorje: What Does the Church Say?* Santa Barbara, CA: Queenship Publishing Company, 1995, revised edition, 1998.

Manifold, Deirdre. *Fatima and the Great Conspiracy.* Galway, Ireland: The Militia of Our Immaculate Mother, 1982.

Manuel, David. *Medjugorje Under Siege.* Orleans, MA.: Paraclete Press, 1992.

Maria Lucia of Jesus and of the Immaculate Heart, Sr. *How I See the Message.* Coimbra, Portugal: Carmel of Coimbra and the Secretary office of the Shepherds, revised edition, 2007.

Marin, Jacov. *Queen of Peace in Medjugorje.* Milford, OH: Riehle Foundation, 1989.

Martins, Antonio S.J. *Fatima: Way of Peace.* Devon, Chulmleigh: Augustine Publishing Company, 1989.

Martins, Fr. Antonio Maria, S.J. and Fox, Father Robert J. *Documents on Fatima and the Memoirs of Sister Lucia; Pictorial Documentary & Historical Update.* Hanceville, AL: Fatima Family Apostolate, 2001.

McFadden, Eleanor. *Words of Our Lady: Medjugorje Messages* (*Map Form*). Dublin, Ireland: Eleanor McFadden, 2000.

McGlynn, Fr. Thomas. *Vision of Fatima.* Manchester, NH: Sophia Institute Press, 2017.

McKenna, Thomas J. *The Fatima Century*. San Diego, CA: Catholic Action for Faith and Family, 2017.

McNamara, Joseph E., ed. *Medjugorje-The Sunset and the Need for Prayer Groups*. Milford, OH: Riehle Foundation, 1990.

Medjugorje, A Friend of. *Look What Happened While You Were Sleeping*. Sterret, AL: Caritas of Birmingham, 2007.

Medjugorje,.Org. *The Medjugorje Messages: 1981-2013*. DeKalb, IL: The Medjugorje Web, 2013.

Meyer, Gabriel. *A Portrait of Medjugorje*. Studio City, CA: Twin Circle Publishing Company, 1990.

Michel, Frère de la Sainte Trinité. *Fatima Revealed…and Discarded*. Chulmleigh, Devon: Augustine Publishing Company, 1988.

——. *The Whole Truth About Fatima, Volume I, Science and the Facts*. Buffalo, NY: Immaculate Heart Publications, 1983.

——. *The Whole Truth About Fatima, Volume II, The Secret and the Church*. Buffalo, NY: Immaculate Heart Publications, 1989.

——. *The Whole Truth About Fatima, Volume III, The Third Secret*. Buffalo, NY: Immaculate Heart Publications, 1990.

Mikulich, Fr. Milan O.F.M. *The Apparitions of Our Lady in Medjugorje*. Portland, OR: Orthodoxy of the Catholic Doctrine, 1984.

Miller, Rev. Frederick L., ed. *Exploring Fatima*. Washington, NJ: AMI Press, 1989.

Minutoli, Armando. *Medjugorje: A Pilgrim's Journey*. Medford, NY: The Morning Star Press, 1991.

Miravalle, Mark, S.T.D. *Heart of the Message of Medjugorje*. Steubenville, OH: Franciscan University Press, 1988.

——. *Introduction to Medjugorje*. Goleta, CA: Queenship Publishing, 2004.

——. *The Message of Medjugorje*. Lanham, MD: University Press of America, 1986.

Morin Jerry. *To the World: A Conversion Story.* Des Moines, IA: Respond Ministry, Inc. Publications, 1998.

Mulligan, James. *Medjugorje: What's Happening?* Brewster, MA.: Paraclete Press, 2008.

Murphey, Guy, O.P. *The Weapon of Medjugorje*. Hillside, IL: Totally Yours, 2006.

Nichols, Aiden, O.P. *Rome and the Eastern Churches: A Study in Schism*. Collegeville, MN: The Liturgical Press, 1992.

Nolan, Denis. *Medjugorje: A Time for Truth, A Time for Action*. Santa Barbara, CA: Queenship Publishing, 1993.

——. *Medjugorje and the Church*. Goleta, CA: Queenship Publishing Company, 1995.

O'Carroll, Michael, CSSp. *Is Medjugorje Approved?* Dublin, Ireland: Veritas Publishers, 1991.

——. *Medjugorje: Facts, Documents, Theology.* Dublin, Ireland: Veritas Publishers, 1986.

O'Conner, Edward D., C.S.C. *I Am Sending You Prophets; The Role of Apparitions in the History of the Church.* Goleta, CA: Queenship Publishing, 2007.

——. *Marian Apparitions Today.* Santa Barbara, CA: Queenship Publishing Company, 1996.

O'Connor, Fr. John O.S.A. *Medjugorje: The Story and the Message.* Galway, Ireland: Marian Promotions, 1989.

——. *Medjugorje: Where the Cock Crows and the Birds Sings.* Galway, Ireland: Marian Promotions, 1986.

Odell, Catherine M. *Those Who Saw Her.* Huntington, IN: Our Sunday Visitor Publishing Division, 1986.

O'Leary, Finbar. *Meeting with our Lady of Medjugorje: With Prayer Group Messages from Ivan, Marijana, Marija, and Jelena.* Dublin, Ireland: Columba Books, 2014.

——. *Vicka: Her Story.* Dublin, Ireland: The Columba Press, 2015.

O'Neil, Michael. *Exploring the Miraculous.* Huntington, IN: Our Sunday Visitor, 2015.

O'Reilly, Bill and Dugard, Martin. *Killing the Rising Sun.* New York, NY: Henry Holt and Company, 2016.

O'Sullivan, Desmond and O'Carroll, Fr. Michael., CSSp. *The Alliance of the Hearts of Jesus and Mary: Testimonies.* Dublin, Ireland, 1997.

Owen, Hugh. *The Light Comes from the East.* Mount Jackson, Virginia: Hugh Owen, 2015.

Paolini, Solideo. *Fatima: Do Not Despise Prophecies.* Tavagnacco, Italy: Edizioni Segno, 2005.

Parsons, Heather. *A Light Between the Hills.* Dublin, Ireland: Robert Andrew Press, 1994.

Pavicic, Darko. *Medjugorje: The First Seven Days.* Cocoa, FL: Catholic Shop, LLC, 2022.

Pelletier, Joseph, A.A. *The Queen of Peace Visits Medjugorje.* Worcester, MA.: Assumption Publications, 1985.

——. *The Sun Danced at Fatima.* Garden City, NY: Image Books, Doubleday, 1951.

Pervan, Tomislav, O.F.M. *Queen of Peace: Echo of the Eternal Word.* Steubenville, OH: Franciscan University Press, 1986.

Petrisko, Thomas W. *Call of the Ages*. Santa Barbara, CA: Queenship Publishing, 1996.

——. *Fatima's Third Secret Explained*. Pittsburgh, PA: St. Andrew's Productions, 2001.

——. *Inside Heaven and Hell*. Pittsburgh, PA: St. Andrew's Productions, 2000.

——. *Inside Purgatory*. Pittsburgh, PA: St. Andrews Productions, 2000.

——. *Living in the Heart of the Father*. Pittsburgh, PA: St. Andrew's Productions, 2013.

——. *The Fatima Prophecies: At the Doorstep of the World*. Pittsburgh, PA: St. Andrew's Productions, 1998.

——. *The Last Crusade*. McKees Rocks, PA: St. Andrew's Productions, 1996.

——. *The Miracle of the Illumination of All Consciences*. Pittsburgh, PA: St. Andrew's Productions, 2000.

——. *The Mystery of the Divine Paternal Heart of God Our Father*. Pittsburgh, PA: St. Andrew's Productions, 2015.

——. *The Sorrow, the Sacrifice, and the Triumph*. New York: Simon and Schuster, Inc., 1995.

Pilgrim Virgin Committee. *Our Lady of Fatima: Our Mother Comes to Us*. Asbury, NJ: Pilgrim Virgin Committee, 1998.

Pirjevec, Joze. T*ito and His Comrades*. Madison WI: University of Wisconsin Press, 2018.

Plunkett, Dudley. *Queen of Prophets: The Gospel Message of Medjugorje*. New York: Doubleday, 1992.

Proctor, Jim d'Urfe. *Sailing Beyond the Sea*. Santa Barbara, CA: Queenship Publishing Company, 1996.

Pronechen, Joseph. *The Fruits of Fatima: A Century of Signs and Wonders*. Manchester, NH: Sophia Institute Press, 2019.

Rangers, Christopher, OFM Cap. *The Youngest Prophet: The Life of Jacinta Marto, Fatima Visionary*. New York: Alba House, 1986.

Reader's Digest, the eds. *Reader's Digest Illustrated Story of World War II*. Pleasantville, NY: The Reader's Digest Association, Inc., 1969.

Remnick, David. *Lenin's Tomb: The Last Days of the Soviet Empire*. New York: Random House, 1993.

Riehle Foundation, the eds. *A Man Named Father Jozo*. Milford, OH: The Riehle Foundation, 1989.

Richard, Abbe M. *What Happened at Pontmain?* Washington, NJ: Ave Maria Institute, 1971.

Riehle Foundation, the eds. *Medjugorje and Meditations, Witnesses, and Teachings.* Milford, OH: The Riehle Foundation, 1988.

Rooney, Lucy, S.N.D. and Faricy, Robert, S.J. *A Medjugorje Retreat.* New York: Alba House, 1989.

——. *Mary, Queen of Peace.* New York: Alba House, 1984.

——. *Medjugorje Journal.* Essex, England: McCremmon Publishing Co., Ltd., 1987.

——. *Medjugorje Unfolds.* Steubenville, Ohio: Franciscan University Press, 1985.

——. *Medjugorje Up Close.* Chicago, IL: Franciscan Herald Books, 1985.

Rosage, Msgr.David E. *Mary, Star of the New Millennium: Guiding Us to Renewal.* Ann Arbor, MI: Servant Publications, 1997.

Rosenbaum, Ron. *How the End Begins: The Road to a Nuclear World War III.* New York, NY: Simon and Schuster, 2011.

Ruane, Rev. Gerald P., and Williams, Ruthann, op. *Thank You for Hearing My Call: Living the Messages of Medjugorje.* Caldwell, NJ: Sacred Heart Press, 1990.

Rupčić, Fr. Ljudevit. *Medjugorje in the History of Salvation.* Zagreb, Yugoslavia: Duvno, 1988.

Rupčić, Dr. Ljudevit and Nuic, Dr. Viktor. *Once Again, The Truth About Medjugorje.* Zagreb, Croatia: K. Kresimir, 2002.

Rupčić, Ljudevit. *The Truth About Medjugorje.* Yugoslavia: Lubiski-Hume, 1990.

Rutkoski, Thomas. *Apostles of the Last Days: The Fruits of Medjugorje.* Evans City, PA: Gospa Missions, 1992.

Santos, Lucia dos. *Fatima in Lucia's Own Words: Sister Lucia's Memoirs.* [Edited by Fr. Louis Kondor, SVD]. Translated by Dominican Nuns of the Perpetual Rosary. Fatima, Portugal: Postulation Centre, 1976.

——. *Fatima in Lucia's Own Words II: Sister Lucia's Memoirs, Volume II.* Edited by Fr. Louis Kondor SVD. Translated by the Dominican Nuns of the Perpetual Rosary (Fatima) and the Dominican Nuns of Monteiro de Santa Maria (Lisbon). Fatima, Portugal: Secretariado dos Pastorinhos, 1999.

Schweizer, Peter. *Victory: The Reagan Administration's Secret Strategy that Hastened the Collapse of the Soviet Union.* New York: Atlantic Monthly Press, 1996.

Seewald, Peter. *Benedict XVI-Light of the World: The Pope, the Church and the Signs of the Times.* San Francisco, CA: Ignatius Press, 2010.

Sharkey, Don. *The Woman Shall Conquer.* Libertyville, IL: Franciscan Marytown Press, 1954.

Schiffer, Hubert F. SJ. *The Rosary of Hiroshima.Washington*, NJ: The Blue Army, 1953.

Shamom, Rev. Albert J.M. *The Power of the Rosary*. Milford, OH: The Riehle Foundation, 1990.

Siguenza, Eduardo. *John Paul II: The Pope Who Understood Fatima*. Goleta, CA: Queenship Publishing Company, 2007.

Singleton, Fred. *A Short History of the Yugoslav Peoples*. Cambridge: Cambridge University Press, 1985.

Sister Lucia of Jesus and of the Immaculate Heart. *'Calls': From the Message of Fatima*. Still River, MA: The Ravengate Press, 2001.

Sivric, Fr. L.O.F.M. *The Hidden Side of Medjugorje*. Quebec, Canada: Psilog, Inc., 1989.

Snyder, Timothy. *Bloodlands: Europe Between Hitler and Stalin*. New York: Basic Books, 2010.

Socci, Antonio. *Mistero Medjugorje*. Milan, Italy: Piemme Edizioni, 2013.

——. *The Fourth Secret of Fatima*. Fitzwilliam, NH: Loreto Publications, 2006.

——. *The Secret of Benedict XVI*. Brooklyn, NY: Angelico Press, Ltd., 2019.

Soldo, Mirjana. *My Heart Will Triumph*. Cocoa, FL: CatholicShop Publishing, 2016.

Srouji, Jacqueline. *Mystic Medjugorje*. Nashville, TN: St. Francis Press, 1988.

Stromberg, Johannes Maria. *Our Blessed Mother Leads Her Children Out of Sarajevo*. Santa Barbara, CA: Queenship Publishing Company, 1993.

Sullivan, Randall. *The Miracle Detective*. New York: Grove Press, 2004.

Symonds, Kevin. *On the Third Part of the Secret of Fatima*. St. Louis, MO: En Route Books and Media, 2017.

——. *Pope Leo XIII and the Prayer to St. Michael*. Boonville, NY: Preserving Christian Publications, 2018.

Talbott, Strobe. *The Russians and Reagan*. New York: Vintage, 1984.

Tardo, Russell K. *Apparitions at Medjugorje: Divine of Demonic?* Kenner, LA: Faith Word Publications, 1989.

Thavis, John. *The Vatican Prophecies: Investigating Supernatural Signs, Apparitions, and Miracles in the Modern Age*. New York, NY: Viking Press, 2015.

Terelya, Joseph, with Brown, Michael. *Josyp Terelya: Witness to the Apparitions and Persecution in the U.S.S.R.* Milford, OH: Faith Publishers, 1991.

The New American Bible. Wichita, KS: Catholic Bible Publishers, revised edition, 1994-95.

Thull, Andrew, ed. *What They Say About Medjugorje 1981-1991: A Contemporary Mystery*. Cincinnati, OH: Precision Built Corporation, 1991.

Tindal-Robertson, Timothy. *Fatima, Russia & Pope John Paul II*. Still River, MA: The Ravengate Press, 1992.

Toye, Charles. *Miracle of the Sun at Medjugorje*. Reading, MA: Send Your Spirit Prayer Ministry, 1988.

——. *Prayer of the Heart from Our Lady of Medjugorje*. Reading, MA: Send Your Spirit Prayer Ministry, 1987.

Trinchard, Fr. Paul. *The Awesome Fatima Consecrations*. Metairie, LA: META, 1992.

Tutto, Fr. George. *Medjugorje: Our Lady's Parish*. East Sussex, England: Medjugorje Information Service, 1985.

Two Friends of Medjugorje. *Words from Heaven*. Birmingham, AL.: St. James Publishing, 1990.

Ulicny, Joan. *A Greater Vision: Back from Abortion*. Santa Barbara, CA: Queenship Publishing Company, 1995.

Varghese, Roy Abraham. *Great Thinkers on Great Questions*, Oxford, England: Oneworld Publications, 1998.

Venancio, Most Rev. Joao, D.D., Bishop of Leiria-Fatima, ed. *A Heart for All: The Immaculate Heart of Mary in the Apparitions at Fatima*. Washington, NJ: AMI Press, 1972.

——. *Lucia Speaks on the Message of Fatima*. Washington, NJ: AMI Press, 1968.

Vlašić, Fr. Tomislav, O.F.M. *Our Lady Queen of Peace, Queen of Apostles is Teaching Us the Way to the Truth and Life at Medjugorje, Yugoslavia*. East Sussex, England: Peter Batty / Pika Print Limited, 1984.

Vlašić, Tomislav, O.F.M., and Barbarić, Slavko, O.F.M. *Abandon Yourselves Totally to Me*. Milan, Italy: The Association of the Friends of Medjugorje, 1985.

——. *I Beseech You, Listen to My Messages and Live Them*. Milan, Italy: The Association of the Friends of Medjugorje, 1987.

——. *Open Your Hearts to Mary*. Milan, Italy: The Association of the Friends of Medjugorje, 1986.

——. *Pray with Your Heart*. Milan, Italy: The Association of the Friends of Medjugorje, 1986.

Wallace, Mary Joan. *Medjugorje: Its Background and Messages*. Huntington Beach, CA: Follow Me Communications, 1989.

Walsh, William Thomas. *Our Lady of Fatima*. New York: Image Books, Doubleday, 1947.

Watkins, Christine. *Full of Grace*. Miraculous Stories of Healing and Conversion Through Mary's Intercession. Notre Dame, IN: Ave Maria Press, 2010.

Weible, Wayne. *A Child Shall Lead Them*. Brewster, MA: Paraclete Press, 2005.

——. *Letters from Medjugorje*. Orleans, MA: Paraclete Press, 1991.

——. *Medjugorje: The Last Apparition. How It Will Change the World.* Hiawassee, GA: New Hope Press, 2013.

——. *Medjugorje: The Message.* Orleans, MA: Paraclete Press, 1989.

——. *Medjugorje: The Mission.* Orleans, MA: Paraclete Press, 1994.

——. *The Final Harvest: Medjugorje at the End of the Century.* Brewster, MA: Paraclete Press, 1999.

Weigel, George. *The End and the Beginning.* New York: Image Books, Doubleday, 2011.

——. *Witness to Hope: The Biography of Pope John Paul II.* New York: Harper Perennial, 2004.

West, Rebecca. *Black Lamb, Gray Falcon: A Journey Through Yugoslavia.* New York, Viking Press, 1941.

White, Lottie. *I Will Save the World: Mary's Promise.* Pittsburgh, PA: FEB Company, 1979.

Williams, Alfred W. and Elizabeth, the "Blue Army Betty." *Gems of Wit and Wisdom: Supplement of Two Hearts of Wit and Wisdom.* Cape Coral, FL: Alfred and Elizabeth Williams, circa 1990.

——. *Two Hearts of Wit & Wisdom.* Cape Coral, FL: Alfred and Elizabeth Williams, 1990.

Yakovlev, Alexander. *A Century of Violence in the Soviet Union.* New Haven, CT: Yale University Press, 2004.

Yeung, Andrew Jerome. *Our Lady Speaks from Medjugorje.* Toronto, Ontario: The Ave Maria Centre for Peace, 2005.

——. *The Way to Medjugorje, Yugoslavia.* Toronto, Ontario: The Ave Maria Centre for Peace, 1984.

Zimdals-Swartz, Sandra L. *Encountering Mary: From La Salette to Medjugorje.* Princeton, N.J.: Princeton University Press, 1991.

NEWSPAPERS, PERIODICALS AND WEBSITES, 1981-2021

1. *Fatima International*, London, England.
2. *Medjugorje Gebetsaktion*, Vienna, Austria.
3. *Medjugorje Sentinel*, New South Wales, Australia.
4. *The Medjugorje Star*, New Orleans, LA.
5. *Via Ad Pacem*, Auburn, NY.
6. *Children of Medjugorje Newsletter,* Notre Dame, IN.
7. *The Spirit of Medjugorje*, Erie, PA.
8. *The Pilgrim*, Voorhees, NJ.
9. *Queen of Peace Center Update*, Dallas, TX.
10. *Medjugorje Torino*, Torino, Italy.
11. *Theotokas News*, Toledo, OH.
12. *Hawaii Catholic Herald*, Honolulu, HI.
13. *Mary's People*, Studio City, CA.
14. *Mary's Mantle*, Yonkers, NY.
15. *The Medjugorje Messenger*, London, England.
16. *Orthodoxy of the Catholic Doctrine*, Portland, OR.
17. *The Mir Response*, New Orleans, LA.
18. *Medjugorje: Queen of Peace Newsletter*, Notre Dame, IN.
19. *Queen of Peace Journal*, Poughkeepsie, NY.
20. *30Days*, Rome, Italy.
21. *Our Sunday Visitor*, Huntington, IN.
22. *Catholic Counter-Reformation in the 20th Century*, Paris, France.
23. *The Wanderer*, Saint Paul, MN.
24. *Evangelist*, Albany, NY.
25. *Glas Koncila, Catholic Newspaper*, Yugoslavia.
26. *Guardian,* London, England.
27. *Catholic Worker*, New York, NY.
28. *Furrow*, County Kildare, IE.
29. *Catholic Twin Circle*, Los Angeles, CA.
30. *Month*, London, England.

31. *Mary's Newsroom*, Pittsburgh, PA.
32. *Libre Belgique*, Belgium.
33. *Queen of All Hearts*, Bay Shore, NY.
34. *Fidelity*, South Bend, IN.
35. *Catholic Standard and Times*, Philadelphia, PA.
36. *London Times*, London, England.
37. *Philadelphia Inquirer*, Philadelphia, PA.
38. *US News and World Report*, Washington, D.C.
39. *Time Magazine*, New York, NY.
40. *Tablet*, London, England.
41. *Criterion*, Indianapolis, IN.
42. *Our Lady Queen of Peace Newsletter*, Chicago, IL.
43. *Echo of Mary Queen of Peace*, Treviso, Italy.
44. *Caritas of Birmingham*, Sterret, AL.
45. *ABC News (20/20)*, TV News Network, New York, NY.
46. *Queen of Peace Newsletter*, Coraopolis, PA.
47. *Center for Peace-West Newsletter*, Portland, OR.
48. *Medjugorje Queen of Peace Newsletter*, Las Vegas, NV.
49. *Weible Columns: Medjugorje Newsletter*, Myrtle Beach, SC.
50. *Words of Our Lady*, Dublin, Ireland.
51. *New York Times*, New York, NY.
52. *Michigan Catholic*, Detroit, MI.
53. *Miami Herald*, Miami, FL.
54. *Cincinnati Enquirer*, Cincinnati, OH.
55. *Newsweek Magazine*, New York, NY.
56. *Medjugorje Magazine*, Riverside, IL.
57. *Our Lady Queen of Peace Newspaper*, McKees Rocks, PA.
58. *Voice of the Sacred Hearts*, Dover, DE.
59. *Crusade Magazine*, Hanover, PA.
60. *Pro Ecclesia Magazine*, New York, NY.
61. *HLI Reports, Front Royal*, VA.
62. *Echo from Medjugorje*, Italy.
63. *St. Louis Review. St. Louis*, MO.
64. *Reader's Digest*, Pleasantville, NY.
65. *L'Osservatore Romano*, Vatican City, Rome, Italy.
66. *Queen of Peace Newsletter*, St. Laurent, Quebec, CA.
67. *Columbia*, New Haven, CT.
68. *Providence Journal*, Providence, RI.

69. *Marian Helper Bulletin*, Stockbridge, MA.
70. *Texas Catholic*, Dallas, TX.
71. *Catholic Herald*, London, England.
72. *New Covenant*, Ann Arbor, MI.
73. *Signs and Wonders for Our Times*, Herndon, VA.
74. *Our Lady's Courier*, Fairview, PA.
75. *Catholic Family News*, Niagara Falls, NY.
76. *Priests and People*, London, England.
77. *The Marian Library Newsletter*, Dayton, OH.
78. *Catholic Telegraph*, Cincinnati, OH.
79. *National Catholic Reporter*, Kansas City, MO.
80. *Soul Magazine,* Washington, NJ.
81. *Spectator.* London, England.
82. *Liquorian*, Liquori, MO.
83. *Catholic Almanac*, Huntington, IN.
84. *America*, New York, NY.
85. *Catholic Digest*, Saint Paul, MN.
86. *Good News*, Wales, UK.
87. *Omni Magazine*, New York, NY.
88. *The Catholic Thing*, https:wwwthecatholicthing.org.
89. *Immaculata Magazine*, Libertyville, IL.
90. *Crisis: Politics, Culture & the Church*, Washington, D.C.
91. *Divine Mercy Messenger*, Erie, PA.
92. *Dallas Morning News*, Dallas, PA.
93. *Mystic Post*, https://mysticpost.com.
94. *The 101 Times*, Asbury, N.J.
95. *The Triumph*, Buffalo, NY.
96. *LifesiteNews*, https://lifesitenews.com.
97. *Spirit Daily*, Palm Coast, FL.
98. *Catholic Times*, Columbus, OH.
99. *Saint Anthony Messenger*, Cincinnati, OH.
100. *Medjugorje: Its Time Newspaper*, Weyburn, Saskatchewan.
101. *National Catholic Register*, Los Angeles, CA.
102. *Sunday Times Magazine*, London, England.
103. *LAF News*, Washington, NJ.
104. *Washington Post*, Washington, D.C.
105. *Orlando Sentinel*, Orlando, FL.
106. NBC News (*Inside Edition*), [TV news], New York, NY.

107. *Listener*, London, England.
108. *Cincinnati Post*, Cincinnati, Ohio.
109. *Long Island Catholic.* Long Island, NY.
110. *Dedicated Decades*, Dickinson, Texas.
111. *Insight* (*Washington Times*), Washington, D.C.
112. *International Herald Tribune*, London, England.
113. *Salem News*, Salem, PA.
114. *Homiletic and Pastoral Review*, St. Louis, Mo.
115. *La Vita Populo*, Treviso, Italy.
116. *Marian Observer*, Berkeley, MI.
117. *Clarion Herald*, New Orleans LA.
118. *Dayton Daily News*, Dayton, OH.
119. *Lamplighters Bulletin*, Ottawa, CA.
120. *South Bend Tribune*, South Bend, IN.
121. *Arizona Republic*, Phoenix, AZ.
122. *The Catholic Review*, Baltimore, MD.
123. *Medjugorje Center Newsletter*, Kansas City, MO.
124. *Leaves*, Detroit MI.
125. *The Children of Mary Center for Peace Newsletter*, Mossyrock, WA.
126. *Pittsburgh Center for Peace World Report*, McKees Rocks, PA.
127. *Gospa Missions Catholic News Periodical*, Evans City, PA.
128. *Inside the Vatican*, Front Royal, VA.
129. *Church Militant*, www.churchmilitant.com.
130. *The Spirit and the Word*, Providence, RI.
131. *One Peter 5*, https://onepeterfive.com.
132. *The Mir Recorder*, Middlesex, England.
133. *Medjugorje USA*, https://www.medjugorjeusa.org.
134. "*Hvaljen Isus I Marija* (*Praised Be Jesus and Mary Newsletter*), Wayne, PA.
135. *The Fatima Crusader*, Constable, NY.
136. *Medjugorje*, Nashville, TN.
137. *Medjugorje Monthly*, London, England.
138. *Medjugorje Herald*, Galway, Ireland.

VIDEOS
AND DOCUMENTARIES

1   *Medjugorje: Our Mother's Last Call with Sister Emmanuel.* Children of Medjugorje: Notre Dame, IN.,1997.
2   *The Madonna of Medjugorje.* Franciscan University Press, Steubenville, OH.,1997.
3   *Medjugorje: Responding to the Call from the Heart.* Respond Ministry, Inc,1991.
4   *Apparitions at Fatima.* EWTN Global Catholic Network, 1994.
5   *Medjugorje, Queen of Peace: A Message of Peace by the Karminski Family.* Wayne, PA, 1984.
6   *The Message of Medjugorje.* Wayne Weible, 1992.
7   *Medjugorje: Transforming Your Heart.* Marian Communications, LTD, 1988.
8   The *Little Shepherds of Fatima.* Fatima Productions, 1981.
9   *Madonna of Medjugorje.* BBC, Everyman / Westenhanger Film, London, UK, 1985.
10 *Prophecy in the New Times.* MaxKol Productions, Herndon, VA, 1996.
11 *The Triumph of the Immaculate Heart of Mary: Volume I: Medjugorje.* Gray Haven Films, Diamond Bar, CA.,1994.
12 *Medjugorje in the New Millennium.* QOP Productions, Sean Patrick Bloomfield,2002.

RECOMMENDED
READING / VIEWING

FATIMA

1. *Fatima: In Lucia's Own Words Vol.I & II*...Sr. Maria Lucia of the Immaculate Heart
2. *A Pathway Under the Gaze of Mary*...Carmel of Coimbra / World Apostolate of Fatima
3. *The Whole Truth About Fatima*...Frere Michel de la Sainte Trinite
4. *Fatima: The Great Sign*...Francis Johnston
5. *Our Lady of Fatima*... William Thomas Walsh
6. *Two Hours with Sister Lucia*...Carlos Evaristo
7. *Meet the Witnesses*...John Haffert
8. *Fatima: From the Beginning*...John De Marchi
9. *The Secret of Fatima*...Joaquin Maria Alonso, C.M.F.
10. *The Fourth Secret of Fatima*...Antonio Socci
11. *Fatima for Today*...Fr. Andrew Apostoli, C.F.R.
12. *On the Third Part of the Secret of Fatima*...Kevin J. Symonds
13. *Fatima Mysteries*...Grzegorz Górny and Janusz Rosikoń
14. *The Last Secret of Fatima*...Cardinal Tarcisio Bertone
15. *1917: Red Banners, White Mantle*...Warren H. Carroll
16. *The Fatima Prophecies*...Thomas W. Petrisko
17. *A Heart for All*...Most Reverend Joao Venancio, D.D, (ed.)
18. *Rediscovering Fatima*...Reverend Robert J. Fox
19. *The Youngest Prophet*...Christopher Rengers, OFM Cap.
20. *Calls from the Message of Fatima*...Sister Lucia of Jesus and the Immaculate Heart
21. *More About Fatima*...Reverend V. Montes De Oca, C.S.Sp.
22. *Documents on Fatima &the Memoirs of Sister Lucia*...Father Antonio Maria Martins, S.J.
23. *Fatima in Twilight*...Mark Fellows
24. *The Devil's Final Battle*...Father Paul Kramer (ed.)

MEDJUGORJE

1. *My Heart Will Triumph*...Mirjana Soldo
2. *Medjugorje: The First Seven Days*...Darko Pavičić
2. *The Visions of the Children*...Janice T. Connell
3. *Queen of the Cosmos*...Jan Connell
4. *Apparition Hill* (Documentary)...Sean Bloomfield
5. *Is the Virgin Mary Appearing in Medjugorje*...René Laurentin and Ljudevit Rupčić
6. *The Miracle Detective*...Randall Sullivan
7. *A Thousand Encounters with the Blessed Virgin Mary in Medjugorje*...Fr. Janko Bubalo
8. *Medjugorje: A Time for Truth, A Time for Action*...Denis Nolan
9. *Medjugorje: Facts, Documents, Theology*...Michael O'Carroll, CSSp
10. *Spark from Heaven*...Mary Craig
11. *Medjugorje: The 90's*...Sister Emmanuel Maillard
12. *What They Say About Medjugorje*...Andrew B. Thull, (Editor)
13. *Medjugorje Testament: Hostility Abounds, Grace Superabounds...* René Laurentin
14. *The Apparitions of Our Lady at Medjugorje*...Svetozar Kraljevic, O.F.M.
15. *Medjugorje Journal*...Lucy Rooney, SND and Robert Faricy, SJ
16. *Words from Heaven*...A Friend of Medjugorje
17. *The Apparitions of Medjugorje*...Ivan Kordic, Ph.D.
18. *Medjugorje: What's Happening?*... James Mulligan
19. *The Medjugorje Messages: 1981-2013*...Međugorje.org.
20. *The Best of the Spirit of Medjugorje: Volume I, 1988-1997*...June Klins

RELATED / MISCELLANEOUS

1. *A Pope and a President*…Paul Kengor
2. *The Embrace of the Gospa*… Larry and Mary Sue Eck,
3. *Saint Michael and the Fatima Connection*…Carlos Evaristo
4. *The Day Will Come*…Michael Brown
5. *The Light Comes from the East*…Hugh Owen
6. *Invited to Light*…John DeMers
7. *The Thunder of Justice*…Ted Flynn
8. *A Heavenly Promise*…Cathy Howe
9. *Rita's Story*…Rita Klaus.
10. *The Final Hour*…Michael Brown
11. *Unity and Victory*…Guy Murphy
12. *Medjugorje: An Affirmation and Defense*…Albert Hebert, S.M.

About the Author

Dr. Thomas Petrisko is the former editor of an international Catholic newspaper and the author of 25 books on health and spiritual topics, including the best-selling, *The Sorrow, the Sacrifice, and the Triumph* (Simon and Schuster, 1995) He has also appeared on or advised numerous newspapers, magazines, radio programs and TV shows such as *The Today Show, Oprah Winfrey, Unsolved Mysteries, Scripps-Howard Productions, CBS-Forces Beyond, Newsweek, Pittsburgh Post-Gazette, The Joan Rivers Show, CBS News-48 Hours, Coast to Coast AM- The Art Bell Show, Hard Copy, Pittsburgh Tribune Review, The Washington Times, Inside Edition ,The Los Angeles Times, The Washington Post* and others. He lives in Ave Maria, Florida, with his wife and six children.

Available to Speak

Dr. Thomas Petrisko is available to come to your Church or organization to speak. He is also available to do radio, television, internet and print media interviews. If you desire to schedule him, please call St. Andrews Productions at 412-787-9735 or email your request at standrewsproductions@yahoo.com.

[Thomas Petrisko writes a freelance subscriber email (digital) newsletter for **Substack** (see **substack.com**), under the title **Consider the Fig Tree**. It deals with Catholic themed issues including prophecy, mystics, apparitions, saints, miracles, contemporary news, related Church events, and excerpts from his books that are relevant to the times at hand.]

www.ingramcontent.com/pod-product-compliance
Lightning Source LLC
Chambersburg PA
CBHW020752290625

28867CB00003B/52